WALKING AND EATING IN
PROVENCE

JAMES LASDUN & PIA DAVIS

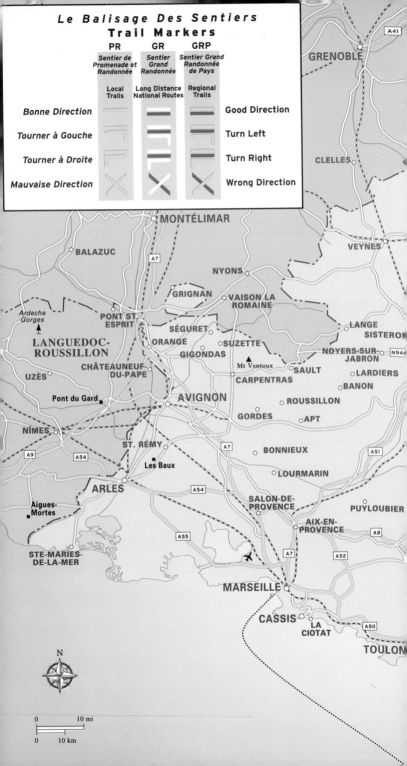

RHÔNE-ALPES

PROVENCE

MODANE

TURIN

BRIANÇON

PINEROLO

FRANCE

ITALY

GAP

CUNEO

PROVENCE

Col di
Tenda Pass

DIGNE

CASTERINO

ST. AUBAN

MÉAILLES

ANNOT

SAORGE

CASTELLANE

SOSPEL

AIGUINES

VENCE

Grand
Canyon
du Verdun

ST. PAUL-DE-VENCE

EZE

MENTON

MONACO

NICE

VILLEFRANCHE-
SUR-MER

GRASSE

BIOT

Ligurian Sea

CANNES

ANTIBES

Côte D'Azur

FRÉJUS

ST. RAPHAËL

ST-TROPEZ

LE LAVANDOU

Mediterranean   Sea

Iles D'hyeres

© AVALON TRAVEL

W e arrived in Provence in March. The mistral was blowing; the rugged mountains around us were brown and
gray. The villages, perched watchfully on their hilltops, were
mostly silent. For a good month we seemed to have the farmland
and mountain country entirely to ourselves. What we noticed
more than anything at that time was the stoniness of the landscape and the monumental human endeavor to work with or
around or against this. Great mounds of stones, *clapas* or *clapi-
ers,* sit piled in the fields, testament to the unending effort to
keep the soil workable. Ancient pathways of stones—*chemins ca-
ladés*—with each stone set in perfect formation, edge-on into the
earth, make the often steep ascents to the hilltop villages navi-
gable at even the muddiest time of year. Beautifully constructed
stone walls, sometimes two in parallel with a *chemin calade* between them, twist and turn over the jagged contours of the hills,

marking the boundaries of sheep and goat pastures. Stone vernacular architecture, in the form of fortified farmhouses, domed *bergeries* (sheepcotes), or the old shepherds' shelters known as *bories,* dot the landscape. The latter evolved centuries ago into a sophisticated folk art: little hand-built miracles of drystone construction, with endless varieties of domed, vaulted, corbeled, or pitched roofs on their conical walls, suggesting exactly the same kind of competitive originality that produced, at the other end of the social scale, the fairy-tale castles of the Loire. A prodigious number of these buildings have fallen into ruin, adding their own eerie note to the atmosphere.

In April farmers appeared in the fields. The dead-looking vine stocks, standing like rows of black candelabras, sprouted jets of green leaf. The even deader-looking lavender shrubs, which thrive on the stoniest soil, turned bluish green. Cornstalks rose

from the dirt. The almond orchards blossomed, then the cherries; white and pink. The landscape revealed its second characteristic: an amazing variety and abundance of wildflowers, unfolding in successive waves of color all through the spring and early summer. Primroses and purple starry hepatica covered the shaded banks of streams in the Lubéron mountains. Several types of orchid and blue gentian appeared in the high meadows of the Lure and the Alpes Maritimes. The long-stalked pink flowers dangling from every crevice of the white-rocked Dentelles de Montmirail were valerian. Poppies were allowed to grow thickly among the wheat and long-tasseled oats in the dreamy farmland outside Apt. Roses bloomed at the end of vine rows north of Nice. Gold-flowering broom opened in a sustained, continuous explosion over the entire landscape from late April till early summer. And when the lavender—wild or cultivated—flowered in June, we knew it by its intense fragrance before seeing its vivid purple blossoms.

Even when it wasn't flowering, much of the vegetation we passed through on these walks consisted of a highly aromatic brush of juniper, rosemary, boxwood, and wild thyme, known as *garrigue*. Much of the landscape was also sheep-farming country, with large flocks still herded up to the high grasslands for the summer *transhumance,* which of course added its own elemental aroma as well as providing the best soundtrack we could have asked for on any walk: the tinkling of sheep bells.

Provence is the main component in the "Mediterranean" identity of France, but travelers expecting the

easy golden charm of Italy or Greece may find themselves surprised by its altogether harsher, more austere beauty, at least in its interior. Even in spring and summer, when the colors come in, there's something savage and blazing about the parts of it that remain wild. You can see why a temperament such as Van Gogh's might have found it congenial.

Any walk you take in this landscape is going to be a departure from the usual tourist routine—the scripted, often harried trajectory from museum to museum, church to church, restaurant to restaurant. A large part of our original inspiration for this series was to find a more natural way to experience the cultural and gastronomic pleasures of these places. There's something deeply satisfying about arriving on foot at a town or village, having spent a day or even just a few hours traversing spectacular countryside. You get a firsthand, bodily sense of the natural context out of which these man-made monuments arose. You experience for yourself the pace and rhythms of the lives that brought them into existence. And at the most basic level, you work up the kind of appetite that actually enables you to appreciate the great food and wine that await you at your destination.

Contents

To Leo and Violet,
indefatigable adventurers

Introduction

Walking

Ten years ago we published a guidebook dedicated to what we considered to be one of life's great, unsung combinations of pleasure: walking and eating. It focused on Tuscany and Umbria, but our hope was always to extend it into a series, and Provence, with its equally beguiling landscapes, wine, and cuisine, was always our first choice for the next volume.

Unlike in Italy, where we had difficulty finding any walking guides at all, even in Italian, there are numerous walking guides to all parts of France. The French are great walkers; their vast local and national networks of *sentiers* (footpaths) and GR *(grandes randonnées)* long-distance hiking trails are mostly well maintained and blazed, and the whole country has been mapped in detail by the Institut Geographique National (IGN) on the 1:25,000 scale most useful for walking.

The problem is almost the reverse of that of Italy: too much information, which makes the question of where to go, where to avoid, and which routes to choose almost as hard to answer. Many of the guidebooks simply direct you from one well-known town or village to another, along the most obvious GR paths connecting them. On paper it looks compelling, but since these paths sometimes converge for long stretches with busy minor roads, and often pass through large areas of built-up sprawl, the experience can be disappointing. And even the better walking guides tend to ignore the questions of food and wine that, in our opinion, are indispensable elements of a great day out walking in the country. So again there appears to be a significant gap in the available literature, and again we offer this book in the hope of filling it.

As in our first guide, our criteria for including a walk are very simple: The walk must go through largely unspoiled countryside and there must be somewhere en route (or at the final destination) where you can enjoy a good meal. If it takes in something of cultural interest such as a medieval monastery or Roman aqueduct or Bronze Age rock carving, all the better, and if it leaves from or arrives at a place where you might want to spend a night or two—a hilltop village of exceptional beauty, say, or a gorgeous remote farm/auberge—then better still. Best of all is when it offers something of all these elements, and much of the time we spent researching this book was devoted to finding as many of the latter as possible.

Provence occupies the southeast corner of France, a sizeable slab of mountain ranges, plains, and coast, covering more than 31,000 square kilometers, stretching from the Rhône in the west to the Italian border on the east. It isn't all idyllic, of course. This has always been contested territory. The Romans grabbed it for a province—"provincia"—2,000 years ago. From the barbarian invasions after the fall of the Roman Empire, through the religious wars of the Middle Ages, to the Nazi occupation during the Second World War, it has seen more than its share of violence, and much of what we now find picturesque—watchtowers, walled towns, houses built into cliff caves, the World War II gun emplacements near Sospel that have become tourist attractions in their own right—is the direct result of this. Whether the depredations of our own time, done in the name of peace and prosperity rather than war, will attract tourists of the future seems more doubtful. Will the miles of un-checked sprawl running around so many of the better-known towns and villages ever seem enticing? Will people one day visit the lines of gigantic pylons slashing across otherwise pristine val-leys, the way they now visit the aqueduct of the Pont du Gard? Call us old-fashioned but we don't see that happening, and we took great pains to spare our readers these kinds of sights.

In many ways this made our work easier. A series of recces by car eliminated a large number of allegedly charming rural areas that turned out to have passed the critical point of suburbaniza-tion. Major cities such as Avignon and Arles were simply out of the question as far as trying to incorporate them into any kind of enjoyable walk (walking inside them is another matter, but you don't need this book for that). Certain major historic sites out in the country, such as the Abbey of Sénanque, were natu-ral candidates for inclusion on a walk; others turned out to be strictly "drive-bys": more satisfactorily visited by car. The notori-ously overdeveloped Riviera seemed a pointless place to look for walks, though we did try, and we almost included a couple of well-intentioned, intermittently pleasant coastal trails that have been set up around Cap d'Antibes and Cap Ferrat, but we de-cided in the end that there was too much about them that didn't quite work. They're easy to find, though, if you're in the area and want a bracing seaside stroll. Farther to the west, however, between Cassis and Marseille, there's a protected area of fjord-like inlets called the Calanques, and we found two gorgeous walks there.

In eliminating large areas, the effects of modern develop-ment also forced us to explore some out-of-the-way corners of Provence in more depth than we might have otherwise, and this proved extremely worthwhile. The Roya and Bevera valleys up near the Italian border were a revelation for us: peaceful, beauti-ful towns and villages set in dramatic mountain scenery with the rich wilderness of the Mercantour national park nearby. (One of our favorite walks, the Casterino Ring Walk, goes into this park.) So too were some of the villages above Nice, where the presence of a narrow-gauge railway, the Train des Pignes, adds the fun of an old-fashioned train ride to the itineraries.

We can't claim that this is anything like a comprehensive guide to walking in Provence. We did try to cover the full range of its different kinds of geographies, but there are without doubt great walks and indeed whole areas that we've neglected. On the other hand, we see this as an ongoing project, and just as we've done with our Italy book, we fully intend to explore this glorious corner of the world further in future editions.

Eating

The popular idea of Provençal food is of a kind of ultimate cuisine of the sun, bursting with the flavors and colors of vine-ripe tomatoes, yellow peppers, violet aubergines (eggplants), and pungent black olives. There is some truth to this, especially if you visit in the summer when those quintessentially Mediterranean elements come into season. But since you're unlikely to be walking in Provence at that time of year (it's too hot), you should bear in mind that there is another side altogether to the cooking of this region.

Provence, as Peter Mayle writes, is a cold country with a high rate of sunshine. The culinary traditions are accordingly rather heavier and meatier than you might expect. Slow-cooked, rib-sticking dishes predominate. Most restaurant menus feature a version of the incredibly hearty olive-flavored beef stew known as daube, often served with polenta. Egg yolk-and-flour–thickened *blanquettes* of lamb or goat are popular in the mountains. Casseroles and fricassees of rabbit (*lapin*), strongly flavored with the wild herbs of the ubiquitous *garrigue,* are common, as are tripe dishes, notably the Provençal classic, *pieds et paquets.* The latter—literally "feet and packages"—consists of a sheep's tripe stuffed with garlicked salt pork, cooked overnight in white wine and tomato, served with a lamb trotter alongside it. It can be an alarming sight if you're not used to it, but it can also be extremely tasty in its gelatinous way. Much of Provence is hunting country, and you'll often find game on the menu: wild boar, hare, partridge, even, alas, the occasional songbird. At one time pigeons and doves

Restaurant Practicalities

Almost all restaurants in Provence offer daily *menus*, usually posted somewhere outside the restaurant. There are usually two or three different prices. The *menus* give a list of courses comprising a full meal. Sometimes each *menu* option will also give course options, a choice between two or three different entrées (entrée in France is the starter course, not the main course as it is in the United States and United Kingdom), two or three main courses, and two or three desserts. As the *menu* prices increase, the restaurant is offering either more food or food that costs more to serve (for example, a steak main course versus an omelette main course).

Even though *menus* are offered, you can almost always order à la carte single items. What we would call a menu (the menu you are handed by a waiter, with all the offerings and prices on it), in France is called the *carte*.

Always check your bill before paying. This goes for shopping at the market too. We were overcharged again and again.

The service charge or tip, *service*, is included in your bill, unless stated otherwise. If the service was good, it's customary to leave a few extra euros, another 5 percent of your bill or so.

We emphasize the importance of making restaurant reservations ahead of time if you possibly can. The reason it's so important is that in many of the villages from which our walks are based, the restaurant listing we give is the only restaurant in the village. If it's full, or closed, then what? The people who answer the phone at most restaurants speak at least enough English to take your reservation. Don't be scared.

were widely raised for food (you'll pass plenty of slope-roofed stone dovecotes or *pigeonniers* out in the fields). They're less common now, but if you do see pigeon on the menu it tends to be very good: succulent and richly gamey. For the less adventurous there is usually a steak of some kind to be had and often a roast *carre* (crown) of lamb or pork.

None of this will sound terribly enticing to vegetarians or even to people who don't like to eat a lot of meat. There's a curious conundrum here. The markets of Provence are spectacularly good, overflowing with every kind of salad green, every variety of asparagus, artichoke, melon, aubergine, and so on, all of it of a superb quality. But remarkably little of this vegetable abundance finds its way into the restaurants, many of which seem to be stuck in a bygone culinary era. Salads tend to be minimal and are generally not considered worth serving unless they are liberally sprinkled with *lardons* (small chunks of bacon) or bits of chicken gizzard—*gézier*—or, in the case of the *salade niçoise*—chunks of tuna. Side dishes are seldom a strong point, as you'll discover after a few blandly eggy *tians* of courgette (zucchini) or aubergine. Artichokes, if you're lucky enough to find them on the menu, are likely to come in the form of a *barigoule*—stewed with sausage meat, bacon, and garlic. Ratatouille—invented in Provence—can be marvellous in summer when the requisite aubergines, courgettes, and tomatoes are ripe, but out of season it can be very disappointing. And finally, be prepared for the question "Do you have anything vegetarian?" to be answered with either "Yes, fish," or "No, are you ill?"

But don't despair. Many restaurants will go out of their way to accommodate your needs, especially if you call ahead. We were particularly lucky on this score with some of the Bistrots de Pays we visited, where the interest in reviving local culinary traditions seems to go hand in hand with a more inventive approach to vegetables. Omelettes are usually an option in even the most die-hard carnivore establishments, and they are almost always beautifully prepared, brimming with fresh herbs and cheese, or truffles when these are in season. Pasta crops up with increasing frequency as you approach Nice (which used to belong to Italy). Most restaurants have a selection of local cheeses—usually goat or sheep—on hand, and these are usually excellent. Unless you're in a large town, you won't find much in the way of non-French restaurants (the French are deeply loyal to their own cuisine). The exception is pizzerias, which abound and which, allowing for the inevitable gallicization (crème fraîche, for example, instead of mozzarella), can provide a highly satisfactory break from the mounds of flesh.

In common with the meat dishes, the great Provençal seafood specialties emphasize heat, richness, and substantiality. You can find simple, delicious grilled fish anywhere along the coast, but this is the birthplace and only true home of bouillabaisse and its cousin, bourride, and it would be perverse to leave Provence without sampling these epic dishes. Every restaurant and cookbook will give you a different definition of each and a different set of distinctions between them. Suffice it to say that they are both enormous concoctions of Mediterranean fish, including but by no means limited to *rascasse* (sea scorpion), *rouget* (red mullet), *loup de mer* (sea bass), as well as conger eel and various members of the lobster and crab family, cooked in a saffron-flavored bouillon along with dried orange peel, olive oil, tomatoes, and fennel, and served over toasted bread with grated emmenthal and a bowl of thick *rouille* made of copious amounts of crushed garlic, red pepper, bread crumbs, and olive oil, for stirring into it. Some authorities state that the bourride differs from the bouillabaisse in being made with only white-fleshed fish, and having no shellfish or saffron in it, but there is no consensus on this. Whatever the case, a decent version of either can be a blissful and unforgettable experience.

If you're any distance from the coast, fish and seafood are generally to be avoided, though there are a couple of notable exceptions. First is the dependably fabulous dish known as *brandade de morue,* in which salt cod is pounded with garlic, boiled potatoes, and olive oil and served with bread. Second is aioli. Many cafés and restaurants serve this as a Friday special, and it tends to be a large, festive affair: a platter of boiled potatoes, cauliflower, carrots, eggs, shellfish (or sometimes snails), and pieces of sautéed fish (usually cod) surrounding a large bowl full of intensely garlicky mayonnaise, the deliberate blandness of the former acting as the perfect foil to the extreme pungency of the latter.

The fact that *île flottante* ("floating island") seems to be the favorite restaurant dessert in Provence probably tells you all you need to know about Provençal desserts. So unless you have a hankering for that nursery pudding of whipped egg white floating on custard or crème anglaise, your best bet (with exceptions, of course) is generally to head to a patisserie at this stage of the meal and treat yourself to some of the pastries that here, as in all of France, are reliably delicious.

A FEW NOTES ON THE LOCAL BEVERAGE

Provence, the geographical area covered by this book, includes not only the official AOC wine area of Provence, but also that of the southern section of the Côtes du Rhône. A Côtes du Rhône is usually an easy, lightly colored red, with some element of grenache sweetness running through it, or a full-bodied white of rather pedestrian qualities. As France's second-biggest AOC, it covers a lot of land and necessarily runs the gamut of quality. The bulk of Côtes du Rhône on the market comes from hot, sunny Provence and is marked more by its lightness and fruit than by its finesse. Nonetheless, you can find excellent examples made by inspired winemakers with an accommodating parcel of land, and

Vins d'Appellation d'Origine Contrôlée

Vins d'Appellation d'Origine Contrôlée, or **AOC,** is the main category of the French wine regulatory system; its basis is the notion of *terroir* (a sense of place). The appellations are based principally on geographical boundaries but also regulate other particulars of the wines, such as grape varieties, yields, cultivation and wine-making parameters, and minimum aging requirements. The point of the system is to produce wines whose scents and tastes are unique to that particular place on earth: when you buy an AOC bottle of wine, you are buying (ideally) the scents and flavors of that particular place, that particular *appellation.*

one drinks them often with pleasure. The Côtes du Rhône-*Villages* AOC is for areas within the huge swath of territory covered by the Côtes du Rhône AOC that have been awarded a promotion. There are 96 communes that can use this AOC straight, and 16 of the best can also add their village name.

Châteauneuf-du-Pape (with its own AOC) is the star here, but for the best ones you'll pay astronomical prices. One might argue the most important legacy of the papal encampment at Avignon are the vines planted at Châteauneuf in the 14th and 17th centuries (popes certainly weren't going to be drawing the line at luxury palaces). The 30 or so top domaines make the wine that makes the reputation, and with the other 90 or so other domaines you're taking your chances. The 13 grape varieties allowed in this AOC make for wide variety in the wines, and despite other AOC requirements such as low yield and hand harvesting, there are still plenty of dud wines here. The best are delicious, full bodied, well structured, powerful, and complex. The lesser-known whites are also sublime. The whites can be drunk wherever you find them, but the reds, though ready to accommodate the impatient drinker at three years, are best aged a decade or two. Among the best are certainly Rayas, Vieux Télégraphe, Beaucastel, Bosquet des Papes, Les Cailloux, Font-de-Michelle, and Péfau.

It's the rare occasion we can afford a top-notch Châteauneuf, but we're perfectly happy with Châteauneuf's friends and relations, Gigondas, Vacqueyras, and Rasteau. To be able to walk the 50 meters from the village fountain at Gigondas into the tiny Bouissière sales room and buy a great Gigondas for €11 could be grounds for relocating. The Bouissière bottles have a wonderful label picturing the beautiful Dentelle Mountains.

Gigondas is also strong and full bodied, often described as "peppery," though it wouldn't strike us that way.

Vacqueyras is very like Gigondas but with a finer structure and—so far at least—a lower price tag. Both of them improve with aging to the point of bearing a strong resemblance to their papal cousin. If you can, try to have at least five years on them, though the more the better.

Rasteau was a new discovery for us, introduced at Le Bistrot de la Lavande in Lardiers. The Domaine La Soumade was the first really good bottle of wine we had on the trip after three weeks of drinking in the Lubéron. These wines taste deeply *French,* in a way the wines of the Lubéron never manage. (We've listed our favorite producers from these three villages— Gigondas, Vacqueyras, and Rasteau—in the *Wine and Lace* chapter.)

Beaumes-de-Venise is widely considered France's best dessert muscat. Our choices here would be to do the Suzette walk (in the *Wine and Lace* chapter) and stop by the organic producers listed therein and do some tasting. Otherwise, worthy producers are St.-Sauveur, Coyeux, Durban, Jaboulet, Pigeade, and Vidal-Fleury.

The huge AOC Côtes de Provence covers areas that have absolutely nothing in common geologically or climactically and so dictates grape varieties in an almost arbitrary combination. Here, as in the Côtes du Rhône, you can find the full gamut of quality. Most of the wine people drink in Provence is rosé: People are on vacation and they feel good sitting in a café drinking rosé—the color is pretty. But most of the Provençal rosé is insipid at best. There are exceptions—notably Bandol rosés—but if you care, you'll seek them out, and otherwise, if you enjoy what's in your glass, that's what matters.

Meanwhile, if you go down to Cassis—or even if you don't—be sure to try the Cassis whites, which make such a marvelous accompaniment to fish and bouillabaisse.

Finally, the best wine in the Provence AOC is Bandol, a small AOC of eight villages making splendid and vigorous reds primarily from mourvèdre grapes—this is one of the few places in the world where they can ripen properly. The rosés are made from the young vines and are incomparable. In a long rosé-drinking history, we have never found a rival. If you like dry rosé, try to drink a few different Bandols while you're in Provence; any restaurant wine list that takes itself seriously should have one on it. Our favorite is Domaine Tempier, but we also loved some Bunans which we found—oddly enough—when we came home. But the reds need a decade on them at least; you could find a bottle that old in a restaurant, or bring some home and store it in your basement. Low yields and hand harvesting are required for the AOC. Good producers besides the two above include Pibarnon, La Suffrène, Lafran Veyrolles, Jean-Pierre Gaussen, Gros' Noré, and Tour du Bon.

Whatever you do where wine is concerned, don't get overwhelmed; you're here to enjoy yourself. The best advice we can give is to drink the wine that's around you and enjoy it. Remember you can seldom go wrong with a Bandol rosé. Ditto Gigondas, Vacqueyras, and Rasteau.

If you're a little more interested, and going out near Banon, you could make a dinner reservation at le Bistrot de la Lavande in Lardiers and orient yourself to wine there. Certainly visit la Cave de Septier in Apt (see *Walk 21, Viens Ring Walk* in the *Banon and the Lure* chapter), to do some tasting and buying; it has an excellent selection. Get the staff's recommendations—they speak English, and they're extremely knowledgeable, and nice. Cast your net across the other side of the Rhône and try some Tavel rosés—there's an AOC for it.

If you're a little more interested than that, drive around to some domaines and taste their wines. If you do the Dentelles walks, by all means check out some of our favorite producers there, and don't forget the sweet wines of nearby Beaumes-de-Venise.

Enjoy!

Planning Your Trip
CLIMATE AND WHEN TO GO

You can always find a place to walk in Provence, whatever the time of year. At its extremes, winter and summer, your options will be more limited—along the coast in winter, high up in the mountains in summer. Because we're talking about a relatively contained surface area, the biggest differences in climate are a factor of altitude, and Provence runs from sea level at the coast to upward of 9,000 feet in the northeast part of the province. The only really flat terrain is near the western border by the

Rhône; from there the landscape becomes increasingly rugged as you move east, with the northern areas more mountainous than the southern areas. Something for everyone, at all times of year.

Having said that, if you can take your pick, spring may be the nicest time for walking, when the leaves have come out and the vegetation is still green from the winter's rains. Wildflowers are abundant and the fields full of bright red poppies are one of the most beautiful things you'll see in Provence. The sun is warm but not yet oppressive, and the light is bright and usually shining, though April and May have a history of being the wettest months. With global warming, though, historical patterns are up in the air (so to speak); we had nearly a week of rain in May, and other than that, never more than a day of rain once in a while from the end of February through the end of June. (There are always plenty of the cultural sites to visit when it's too rainy to walk.) The fields stayed green all through June as well, which locals said was somewhat unusual. In spring the widest possible area has temperatures conducive to walking, with the added advantage of being pretourist season. Some of the smaller restaurants are on limited opening schedules until Easter (Pâcques), but in most respects being out of the "season" is only to your advantage. May and early June are possibly the best time of all; the broom is blooming profusely, local produce is beginning to come in by then, and apricots such as we've never encountered in the States (juicy as peaches, deep yellow/orange with the pink blush) in from Spain. June is the turning point for comfortable any-time-of-day walking, though; sometime in June summer is likely to set in and then, as in July and August, poolside is probably where you'd rather be for most of the day.

September sees life return to normal, and by October the temperature is again fabulous for walking, and those storms that tend to blow up also tend to blow away quickly. Wild berries, local harvests, gentians, and changing leaves are further inducements to vacation here in autumn. By November the weather is cold and wet, and many businesses (particularly hotels) are shut.

If you're thinking of very early spring, March for example, when the days can be sunny and in the low 70s already (if you're not too high up), bear in mind the mistral. The mistral is the cold, dry north wind that blows for days at a time down the Rhône valley corridor through western Provence, whenever

INTRODUCTION

there's a depression out over the ocean. Refreshing in the summer, in winter it gives the impression of penetrating everything, everywhere. Winds can reach 50–60 mph (with a record 170 mph at the summit of Mont Ventoux). On the job an average of 120 days a year at Orange and 90 days a year at Marseille, it blows mostly in the winter and spring, and without it, the Rhône valley would be a humid bog.

If you've never lived through three days of nonstop wind of this magnitude, it's really something to experience. What eventually makes the impression is its sheer relentlessness, the way it never gives up. At home, windstorms come and go, and they tend to die down after a night of hard blowing. Not the mistral. Its relentlessness, the noise that never quiets, becomes irritating after the novelty wears off, so much so that "the mistral" has been used—on occasion successfully—as an excuse for murder.

WHAT TO TAKE AND WHAT TO WEAR

One of the reasons walking is so easily incorporated into a vacation of any kind is you don't need a lot of special equipment. Most of what you need for walking you'd probably be bringing anyway. All that's really indispensable is a pair of sturdy walking shoes with good soles. They don't have to be hiking boots, but the paths in Provence tend to be stony and good soles, like the ones that used to be found only on hiking boots but are now on all kinds of "sport" shoes, make all the difference comfortwise. They're more shock absorbent and give a better grip. If you're reading this book, chances are you're already walking at home, so you have comfortable shoes and socks. If not, get some before you go, and break them in before you leave on your trip. You'll find they're great for sightseeing as well, which tends to be a walking activity of sorts. It's nice, but certainly not essential, to have good walking socks that wick away sweat.

That takes care of indispensable. Highly desirable are a small day pack, a reusable bottle, sunscreen, multipurpose knife (e.g., Swiss Army knife), and hat. Let's take them one by one:

Day pack: This is the kind kids carry their stuff in to school. If you don't already have one, they're sold at sporting goods stores, department stores, discount stores, and of course online. You could also consider borrowing one; most people who have kids probably have an extra one lying around. It doesn't take up

Packing for Overnight Walks

Everything you need for a walk of two or three days can fit easily into your day pack. If you're going out for longer, you could consider a bigger pack or having a little laundry done along the way (or doing it yourself), or just stuffing a few more shirts and pairs of underwear into your day pack. (For more on leaving your main luggage behind, see the *How to Use This Book* chapter.)

You'll want to carry the least weight possible; one way to do this is to make clothes serve dual functions when you can. So, for example, the clean T-shirt you change into on your arrival in "town" after your first day's walk becomes your walking T-shirt on the second day. Same with underwear. Your walking pants or shorts remain the same every day (as, potentially, could your socks), but you'll need an "evening" pair of pants or skirt, or a dress. Silk and linen are lightweight and respond fairly well to being crumpled up in a pack, and we found trousers or a skirt of one of these materials served well as evening attire. Remember, it's only for a few days.

Sandals can be a very lightweight evening shoe. If you don't have them at home, you can buy an inexpensive lightweight pair at the market. They don't need to be sturdy, as you'll be wearing them only in the evening, when you'll mostly be sitting down. One exception to this is if you stay somewhere outside the village and decide to walk into town.

To round out the look: your lightweight windbreaker/anorak or sweater.

If it's cold you may need to augment or otherwise adjust this list, maybe with a pair of long underwear, some gloves, and a warm hat. Let common sense be your guide.

The only other things you need to pack are your minimum toiletry requirements (for a couple of nights, do you really need any more than a toothbrush, toothpaste, and comb?), maybe a book in case it rains, your money, and your passport.

much room if you want to pack it, but why not use it as your carry-on luggage?

Reusable bottle: Here's an important purchase, something you can really use—and not just for the trip. In 2006 Americans alone tossed more than *22 billion* empty plastic bottles in the trash (or on the ground). That bottle production alone (to say nothing of the cost of transporting them to your local store), takes 1.5 million barrels of oil during the course of one year.

People think that bottled water is somehow safer or healthier than tap water, but a 1999 Natural Resources Defense Council study found that, with required quarterly testing, tap water may be even of a higher quality than bottled, which is tested only annually. This may make it only a waste of money and natural resources, but when these water bottles (which are the ones with the number 1 in the triangular recycling imprint on the bottom) are reused, which they commonly are, they can leach chemicals such as DEHA, a known carcinogen, and benzyl butyl phthalate (BBP), a potential hormone disrupter. Because the plastic is porous you're also likely to take in plenty of bacteria with your water if you refill your number 1 plastic bottles.

As for reusable plastic bottles, the debate continues as new studies emerge over the safety of bisphenol A (BPA), a hormone-disrupting chemical known to leach out of the number 7 polycarbonate plastic used to make a variety of products, including the popular Nalgene Lexan water bottles.

Why not try a lightweight metal water bottle that can handle a variety of liquids, even acidic fruit juices, and won't leach chemicals into your drink? "Klean Kanteen" (www.kleankanteen.com) makes a lightweight, durable, chemical-free stainless steel bottle, and "Sigg" (www.mysigg.com or google "sigg bottle" for discount sites) makes aluminum bottles with a taste-inert, water-based epoxy lining, in a wide range of decorative surfaces. Besides saving you money, being less environmentally taxing, and protecting your health at home, on the trail in Provence they are incredibly convenient for collecting water at the numerous fountains you'll come across. Almost every village has a communal fountain, and unless there's a notice saying otherwise, the water is safe for drinking. It's not only safe, but some of the best water you'll get anywhere—especially when you get up into the mountain villages.

Sunscreen: The sun is *very* intense in Provence, even if it's not hot. If you keep the sunscreen in your day pack, you'll always have it.

Multipurpose knife: It's nice to have a knife for picnics, and consider its being one with a blade, a bottle opener, and a corkscrew. And maybe not much else, as additional gadgets add unnecessary weight. Swiss Army knives are very good quality and widely available. You can also buy a knife in Provence, either at a hardware or kitchen store or at one of the larger towns' outdoor markets, and then when you get home you'll have yourself a pleasing and utilitarian memento. The two excellent brands we saw most often were the Opinel and the Laguiole. The Opinel is less expensive, but either one is a pleasure to own.

Hat: Another pleasure, another memento: finding the perfect hat at the market. All of the larger town markets will have a big hat booth. Straw hats (with a brim to keep the sun off your face and neck) are perfect for walking; the weave lets the air circulate.

And finally…. comfortable clothes for the season, with a light-weight sweater or some kind of long-sleeved overshirt, even if it's warm out when you start on the walk. The weather can change surprisingly rapidly. For this reason, it's also a good idea to carry a lightweight rain jacket or anorak. If you're fairly certain it's going to rain, and you're still determined to walk, a small umbrella carried in your day pack or hung from its side would not go amiss.

A miniature pocket dictionary always comes in handy unless your French is stellar. A compass is a nice thing to have and so is a map. We also always carried a small roll of toilet paper. A plea on this point: How much more difficult is it to make a little impression in the dirt with a stick, put your toilet paper in it, and throw a rock (plentiful in this part of the world) on top, than it is to just leave your toilet paper in the middle of the trail as a reminder to everyone who will pass for the next three months of how awful is the presence of Man?

USING THE TOURIST OFFICES

The tourist offices are a wealth of information during the planning stages of your trip as well as "on the ground." The people who staff them almost always speak English, which can be a tremendous relief, and in most cases seem really pleased to help.

Two of the most useful services the tourist offices can provide are help with public transport information and local accommodation.

During the planning stages, tourist offices—and their websites, which almost always offer an English version (click on the British flag icon)—can provide so much information about the area. Their accommodation listings can be particularly helpful, especially in the smaller villages (which tend to be our bases). If you have specific questions that aren't answered on the website, you can email them—there's always an email link on the website; they are generally very good about responding promptly.

On the ground (and also in the planning stages), one of the best uses of tourist offices is having them decipher the local public transport. Local bus schedules (if there *is* a local bus) can be difficult to interpret. They're usually based around the school schedule and market, with different schedules during school-time, non-schooltime, Wednesdays, Sundays, and so on. It's much easier to ask for help.

Another useful service they provide—if you don't speak

INTRODUCTION

Gîtes de France Online

Here are some tips on using the Gîtes de France website:

- Go to www.gîtes-de-france.com

- Along the top of the page, click on the type of accommodation you're looking for: "chambres d'hôtes," "gîtes d'étape – séjour," or "gîtes ruraux" (houses by the week).

- Choose the "Région" from the drop-down menu. Your region is "Provence-Alpes-Côte d'Azur." (You'll often see in French websites or publications the acronym PACA, which stands for this region.)

- Choose the "Département" from the drop-down menu. There are no walks in this book from 05 (Hautes-Alpes), and only the three walks based in Aix are in 13 (Bouches-du Rhône). If you're not sure which département the town you're thinking about is in, you can look on a map or google the town's name to find out.

- "Commune" means the town or village you want to look in, if you want to narrow it down to that degree.

- The box "Dans un rayon de" means the radius from the *commune* (village) you'll consider. If you don't have a car, you'll want to choose "sur place."

French very well—is making calls for you. If you're feeling uncertain of your ability to make an arrangement—for a *chambres d'hôte* for example—you can ask them to call for you.

Tourist offices have information on all the local goings-on and offerings, so checking in there can also alert you to a free concert or other event you might not otherwise know about. They can also advise where to do things such as rent bikes or arrange for a pony trek. If you ever feel at loose ends about your practical matters, think of the tourist office.

Use the tourist offices! That's why they're there. Remember they (almost always) speak English, so don't hesitate to call.

TRANSPORTATION

Using public transportion costs less and is environmentally preferable, but it does take more time. Almost all the towns that serve as bases for our walks are served by some kind of public transport, usually a bus, but there are a few—particularly in the Banon chapter—that don't have even so much as a local bus. An interesting phenomenon we found in a few places is the "by reservation" bus, a shuttle bus that will come for you by reservation. Where we've found them we've noted them in the appropriate *Logistics* sections.

Generally trains are best for longer-haul trips, with buses taking over for the local segment. We've listed whatever local public transport exists in the *Logistics* section of each walk. We've also tried to include phone numbers for taxi services where they exist. Sometimes these numbers are cell phone numbers and you might get the driver directly, but try—if at all possible—to make your arrangements ahead of time, at least to the extent of making contact and establishing the possibility of service in principle.

Two of the chapters in this book (the *Train de Pigne* and *Northeast Kingdom* chapters) are centered around trains, the former being an old-fashioned narrow-gauge train. You don't need a car to do most of the walks in either of these chapters, but each of them has one walk that requires a car or other arrangements (such as a taxi or hitching).

As mentioned, if you're using public transport, don't hesitate to ask the tourist office for help, either by dropping in or phoning, or even emailing if that's more convenient in a particular situation. Bus and train schedules can be confusing at first, and how could one expect otherwise, when to begin with a bus is called a *"car"* in French. Phrases such as *en semaine* can be tricky: You'd think it means Monday–Friday, but it's Monday–Saturday. Often there's no bus at all on Sunday, and as mentioned above, schedules differ depending on whether school is in session *(période scolaire)* or not. Larger towns usually have a *gare routière* (bus station), but not all the bus companies necessarily leave from it. That's why it's good to let the tourist office staff help you get the hang of it.

Having said that, the national railway line SNCF has a great online site, www.ter-sncf.com/paca/index.asp, where you can enter your "from" and "to" locations and see all the pertinent train information—schedules, fares, booking, and so on.

To interpret a local bus schedule it helps to know when school vacations take place, since the schedules always refer to these periods as *scolaire* or *non-scolaire*. (Being aware of school vacations, when French families may take the opportunity to travel, is also useful in terms of anticipating increased demand on tourist services generally—such as heavier hotel and restaurant bookings.) For a rough idea, the following are the school vacation periods in the Vaucluse for the 2007–2008 school year:

- Vacances de Toussaint: October 28–November 7
- Vacances de Noel: December 23–January 6
- Vacances d'Hiver: February 10–24
- Vacances de Printemps: April 6–20
- Vacances d'Été: from July 4

When reading bus schedules, remember to look at the top and bottom of the column of bus times, to see *which* days of the week the bus operates (it might be one day a week only!), whether it's during schooltime, school vacation, or *annuel,* which is all through the year. *Annuel sf fêtes* means all through the year except *(sauf)* holidays *(fêtes).*

From time to time a taxi can be useful, especially in the case of one-way walks. We've given taxi info if it's been available, but these services have a tendency to come and go. Once you're in a place, you may see a sign with a taxi number on it; otherwise ask the tourist office.

If you'll be driving, you might consider leasing a car if your trip will be a month or longer. Leasing gives you a new car with free insurance and no charge for additional drivers, and though leasing agencies can do a contract for anything longer than 17 days, it's only at about a month that the leasing option ends up costing less than renting. You don't have to return the car to the same location you picked it up, and the agency provides 24-hour emergency service. You need to arrange leases well ahead of time, usually at least four weeks in advance of your trip. We used Auto France and can recommend it highly (800/572-9655, www.auto france.net). Another option is Europe by Car, which does both leasing and rentals (800/223-1516, www.europebycar.com).

ACCOMMODATIONS

If a friend were planning a trip to Provence and asked for advice (or if we were planning our own trip), we'd recommend staying in a variety of *chambres d'hôtes* and taking long walks.

Chambres d'hôtes are basically bed-and-breakfasts, usually in the proprietor's home. Dinner is often available for an extra cost, and in that case the *chambres d'hôte* is offering *table d'hôte.* When meals are offered, there will usually be a half or "demi"-pension (half-board) price, which includes bed, breakfast, and dinner, as well as a standard room price, which includes bed and breakfast only; you pick one or the other. If you do want the dinner meal, make sure to say so at the time you book your room, as the owner will be doing his or her shopping based on who'll be eating. If you'll be wanting a picnic for your onward journey the next day, also request this at the time you make your room reservation, for the same reason.

Chambres d'hôtes are not necessarily a cheaper option than a hotel room; on average they may be priced close to what a two-star hotel would be. But the experience of staying in a *chambres d'hôte* is much more variable than that of a hotel stay. To begin with, *chambres d'hôtes* can be in any kind of home—a rustic farm-house, a village "town house," or even in a château. The rooms themselves also vary widely, many being quite spare, others more like someone's home. Usually the rooms have at least a separate entrance hall, and the proprietors tend to be no more overbear-ing—in the sense of impinging on your privacy—than those of hotels. And sometimes the food—should *table d'hôtes* be an op-tion—is better than the local restaurant's. In some small villages (at least two in this book) a *chambres d'hôte* is in any case the only option. Tourist offices have the complete list of their local *chambres d'hôtes* (if there's no English option on the tourist office's website, click on "Hébergement" for lodging listings) and Gîtes de France (www.Gîtes-de-france.com) has listings by *département,* as well as an annual guidebook that covers *chambres d'hôtes* through-out France. Those *chambres d'hôtes* that are "officially" listed, or in other words, registered with Gîtes de France, will have the or-ganization's green logo somewhere on their premises and be rated from one to four ears of corn *("épis"),* which is a general indication of comfort level and amenities. Gîtes de France also registers *gîtes ruraux* (rural) and *gîtes d'étape* (see below), according them *epis* on a similar basis (*gîtes d'étape epi* ratings go only to three).

If you're interested in a farm stay, an organization called Bi-envenue a la Ferme has farm listings, varying from farms that simply sell honey or some other single item to those that offer meals and/or accommodations. If you're passing through an area that has one of these farms that offer meals, this can be a great eating option. See the website www.bienvenue-a-la-ferme.com (it has an English option). It also produces a guidebook available in bookstores.

We wouldn't want to miss out staying in some *gîtes d'étape* either, and along with the few small hotels we stayed in during our research for this book, they were the favorites with our kids. Kids love them because they have bunk beds, and the *dortoirs* (dormitory-style room) are a change of pace from any other usual sleeping arrangement.

Gîtes d'étape are often run by the local municipality and exist to provide a stopover place on an itinerary, a walking, cycling, or horseback itinerary primarily (and as such, are marked on the IGN 1:25,000 hiking maps), though all the *gîtes d'étape* we stayed in were just as accessible to those arriving by car. They're very reasonably priced, usually less than €15 per night per person (sometimes they require a "membership fee" of a euro or two, sometimes not). Usually they're a free-standing building, often in lovely surroundings, but sometimes they're just part of a large house, as *chambres d'hôtes* are. They tend to be impeccably clean. Many of the *gîtes d'étape* we saw had a couple of *dortoirs* sleeping 6–8 people each, along with a couple of double rooms that were slightly more expensive, but the configuration varies completely from place to place. If they have room to put you by yourselves, they will. In most cases there are basic kitchen and laundry facilities, shared bathrooms, and usually meals. If it's a *gîte d'étape* that serves meals, it will also usually be able to provide you with a picnic for your onward journey the next day (for €5–10; request it at the time of placing your reservation). We've listed them in the *Logistics* section of any walk that has one, because we think more people would use them if they knew about them.

The fee usually includes just a bed and a blanket; sometimes sheets are included in the fee, but if not, they're available for a modest additional sum (usually around €2). If you plan to stay in *gîtes d'étape* often, you might consider buying a sleeping sack (which is basically a sleeping bag made of a sheet, available at camping stores) to avoid the extra charge.

Again, Gîtes de France publishes an annual national guide, *Gîtes d'étape et de séjour.*

Many of the towns our walks are based in have a hotel. All the hotels we've listed are part of the Logis de France organization, which rates them in a similar fashion to that of Gîtes-de-France's ears of corn, but in the Logis case it's fireplaces. We stayed in only two of them (La Brigue and Casterino), but we found them delightful. Usually they have a restaurant as well, and as such will offer a half-pension rate as well as a room rate.

The Logis de France hotels we came across didn't tend to be very big or very fancy, and they were quite reasonably priced.

If the idea of planting yourself in one location for a week or more appeals, the best way of renting a house is through—Gîtes de France! Its website lists houses (this type of accommodation is called *gîte rural*) by *département,* has an English version, and enables you to book online. You'll see its *epis* rating system again here, and the houses run the gamut pricewise, but in our experience (we stayed in six different houses) the price/quality relationship is accurately reflected, and the houses were all clean and comfortable. Expect to pay an extra fee for cleaning, unless you state ahead of time that you will be responsible for the cleaning. The fee is stipulated in your contract and is in addition to the price of the rental. We found the average charge to be €40–60. There's a set amount of electricity and water accorded your stay, which you're unlikely to exceed if you use these resources reasonably. If applicable, heat can also be an additional charge. The owner will meet you at the *gîte* when you arrive; clarify these extra charges with him or her at that time, if you haven't already.

Finally, here are a few generalities that apply to whichever type of accommodation you use. English is spoken—at least enough to communicate the essentials—at most restaurants and lodging places. When phoning, don't hesitate to ask if the other person speaks English if you don't speak French.

Most hotels (and often *chambres d'hôtes*) are happy to provide rooms with extra beds, for three or more people, at a discounted rate.

If you're staying anywhere for more than three days, you can often negotiate a discount, particularly out of season.

For additional accommodations listings see the tourist office websites; click on "Hébergement" if it's not in English (though most sites offer an English option). It's always best—no matter which type of lodging you're considering—to check its website for current prices.

FOREWARNED IS FOREARMED
Closings

Businesses close more often in France than they do in the United States or United Kingdom. Not just the midday closing, but there are more holidays observed in this way and, in the smaller towns at least, more seemingly arbitrary closings. We're in favor of this, as it's obviously a more civilized way to live a life, but let the traveler beware.

Your best line of defense in this regard is the telephone. Make reservations ahead of time whenever possible, and if you've done this *very* far in advance—more than a week, say—it doesn't hurt to call in again closer to the time, especially with the smaller establishments, be they *chambres d'hôtes* or Bistrots de Pays.

Bear in mind that Sunday lunch is a big social occasion. Leaving this reservation until the last minute is a dangerous game.

Phones and Phoning

The country code for France is 33. All phone numbers in France start with a four-digit area code, such as 0492, followed by a six-digit number. Therefore, a number will be given in a format something like: 0492/ 23 45 67. There seem to be several print arrangements for doing phone numbers, but this is how we're doing them. In any case, if you're calling from outside France you drop the "0," so to call the number above you'd dial whatever your overseas access code is (e.g., usually 011 in the United States, 00 in the United Kingdom), followed by 33 492 23 45 67. But within France you'd keep the "0" but drop the country code 33. So: 0492/ 23 45 67.

For cell phones the first two digits of the four-digit area code are 06. Accommodation listings, particularly, often give both a landline and cell number, so if you call a *chambres d'hôte* for a reservation and no one answers, try the cell.

Phoning home from France is cheapest with an international phone card, available at *tabacs*—newsagent-type shops displaying the Tabac sign outside. For calls within France you can buy a domestic calling card at the post office.

Water

Most villages have at least one public fountain. Unless there's a sign stating otherwise, the water is safe to drink. Not only safe, but often great, especially in the mountains. If you've brought your refillable bottle, you're in luck.

How to Use This Book

We have tried to suit this book to a wide variety of purpose and circumstance, as useful to those for whom walking will be a major focus as to those who are tentatively considering a single walk; for those who have a car and those who are car free. In response to feedback from our original book *Walking and Eating in Tuscany and Umbria,* we've oriented the book more toward ring walks—those that return to the same place they began—in most cases without retracing their tracks. Ring walks are more convenient certainly, but walking from village to village is also extremely satisfying, and to that end we have again included some walks of this type, albeit not as many as in the last book. These walks from point A to point B either link up to make multiday walks or can be done as single-day walks by using public transport in one direction.

We've added a third "category" of walk in this edition, which falls somewhere between the other two. Both the Train des Pignes chapter and the Northeast Kingdom chapter use train lines to connect walks. In the Pignes case, it's a touristic narrow-gauge train line, and in the Northeast, the Nice–Turin line running from the Mediterranean Sea northward through Provence into Italy. These chapters, perhaps our favorites in the book, cover a lesser-traveled part of Provence and work well with or without a car.

Walk routes are incredibly well signed in Provence—one of the biggest differences we found between this region and Italy. Whereas in Tuscany and Umbria we thought our biggest contribution was putting together walks that worked from start to finish, a majority of the walks we did in Provence were there before we arrived, well signed, and where the maps said they would be. Our biggest job this time turned out to be finding areas that weren't spoiled by development, but that still had decent food. Not as easy as it might sound.

One practical ramification of this situation is that if you find an area you like, you can easily find additional walks to those in the book. With the IGN 1:25,000 map for the area, you should be able to keep yourself busy almost indefinitely. You can also buy Topo Guides' PR (Promenade & Randonnée) guidebook for the local area, which will give you more walks than are shown on the IGN map itself. These guides are published by FFRP (Fédération Française de la Randonnée Pédestre) in conjunction with the local *département* and IGN, and they cover all of Provence. They're in French, but even if you can't read the directions, you can use the maps. Other guidebooks are just as good; the local tourist office will often have the available selection, and so will newsagents and bookstores.

France is full of marked walking trails, from the long-distance national routes (called *sentiers de grande randonnée,* or GR), to the regional trails (GR *de pays*), to the local paths (*sentier de promenade et randonnée,* or PR, as in the local PR guidebooks mentioned above). Each level of this heirarchy has its own color trail blaze (see diagram), and the paths sometimes overlap. The walks in this book make use of all three types of paths, often combining two—or possibly even all three—in one walk.

The Walks
DIFFICULTY LEVEL

The main differences among any of the walks is the time they take. A six-hour walk is more "difficult" than a three-hour walk, because it goes on longer. For the most part, all the walks

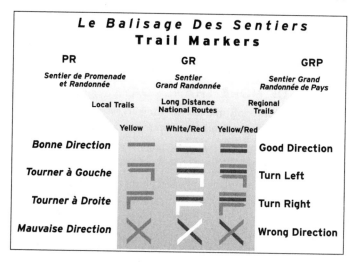

Le Balisage Des Sentiers
Trail Markers

PR	GR	GRP
Sentier de Promenade et Randonnée	*Sentier Grand Randonnée*	*Sentier Grand Randonnée de Pays*
Local Trails	Long Distance National Routes	Regional Trails
Yellow	White/Red	Yellow/Red

Bonne Direction	—	▬	▬	Good Direction
Tourner à Gouche	⌐	⌐	⌐	Turn Left
Tourner à Droite	⌐	⌐	⌐	Turn Right
Mauvaise Direction	✕	✕	✕	Wrong Direction

have sections of flat, rolling, and hilly—sometimes even mountainous—terrain. You should feel exercised by the end, but no Herculean effort or stamina is required. If the walk includes a particular challenge, we've noted it in the walk's introduction.

SINGLE-DAY WALKS

Almost all the walks in this book are ring walks, bringing you back to your starting point at the end of the walk. In the few cases of point A to point B walks, these can be managed either by taking a bus or taxi back to your starting point when you finish the walk, or by taking the bus or taxi to the beginning of the walk and walking back to your car or village accommodation. Another possibility, if you're traveling with someone else who has a car, is to leave one car at each end of the walk. Finally, there's always hitching. While not the ideal way to travel, it does have its advantages. It doesn't require planning, and it's sometimes the quickest way to get where you're going. On the small roads you're likely to encounter in this book, people are more likely to stop for you, and those who do tend to be interested in talking about where you come from, what you're doing, and offering advice to help you do it.

The Bistrots de Pays multiday walk in the Banon chapter is an exception, not lending itself easily to the single-day format. These walks are point A to point B sequential walks (though the three- to four-day series starts and ends in the same village,

Banon), and while they *can* be done as single-day walks, because they're in an area that has very limited public transport, they're easier to do as written.

WALKS OF MORE THAN A DAY

Even if you spend only one day walking across the landscape, rather than rushing around town from one "must-see" to the next, you'll experience a side of the region you never would have otherwise. Many people have written to us saying their memories of the days they spent walking have stayed with them long after their memories of the other days have blurred into one.

A longer walk only makes it better. There's something deeply satisfying about walking from one village to the next across the spectacular countryside lying in between. When you set off without your car (if you have one) and the bulk of your luggage, it's not only your "things" you leave behind but also a time frame and the determination to control every aspect of your experience. Walking from town to town, you open yourself up a little more to what chance sends your way, while at the same time allowing yourself an opportunity to really "get away from it all." The physical pleasure of the walk and the anticipation of the good food and drink awaiting you at your destination (not to mention the cultural perks) are deeply relaxing; not only that, but walking allows you to acquire an appetite, which makes eating all the more enjoyable.

Other than remembering to book your restaurants and accommodations ahead of time, the main thing you need to plan for if you decide to do more than a single day's walk is leaving the bulk of your luggage (and your car if you have one) behind. If you're staying in a *gîte* this is of course a moot point. Otherwise, we usually left our luggage wherever we'd been staying before we left on one of our extended walks. In our experience, hotel proprietors were always very accommodating, storing our bags behind the front desk or in a storage closet, free of charge. These are small hotels, family owned, and as such have a very personal face, someone you can talk to. If you've been staying at a *chambre d'hôtes,* you'll probably know the proprietors there even better than you'd know the hotel owner, and here too, they will generally help you as much as they can. Even a *gîte d'étape* should be able to arrange to keep your bags for a few days.

At the end of our walk we'd bus back to the hotel, often staying the night there again, in which case the hotel had become the "base" for our itinerary. Equally, you could bring your bags ahead to where you'll finish the walk, book yourself in for that future night you'll arrive, and ask the hotel to hold your bags until you arrive.

If you have a car, you can make similar arrangements with your hotel, though in some cases it might charge a fee for this. *Chambres d'hôtes* may be more willing to let you leave your car for free, if they have the room, as they don't have the space constraints of town locations. We left our car overnight in the village's public parking lot both in Vaugines and Lourmarin. We first checked with the tourist office in Lourmarin (Vaugines doesn't have a tourist office, but it just seemed obvious that it would be okay to leave the car there overnight). Don't leave anything valuable in your car.

PRIVATE PROPERTY AND REASONABLE ETHICS

Most of our walks—mainly on "official" paths—pass through private property. "How can this be?" you might ask, as in the United States you'd likely be shot for stepping on someone's *private* property.

Welcome to the civilized world. The French and Italians are not inheritors of the brutish American precept of Man's Home Is His Castle; All Others Keep Out. In its place is a less selfishly oriented recognition of balance between individual and community rights: As long as people are respectful—of the property, people, crops, or livestock—why shouldn't they be able to go for a walk? This civilized attitude is ensconced in and supported by a legal structure for grown-ups, which holds the individual, rather than the landowner, responsible for any accidental injury he inflicts on himself, obviously a more reasonable position.

It's a more generous basis for human relations. Bear in mind your side of the responsibility: It *is* someone's property. Specifically, leave gates as you found them (whether open or shut); don't walk through a cultivated field—stick to the path at all times; don't pick the fruits, vegtables, or flowers (including sampling the grapes in a vineyard or picking wildflowers); don't litter (obviously); don't make undue noise; don't light fires. In other words, treat the property as you would want your own property treated, were you generous enough to share it in this way.

Directions

MAPS

The maps in the book supplement the written directions, give an overview of the walk, and are intended to be sufficient. The IGN maps listed in the *Logistics* section of each walk are more detailed and cover a larger area, so if you feel more comfortable having them, or if you like an area and plan to do more walks in it, by all means buy the IGN map. The blue-bordered IGN maps are basically the same as the Geological Survey maps in the United States and the Ordinance Survey maps in the United Kingdom; the 1:25,000-scale maps are the ones most useful for walking. Many walks—all the long-distance GR routes and many of the regional ones—are superimposed on them in red. Each has a name, indicating in a general way the area covered, and a number. They cost about €9 and are available at newsagents and bookstores. They're easy to get hold of in any village.

ESTIMATING DISTANCES

We chose to use metric distances in the book because all the French maps are based on the kilometer, and the grid lines drawn on the maps show kilometers.

- 1 kilometer = .621 miles
- 1 mile = 1.609 kilometers

An easy way to think of it is that a kilometer (km) is about ⅝ of a mile, and a mile is about 1.5 kilometers.

- 1 meter = 39.37 inches
- 1 yard = 36 inches

Therefore, 1 meter = 1 yard, more or less. We estimated our distances in terms of yards and big footsteps, so when we say something is 10 meters away, rest assured it's just as likely to be 10 yards, and most likely of all to be neither, exactly.

But what about when a distance given is 200 meters (yards)? That's not as easy to visualize as 10 meters (yards). You can either go with a rough estimate of 200 yards, or you can think of it as the time it takes you to walk 200 meters.

We're fairly brisk walkers, and on flat ground it takes us about

10 minutes to walk a kilometer. On the other hand, we've noticed a meandering, leisurely pace common with our friends who aren't big walkers. A kilometer can take them 15 minutes. What about you?

When we've given the time it takes to walk a certain distance, such as 200 meters/yards, we've estimated about 12 minutes for a kilometer on flat ground (a pace our kids, ages 7 and 11 at the time, were also comfortable maintaining). These estimated times are only rough guides; interpret them in light of your own walking style, and take into account the type of terrain, flat or steep. Even so, when we give a range of time (e.g., 7–10 minutes), the time it takes you to do that segment could still be outside that range. But if it took you, say, 20 minutes, you might at that point want to consider whether you were still on the correct path.

Once you decide what rough estimate you're going to use as your minutes-per-kilometer pace, you can "visualize" 200 meters as the time it takes you to walk one-fifth kilometer. If it takes you 10 minutes to walk a kilometer, it will take two minutes to walk one-fifth kilometer or 200 meters. Isn't it nice that there are 1,000 meters in a kilometer? The same equation in yards and miles would require you to divide 5,280 by three, and then multiply that by 200. That must be why the rest of the world uses the metric system.

If you feel confused at all about this, here's a handy reference guide until you get the hang of it:

- *@ 10 minutes per kilometer*

   100 meters = 1 minute

   300 meters = 3 minutes

   .5 km = 5 minutes

   800 meters = 8 minutes

- *@ 12 minutes per kilometer*

   100 meters = just over a minute

   300 meters = 3.5 minutes

   .5 km = 6 minutes

   800 meters = 9.5 minutes

- *@15 minutes per kilometer*

   100 meters = 1.5 minutes

   300 meters = 4.5 minutes

   .5 km = 7.5 minutes

   800 meters = 12 minutes

Remember that these estimated times are the time it takes *without stopping*. That means if you stop—to look at a flower, or your map, or the book—it's going to add to the time it takes to complete that particular stretch. This calculation becomes even more significant when applied to the walk duration time we give at the beginning of each walk. If it says "3 hours," it's not going to take you three hours unless you don't stop for anything—which is never really the case. A three-hour walk can easily take all day, between stopping to look at things, taking little breaks, having a picnic…. Moreover, those durations are only the roughest of estimates, and vary by individual walking paces anyway, as discussed above.

Please use our estimated distances suggestively rather than statement of fact. Unless we went back to measure something with the car, which wasn't usually possible, we weren't measuring with anything other than giant steps and our best guesses.

DOING THE WALKS IN REVERSE

This is generally not a great idea, but if you're a good map reader and have the IGN map, and there's some reason you really want to do it the other direction, go for it. The paths are generally very well signed. The written directions won't be of much use to you, though, as turnoffs and landmarks visible in one direction often go unnoticed when approached from the other side.

USING OUR MAPS AND DIRECTIONS
Ignoring Deviations

When you're on the trail and see another track branching off the one you've been following, if we haven't mentioned it specifically, assume that you don't take it. Usually we haven't mentioned these deviations individually in the text, though occasionally we have given the general advice "ignore deviations." On our maps, these other tracks branching off are marked as little "tabs" leading off the main route. We haven't marked every single one, by any means. Therefore, use them only as a general guide, as one piece of information among others. Sometimes we don't mention a fork when both of its prongs meet up again shortly.

T Junctions

When the directions refer to a "T junction," the junction may not conform to an exact "T" and may in some cases even be interpreted loosely as "meeting another path where you have to turn left or right."

At Time of Writing

Things change. Dirt roads are paved, new roads appear that weren't there before, signs or other markers may be taken down—or put up. No one can anticipate all these changes, but please understand that all directions in this book were accurate at the at the time they were written. If "at the time of this writing" actually appears in the text, it indicates a greater sense of fragility concerning the longevity of the landmark or circumstance being mentioned.

Compass Directions

We sometimes give compass directions, and certainly a compass is a great thing to have in conjunction with the IGN maps. However, we didn't assume that everyone would have a compass, and we've written the directions so that anyone can orient him- or herself by the visual landmarks.

Getting out of a Town

Sometimes figuring out how to get out of a town is the most difficult part of the walk, so we've tried to be very detailed about this. Sometimes we've used the GR trail if there is one, but particularly in the larger towns, the GRs sometimes go through rather ugly built-up areas around the town. You can almost welcome this sign of "civilization" when you've been walking long distances through unspoiled, deserted landscapes between towns, but when you're dealing with a day's ring walk from a town…we tried to do better when the possibility existed.

What Is a *Lavoir?*

All the old villages have a large stone basin that once served as the village's public laundry. It's usually at least somewhat centrally situated and connected to a fountain that still provides drinking water through a spigot. Oddly, though there must be some reason for it, in a land as dry as Provence the spigots are always on and the water is always running. In any case, the *lavoirs* make excellent landmarks, and we use them all through the book.

UPDATING AND OUR WEBSITE

We have done our best to make this guide as accurate as possible, but it is in the nature of places described in a book such as this to be in a constant state of flux. Dirt tracks become paved roads, meadows find gainful employment as vineyards, the village reroutes a local PR trail, restaurants slide downhill, go out of business, or are made redundant by a new competitor.

In the first eight years after the original edition of our *Walking and Eating in Tuscany and Umbria* book was published, many people wrote to us about things that had changed, or to ask if we had any updates to pass on to them before they left on their trip. Some suggested a website for posting these updates, and so was born **www.walkingandeating.com.**

Now this book will be part of the site as well. We hope it will be useful and help keep the book current, and we are deeply grateful when anyone takes the time to pass information on to us. While updates on the walk directions are the most important pieces of information, we also greatly appreciate any feedback on our restaurant or lodging recommendations, discoveries of your own, or just anecdotes about your experiences.

The Walks

Classic Provence: The Lubéron Mountains

In many people's minds (our own included at one time), Provence consists of the Riviera, a few historic towns such as Avignon and Aix, and the Lubéron mountains. The latter is where you come to experience the authentic flavors of *rural* Provence: the small-scale vineyards, the hunting and foraging cuisine of boar, rabbit, mushrooms, and myrtles, the whimsical old drystone shepherd's shelters known as *bories,* the picturesque villages made famous by Peter Mayle, the mountain landscape aromatic with the classic *garrigue* of wild rosemary, thyme, and juniper. . . .

As it happens the Lubéron is indeed an area of great charm. And even though its enormous popularity has led to some serious overcrowding during the high season (July and August), with visitors clogging the small roads and some regrettable suburban sprawl around many of the prettier villages, there are still very few people around in spring, which is good news for walkers. Its reputation, in other words, is deserved: Just remember that there are other, equally attractive regions too.

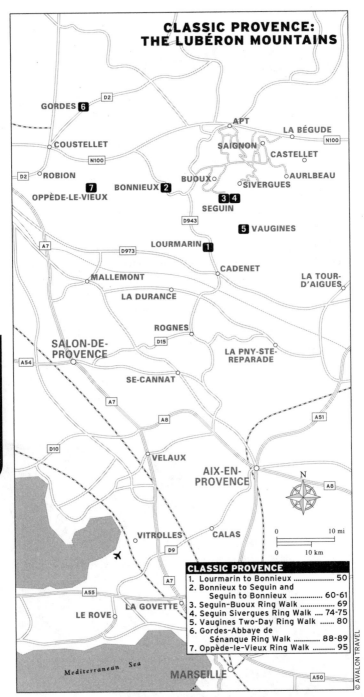

CLASSIC PROVENCE: THE LUBÉRON MOUNTAINS

GORDES **6**   D2

APT

LA BÉGUDE   N100

COUSTELLET   N100   SAIGNON

CASTELLET

D2   ROBION   BONNIEUX **2**   BUOUX   AURLBEAU

OPPÈDE-LE-VIEUX **7**   SIVERGUES

3 4

SEGUIN

D943   **5** VAUGINES

A7   D973   LOURMARIN **1**

CADENET

MALLEMONT   LA TOUR-D'AIGUES

LA DURANCE

ROGNES

SALON-DE-PROVENCE   D15

LA PNY-STE-REPARADE

A54

SE-CANNAT

A7

A8

A51

D10

VELAUX

AIX-EN-PROVENCE

N   A8

0   10 mi

VITROLLES   CALAS   0   10 km

D9

A7

CLASSIC PROVENCE

A55

LE ROVE   LA GOVETTE

Mediterranean Sea   MARSEILLE   A50

THE LUBÉRON MOUNTAINS

© AVALON TRAVEL

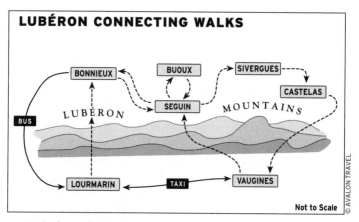

LUBÉRON CONNECTING WALKS

BONNIEUX — BUOUX — SIVERGUES — CASTELAS

LUBÉRON — SEGUIN — MOUNTAINS

BUS

LOURMARIN — TAXI — VAUGINES

© AVALON TRAVEL

Not to Scale

Aside from the highest summit, Mourre Negre, which has been scandalously disfigured by transmission towers, the mountains themselves have been generally well protected from development. Numerous hiking and riding trails crisscross the varied landscape of olive groves, sheep pastures, forests, and towering cliffs. You can cross the whole range from north to south in a day's march, an exhilarating but manageable adventure that we've incorporated into a couple of our itineraries.

We've tried to find walks from the least-built-up villages on each side. These aren't always the most famous, though Vaugines and Lourmarin on the south, and Bonnieux on the north, are generally (and rightly) considered essential viewing. We've also made good use of a less-well-known place on the north side, near Buoux, called Seguin. There's a stunningly situated inn here (and nothing else), set on the idyllic Aiguebrun stream, under spectacular cliffs. There's *gîte d'étape* dormitory accomodation here as well as private rooms. You should make reservations if you plan to stay, but don't despair if it's full as there are other places to stay on all the walks in which we've incorporated it.

In terms of history and culture, the highlights in this chapter are the magnificent Romanesque Abbey of Sénanque near Gordes, and the ancient Fort of Buoux, a dramatic cliff-top refuge with fortifications dating from prehistoric times to the 17th century.

WINE NOTES

The Lubéron has its own AOC, Côtes du Lubéron, so this is one good opportunity to drink the "local." The wines are

THE LUBÉRON MOUNTAINS

perhaps best enjoyed for that very quality—their localness. Easy to drink, inexpensive, and ubiquitous while you dwell in their midst, they never rise to the level of, say, those locals of the Dentelles chapter. While the vineyards, which encircle the Lubéron mountains, are sometimes iconically picturesque—the quintessential, timeless Provençal idyll—their gravel-over-sand terroir produces reds that tend to the slightly thin and tangy, though the whites are possibly more promising.

There are certainly good bottles to be had. While in Lourmarin, check out the Tardieu-Laurent Lubéron, made in conjunction with La Cave à Lourmarin (see *Logistics* under *Walk 1* for more information). If you visit the Tardieu-Laurent cellars just outside Lourmarin, you might enjoy comparing the Lubéron with some other localish wines, such as the Côtes du Rhône Vieilles Vignes (from outside Châteauneuf) and the Vacqueyras Vieilles Vignes, a local in the Dentelles chapter.

Of the less expensive local wines, we can recommend those of Château La Canorgue. You'll find these on most restaurant wine lists in this area, or make a trip to the château to buy them directly. The château was used as the location for Ridley Scott's *A Good Year,* the movie version of Peter Mayle's *A Year in Provence.* More important, the wines of La Canorgue are delicious and organically—in some measure biodynamically—grown for 20 years. We found its straight Château La Canorgue wines (its AOC Côtes du Lubéron) preferable to its other selections. La Canorgue's south-facing slopes are warmer than many others in the Lubéron, and the reds especially are one of the best structured and most articulate of the AOC.

The Constantin-Chevalier wines are also very good (we slightly preferred its white to Canorgue's) and are another popular item on local wine lists. Its château is just outside the village of Lourmarin. (See *Logistics* in *Walk 1* for further contact information.)

To buy a wider range of wines, visit the Cave du Septier in Apt (see *Walk 21, Viens Ring Walk* in the *Banon and the Lure* chapter).

HOW TO USE THE BUS WEBSITE

- Go to www.vaucluse.fr.
- In the search box enter "bus."
- Click on "Réseau Départemental."

- Scroll down to the heading "Quels trajets?" Here you can get a bus route map of the entire region and/or find a list of all the bus routes serving a particular town.

- To see the bus route map: Click on the "Télécharger le plan du réseau de transport interurbain" link.

- To find a list of all the bus routes serving a particular town: Click on the "Rechercher votre trajet interurbain" link. Scroll down to the bottom where it says "Choisissez votre commune" and enter the town name for which you're seeking bus information, and then click "rechercher." Scroll down the page and find all the routes that go through the town you've selected, and when you find the one you want, click on its "voir le fichier" link to see the current schedule.

Another way of getting bus info is by googling "[town name] bus info." Bear in mind that consulting the local tourist office is often the easiest way of finding bus information.

1 Lourmarin to Bonnieux

4 Hours

This is a great day walk across the mountains, connecting two of the most appealing villages in the region. Lourmarin, with its tiny alleys and grand château (where Camus is buried), has a lively market on Fridays. Bonnieux, even prettier (once you get past the modern sprawl below it) has stunning views overlooking both the mountains and the plain below.

A steep but nicely shaded ascent leads to the crests above Lourmarin with increasingly impressive views opening across the Durance valley behind you. Wild rosemary and thyme abound. As you come out of the woods for the final climb to the Cap de Serre, the lack of shade is made up for by the sudden sight of the north side of the Lubéron, a rugged, magnificent landscape, grayish green in spring, with tiny blue hyacinths and the pink clustered florets of rock sanfoin blossoming along the path. To the northwest you'll see the Tour Philippe, a stone tower put up—so the story goes—by a man who fell in love with the wife of a mason, commissioning the husband to build the tower to keep him out of the way and demanding an additional story every time the poor builder thought he was finished.

After a steep downhill scramble, the descent becomes

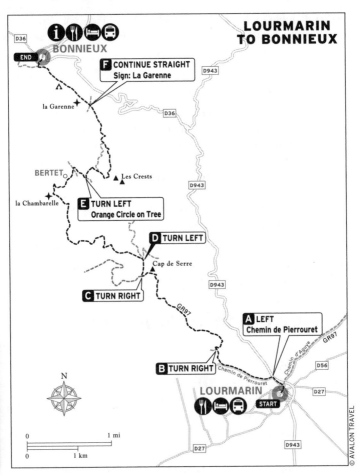

pleasantly gentle, following old farm trails and then entering a rather melancholy wood of thin holm oaks hung with lichen and full of ruined *bories* and overgrown stone terraces. Like the departure from Lourmarin, the entrance to Bonnieux, poised stunningly on its hilltop, is remarkably free of the semiurban clutter that can sometimes spoil one's arrival at even the loveliest of villages.

LOURMARIN FOOD

Several restaurants are in and around this popular village, including one with a Michelin star just a short car ride away, **Auberge la Feniére.** It's a somewhat flossy, fussy establishment (lots of hovering, overdressed waiters) with expensive food, much of which sounded more interesting than it tasted. We were overcharged hugely on our bill; the mistake was profusely apologized for, but it didn't endear the place to us. Part of the La Feniére enterprise, housed in a separate building on the property, is its bistro **La Cour de Ferme.** With *menus* at €35 and a warmer, more relaxed atmosphere, this might be worth checking out, but in the end we felt unable to recommend the main restaurant.

Despite its many restaurants, the village itself proved not to be, for us at least, a culinary high point. Of those restaurants we tried—and we tried several, though not all—none was without its drawbacks. The one we liked best was **La Récréation,** which claims to serve organic food, though there was some doubt as to whether this applied to the whole *menu* or just selected items. It's a *salon de thé* and *créperie* as well as a restaurant and its strong points are its desserts: a towering peach melba with homemade ice cream, an excellent pear crumble. The rest of the food is hit and miss: an impressive-looking but tasteless *tian* of eggplant; a beautifully tender, aromatic dish of slow-cooked lamb. Other items include omelettes and a *magret de canard* with honey and lavender. It's a pleasant place, very popular among the local Anglos, moderately priced with *menus* at €23 and €29, or main courses à la carte from around €16.

If you're just out for a snack, **Le Pan Garni,** just opened by a sweet, very young couple when we were there, does light snacks and takeaways and very nice ice cream.

BONNIEUX FOOD

Like Lourmarin, Bonnieux has more than its share of gourmet (and allegedly gourmet) restaurants. Our own recommendation is **le Fournil,** a serious eatery built into a cliff grotto. Set off against the raw rock face that provides its walls and ceiling, its gleaming touches of chrome and glass (not to mention the laboratory-like tableware) lend the place an interestingly hybrid atmosphere of the prehistoric and the ultramodern. And given a certain technical emphasis in the cooking itself—heavy on foams and ices and other refined preparations—you might be forgiven for thinking you're participating in some strange clinical experiment as you eat here. But it's a very pleasant experiment: The sophistication is generally in the service of the food itself, not just to bedazzle the diner. After a dubious *amuse-*

bouche comprising a warm chestnut drink thickened with foie gras (it tasted like the English bedtime malt drink, Horlicks), we had an extraordinary cold "cappuccino" of asparagus and goat cheese; an interesting bitter caramel-flavored soup built around a *tartare* of *coquilles St-Jacques;* a substantial and excellent dish of roast kid (along with its liver) accompanied by a pimento-flavored "foam," and a turbot with artichoke hearts and more asparagus. The fish was fine but lacked the vivid freshness of seafood eaten at the ocean, and it confirmed our suspicion that saltwater creatures are best avoided in the mountains. The cheese plate included a sensational little roquefort "ice cream." A vegetarian dish—not on the menu but obligingly improvised in the kitchen—had lovely light galettes of chickpea filled with spinach and a very tasty sweet-savory preparation of salsify. Desserts, equally thoughtful and creative, included a lemon-cream timbale as well as excellent homemade sorbets and ice creams. You can eat from a set *menu* of around €40 or à la carte with main courses running around €21.

It was here that we were introduced to the peach-wine aperitif Rinquinquin—a perfect drink for a hot day—and here that we tasted our first bottle of Château La Canorgue, an organic vineyard just outside the village that uses syrah and other local grape varieties to produce fine, clean, focused wines (both the red and the white—less so the rosé) that became our favorite Lubérons.

WINE NOTES

We bought various bottles of wine recommended by a salesperson at **La Cave à Lourmarin,** in the village of Lourmarin, and weren't very favorably impressed. However, we didn't know at the time that the cave is producing a Côtes du Lubéron in conjunction with **Tardieu-Laurent;** this would be worth a try. Tardieu-Laurent is a *négociant* firm; it doesn't actually own any land, but it buys the juice from other winemakers and "brings it up." This it does very attentively, using very low amounts of sulphur (comparatively), leaving the wines on their lees for an extended period, and ultimately hand bottling the wines without fining or filtration. New oak is a mainstay here, but not to the extent of overpowering the grapes. Originally a partnership between Dominique Laurent, a famous Burgundy *négociant,* and Michel Tardieu, a young, ambitious winemaker, the operation is now completely in the hands of Tardieu. If you like the wines of Tardieu-Laurent, and your pockets are deep, its cellars are just outside Lourmarin. There you could also pick up the Côtes du Rhône and Vacqueyras mentioned in the chapter introduction, as well as other wines from all over the Rhône area.

LOGISTICS

If you're doing this point A to point B walk as a day walk (as opposed to a multiday walk connecting to others in this chapter), you'll have to consider how you'll get back to Lourmarin from Bonnieux (or, if you're based in Bonnieux, how to get to Lourmarin to start the walk). Unless you have two cars (to leave one at each end of the walk), you can either take a bus or a taxi, or walk back the next day. (See *Transportation*.)

This walk is a bit longer than our average, and though it's not particularly difficult, you *are* going to climb that mountain range! There is some fairly steep and prolonged climbing. That said, our kids, 7 and 11 at the time, did it with no problem. Make sure you have sturdy shoes.

IGN Map Number and Name
#3243 OT—Pertuis/Lourmarin

Tourist Information
Lourmarin:
  Address: Avenue Philippe de Girard
  Phone: 0490/ 68 10 77
  Website or Email: www.lourmarin.com
  Hours: 9:30–13:00 and 15:00–19:00 Mon.–Sat., 9:30–12:00 Sun.
Bonnieux:
  Address: 7, place Carnot
  Phone: 0490/ 75 91 90
  Website or Email: www.tourisme.fr/tourist-office/bonnieux. htm or www.holidays-in-lubéron.com
  Hours: 9:30–12:30 and 14:00–18:00 Mon.–Sat.

Restaurants
Lourmarin:
  Name: Auberge la Feniére

Address: Route de Cadanet
Phone: 0490/ 68 11 79
Closing Day: All day Mon. and lunch Tues.
Notes: The bistro, La Cour de Ferme, is open evenings Fri.
and Sat. and lunch Sun.
Name: La Récréation
Address: 15, rue Philippe de Girard
Phone: 0490/ 68 23 73
Closing Day: Tues. and Wed. out of season, open every day in
season
Name: Le Pan Garni (snack bar)
Address: Place du Temple
Phone: 0490/ 68 84 43
Bonnieux:
Name: Le Fournil
Address: 5, place Carnot
Phone: 0490/ 75 83 62
Closing Day: Lunch Tues., Mon. and Tues. out of season,
lunch Sat. in summer, closed in winter

Accommodations

Both Lourmarin and Bonnieux have many *chambres d'hôtes* in
addition to their hotels. For additional listings see the tourist of-
fice websites.
Lourmarin:
Name: Le Four à Chaux
Address: 300 meters outside the village, on the D943 toward
Apt/Bonnieux
Phone: 0490/ 68 24 28
Website or Email: www.le-four-a-chaux.com
Type of Lodging: *Gîte d'étape*
Price: €12–28, plus €2 "membership" fee
Notes: Two *dortoirs* of seven and eight people each, plus one
double room with a crib or extra bed are available. English
spoken.
Bonnieux:
Name: La Flambée
Address: Place du 4 Septembre
Phone: 0490/ 75 82 20
Website or Email: jacques.clerici@wanadoo.fr

Type of Lodging: Small hotel (five rooms)/pizzeria
Price: €38–50 per room, extra bed €8, breakfast €5
Notes: Though it doesn't have a website, you can google "la flambee, bonnieux" and see photos.
Name: Le Cesar
Address: Place de la Liberté
Phone: 0490/ 75 96 35
Website or Email: www.hôtel-cesar.com
Type of Lodging: Logis de France hotel
Price: €38–75 per room

Transportation

Between Lourmarin and Bonnieux
  Name: Autocars de Haute Provence
  Phone: 0491/ 49 44 25
  Website or Email: See How to Use the Bus Website section.
  Route Name/Number: Apt–Marseille, #24
  Frequency and Duration: Two per day in each direction, one in the early morning, one in the early evening; 20-minute ride

Miscellaneous Notes

Lourmarin has a good Friday morning market. Market day in Bonnieux is also Friday morning.

You can leave your car for several nights in the public parking lot in Lourmarin, but don't leave anything worth stealing in it.

  La Cave à Lourmarin: 0490/ 68 02 18

  Château La Canorgue: 0490/ 75 81 01; hours are 9:00–19:00 except 9:00–12:00 and 14:00–19:00 Sat. in summer, 9:00–12:00 and 14:30–17:30 in winter, closed Sun. and holidays. From Bonnieux take the road north signed for Pont Julien and watch for the château's signs.

  Château Constantin-Chevalier: 0490/ 68 38 99, www .constantin-chevalier.fr; directions to the château are on the website.

  Tardieu-Laurent: 0490/ 68 80 25, www.tardieu-laurent. com; Les Grandes Bastides, route de Cucuron (i.e., the D27 going in the direction of Cucuron); hours are 8:00–12:00 and 13:30–17:30 Mon.–Thurs., 8:00–12:00 and 13:30–16:30 Fri.

WALK DIRECTIONS

Leaving Lourmarin from the front of the post office, across the street from a playground and a playing field, follow the road (avenue Philippe de Girard) away from town. Walk down toward the intersection where this road meets the larger road (D943). There's a parking lot on your left, and the larger road goes right signed Autres Directions and straight ahead signed to Bonnieux and Apt. Carry on straight ahead (northwest) along the edge of the parking lot. Where the lot ends there's a little road, Chemin de Pierrouret, to the left: Take that Ⓐ. It's well blazed, and there's a way mark, "Chemin de Pierrouret."

Follow this little road for about 15 minutes (1.2 km), and you'll see a way mark on your left, "Pierrouret" (signed to Bonnieux at 11.3 km), and a "right-turn" blaze on a tree on the right side of the road. Leave the road here for the footpath on your right—not the farm track running up along the vineyard, but rather the narrow footpath through trees just to the left of that. You'll see more blazes on the trees as soon as you're on the footpath.

In about five minutes you'll come to a T junction Ⓑ. There's a "right-hand turn" blaze showing you which way to go here, and were you to turn left instead, you'd find the "wrong-way" blaze on a rock. As on most of the GR trails, the signing on this route is very reliable…except when it isn't. Sometimes the signs abandon you at important junctures.

After making the right turn, follow the trail as marked.

About 45 minutes later, trees have given way to shorter scrub; ignore a deviation where the real path bends left. It's marked with a "left-turn" blaze on a tree before the intersection, and a "wrong-way" blaze on a rock if you go the wrong way. A minute later as you reach the top of this hill, the path bends right (you'll see a "right-turn" blaze on a rock).

Keep following the path as marked and in about 20 minutes you'll reach the summit, Cap de Serre. Confirm where you are now (as your next direction depends on it): At this summit, if you go left off the trail, on a little minipath that goes through the scrub straight to the left off the path for about five meters, you'll find a stone marker, about two feet tall, with a "70" carved on it. It's in a tiny clearing at the highest point. There are other minipaths off the main path here too that circle around this summit area, but if you look for that highest spot, you'll find the stone. The stone isn't visible from the main path.

Once you find it, get back on the main path and continue in the direction you were going. Across the valley you can see an isolated tower on a hill, Tour Philippe. Be aware here: Now you have a gentle descent on a nice wide path along the saddle between the summit you just passed and the next hilltop straight ahead. It takes only a minute for the path to bottom out, and there's a blaze on a tree to the left of the path here on the flat.

About 30 paces from the tree, watch for a narrow path striking out to the right; there was a big pile of stone on the left side of the path, across from the right-hand turn. Take this turn **C**.

After a steep descent of about five minutes, you'll intersect a wider path. Continue straight ahead on the downhill narrow path.

Another three- to five-minute descent brings you to a confluence of wider paths, with a way mark, "Vallon des Bourras," in the northeast corner of the junction. There are paths right, left. and straight on. Turn left here **D**.

It's a nice trail here: wide and flat. Another 5–10 minutes later ignore a deviation coming in from the left.

In another 20 minutes or so the path comes to a very short strip of asphalt and a concrete water cistern for fire fighting. About 15 minutes further on you'll pass a beautiful old stone farmhouse (la Chambarelle) with an ugly new addition.

Past the house 15–20 minutes, another similar track joins ours from the right, at what seems to be the end of Chambarelle's driveway. There's a way mark here, "Bertet." Follow the direction to Bonnieux; that is, stay on the main path.

In another minute, where a gravel track comes in from the right ("Les Crests" on a huge boulder in this driveway), you come to another way mark, "Les Crests." Leave the asphalt road here and turn right onto the little footpath, signed on the way mark to Bonnieux.

Pay attention as you begin this footpath, as in about three minutes there's a fork off to the left **E**, which is the correct way to go, but it could be easy to miss if you weren't looking. The blazes on this footpath are primarily an orange circle, and there are also occasional yellow horizontal stripes. At this left forking, there's an orange circle blaze on a tree on the left fork, and an orange "X" on a tree on the right fork, so you'll know to turn left.

Note: The paths here have been modified to accommodate new properties and no longer follow exactly the routes as marked on the IGN map; nonetheless, the paths as marked are easy to follow, as they're well-blazed. We've done our best to indicate the trajectory of the new route on our map, but at these points the verbal directions are—as always—crucial.

Follow the path through scrub forest, blazed with orange circles. There are many *borie* ruins along the route.

In another 3–5 minutes there's another path going off to the left, also marked with orange circles. Continue straight ahead here.

Follow the footpath, which is straightforward from here and well-blazed.

When the footpath ends at a gravel track 15–20 minutes past ❸ (there are two posts here with yellow arrows on them, one at the path end and one on the side of the gravel track), bear left and stay on this gravel track, ignoring deviations.

In about five minutes you'll come to deviations both right and left, the left one being the driveway to "Cabannes." Continue downhill about 10 meters past the Cabannes driveway and take the fork off to the right and ahead (not the lesser fork to the right and behind) rather than going straight on, which is a driveway with the signs Attention au Chien and Propriété Privée. The track is still signed with orange circles and yellow stripes.

The path is flanked by stone walls, soon emerges on a stone outcrop, and then climbs. Stay on the path until, in about 10 minutes, it comes out on a small tarmacked road ❻.

Cross the road to the way mark "La Garenne." There are two choices of path here, straight ahead or off to the right; take the larger path, straight ahead.

In about two minutes there's a blaze on a phone pole on your right. Just before a stone wall on the right, take the smaller footpath downhill and to the right.

In about 10 more minutes you pass a campground on your left, and five minutes later you emerge onto the road at a stop sign at the campground's entrance and a way mark, "St. Gervais."

Turn right here and follow the road up to Bonnieux, passing a playground on your left. Just beyond the playground a low stone wall begins on your left, and just beyond the start of this wall you'll see stairs going up to town: Take these.

At the top follow the road up for about 20 meters to the next set of steps on your left.

At the top of that flight, bend left and come to more steps on your right. Arriving there, you could keep going up through the archway, or turn left here, past the Hôtel-Restaurant Cesar for the bus, across from the Brasserie Les Terrasses.

2 Bonnieux to Seguin and Seguin to Bonnieux

2 Hours Each Way

This is offered primarily as a way for people who've done the Lourmarin to Bonnieux walk to get to Seguin to do more walking from this spectacular spot, possibly all the way to Vaugines (which is a quick bus hop back to Lourmarin). It's also for people who've done the Vaugines to Seguin walk and want to walk to Bonnieux (where you can get a bus back to the south side of the Lubéron).

That said, it's a pleasant enough walk in itself. As you leave Bonnieux there's a certain amount of fairly benign asphalt to negotiate, but after that you're in quiet, wild country for a long stretch, much of it semi-abandoned farmland reverting to the local *garrigue* (scrub). Halfway along (named on the IGN map as "la Tour") you pass a noted local hotel/restaurant, **Auberge de l'Aiguebrun,** which is said to be good, though it's expensive. Some pleasant, open country follows, with glimpses of the superb Romanesque bell tower of the St-Symphorien priory (a private school now, not open to the public). For the last kilometer or so you can take the shady trail along the murmuring Aiguebrun River or (a little easier) go straight in along the quiet road.

AUBERGE DES SEGUINS

This is a splendid old inn, magnificently set below a monumental curtain of sheer, smooth cliffs at the northern edge of the Lubéron, on the only year-round river in these mountains, the Aiguebrun (old Provençal for "murmuring water"). The cliffs have made the place a mecca for climbers. It's also a walker's

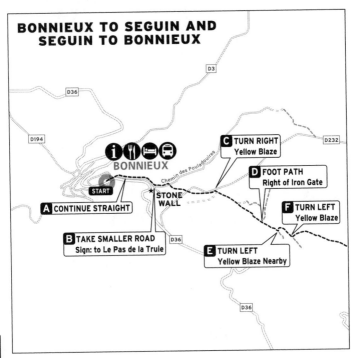

paradise, with marked trails leading through gorges, up stone-terraced valleys, and along high plateaus planted with lavender and olives. The extraordinary ruins of the prehistoric Fort de Buoux are nearby, as are the villages of Buoux itself and Siver-gues, both of which offer modest accommodation if you prefer to base yourself there (though like Seguin, neither of those hamlets has anything so much as a shop).

The auberge is part hotel, with individual rooms (some with part of the rock face serving as a wall), part *gîte d'étape*, with a *dortoir* with 21 places, and a large swimming pool. The restaurant is unpretentious and rustic, with *menus* at €27 and €37 featuring an excellent hearty, olive-flavored daube, a good *estoufado d'agneau* (stuffed lamb) in a sauce of olives and on-ions, and very fresh—if rather small—river trout. Vegetable dishes include gratins of asparagus and zucchini (asparagus in Provence is wonderfully intense in flavor and stands this kind of treatment far better than its English or American coun-terpart). There's a mixed (in every sense) Provençal appetizer with local terrine, chickpeas, and cumin, so-so mushrooms

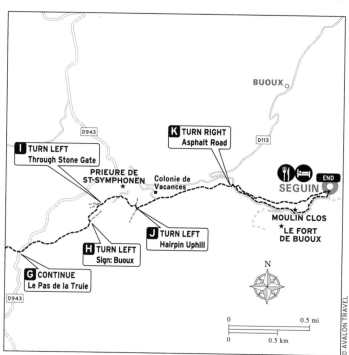

and other seasonal specialties, and several tasty desserts, including a deliciously sweet *clafoutis de poire* (a moist pear cake). All the dishes are available à la carte, with main courses at around €18.

LOGISTICS

Note that the Auberge des Seguins is the only sign of civilization at Seguin. There's no store, no other restaurant. There's no tourist office either, but the manager at Auberge des Seguins is very knowledgeable about the area and speaks English.

IGN Map Number and Name

#3243 OT—Pertuis/Lourmarin

Tourist Information

For Bonnieux listings see Walk 1.

Restaurants

Name: L'Auberge des Seguins

Address: Seguin
Phone: 0490/ 74 19 89 (restaurant)
Name: Auberge de l'Aiguebrun
Address: D943, about midway along this walk route
Phone: 0490/ 04 47 00
Website or Email: www.aubergedelaiguebrun.fr

Accommodations

Name: L'Auberge des Seguins
Address: Seguin
Phone: 0490/ 74 16 37 (hotel)
Website or Email: www.lesSeguins.com
Type of Lodging: Logis de France hotel with separate *dortoir*
Price: Hotel: demipension €50–65 per person; full pension
€73–88 per person; children ages 3–6 half price; supplement for
single occupancy €15; in the *gîte d'étape dortoir:* €36 demipension

Transportation

There is no public transport available to Seguin.

WALK DIRECTIONS

Note: Since the section between **F** and **G** is new, and not on
the IGN map, our mapping of it is necessarily approximate. We
haven't shown any of the intersections, but it's a short section
and the written directions will suffice.

Bonnieux to Seguin

With your back to the Hôtel-Restaurant Cesar, turn right and
follow the road (rue République), passing the fountain carved
with two fish on your left in less than a minute, and about 30
meters/yards beyond on the left is a stairway: Take that.

Follow this cobbled road, in a couple of minutes passing
under a stone arch at the end of the town, at which point the
road surface becomes asphalt. Continue, ignoring a downhill
right fork about 40 meters past the arch, and beyond there walking with a low stone wall on your right. At the end of the stone
wall (about two minutes past the arch), there's an iron cross
in a stone base on your left, and the road forks **A**, continuing
straight or making a hairpin right downhill. Continue straight,
passing a way mark on your left, "Aire des Croix."

Follow this road for about 350 meters (3–5 minutes), until the road forks at a stone wall; bear left onto Chemin des Poudadouires.

In 150 meters or so, you'll come to a way mark, "Les Blayons," where a gravel road turns right off our small asphalt road. Take this gravel road, signed Les Cabanes.

In another few minutes the gravel road comes to a T junction **B** with an asphalt road. Cross the asphalt road and take the smaller asphalt road, by the way mark "Les Cabanes," signed to Le Pas de la Truie.

The asphalt immediately becomes a dirt track, following between two stone walls. In 1–2 minutes the track ends at a house; bear right onto a narrow dirt footpath.

In another 1–2 minutes this footpath comes out to the asphalt road again, and just ahead of you (less than 10 meters), you'll see a smaller asphalt road to the right with a yellow right-turn blaze on a street sign, Chemin du Pas de la Truie. Take this **C**. Ignore a right-hand turn about 25 meters along, where the asphalt ends and the road becomes gravel.

Stay on this road (blazed yellow all along), ignoring all turn-offs, for just more than half a kilometer (6–8 minutes), until it ends at a stone wall with an iron gate **D**. The road makes a left turn here, becoming smaller, but don't go this way; instead take the footpath to the right of the iron-gated driveway.

Follow the yellow blazes along this trail; when you reach a T junction in about four minutes, turn left **E** (yellow blaze nearby).

Be alert here: When you come to a blaze on a rock on the ground, about 37 paces farther on, you'll see a left-hand-turn blaze on a tree to the left of the path. Ten paces farther on is a very small (easy to miss) footpath on your left, heading up to a stone wall and turning right to travel parallel to it **F**. There's a yellow blaze on a tree here. (If you have trouble finding this footpath, another way of looking for it is to count about 155 regular walking paces (or one minute and 40 seconds) from **E**, and you'll see it there on your left.)

The footpath is well blazed in yellow along here (it's a new footpath, not the one shown on the IGN map). In 2–3 minutes the footpath comes out at a dirt and rock track. Turn right on it and then immediately (about seven meters) left onto a farm track (there's a blaze on the left a few meters in).

Again be alert: In less than a minute, watch for a yellow right-hand-turn blaze on a rock on the ground: Six meters farther on, take the footpath bearing off to the right (a yellow blaze on a tree at the entrance).

Stay on this narrow dirt footpath, following blazes and traveling parallel to a stone wall on your left. In a minute or so the footpath crosses over a gravel driveway/road. About three minutes past that gravel driveway, there will be a taller stone wall paralleling you on your right, and the path becomes more rocky. About 10 minutes later, you'll come out at the asphalt road (D943) by a way mark, "Le Pas de la Truie."

From ⓖ you can see the entrance of the Auberge de l'Aiguebrun across the road about 40 meters to the left. Head for that and take its road downhill to the auberge, reached in another 4–5 minutes.

Continue on the road in front of the auberge, passing it on your right. The road almost immediately turns into a gravel track at a huge rock. Follow this path (first passing to the right of a field and then entering a little wooded stretch) for 5–7 minutes: Watch for a turnoff to the left (a left-hand-turn blaze in yellow on a tree to your right, then yellow blazes on stones to the left of the path, and a blue-painted and misspelled ("Bioux") Buoux. Take this left ⓗ.

Stay on this main path for 5–10 minutes, until the path ends (near a multicenturian oak) at a T junction with a gravel road ⓘ. There's a stone entranceway to your left. Turn left here, passing through the stone gate, and then immediately on the other side of the stone gate take the narrow track to your right downhill, signed on a tree to Fort de Buoux and Seguin.

Follow this path downhill, coming to a rustic wood bridge over the Aiguebrun. Continue on the other side, staying on the main path.

In 2–3 minutes the path comes out on a bigger gravel road that is making a hairpin turn; turn right uphill on this. This path makes a right bend, and about 20 meters after the bend, watch for a hairpin left-hand turn off this track and take it ⓙ uphill.

In a minute or less the path forks—both ways meet up in 100 meters or so, but take the right side to give larger clearance to the Colonie de Vacances below. Stay on this path and don't take any paths off it, as this is private property belonging to the *colonie* down on the left; please be considerate and respectful. In about 15 minutes it ends at an asphalt road ⓚ.

Turn right on this road, and in about 15 meters bear left off it, downhill into a parking area. (You also have the option of taking the road here all the way to Seguin. The footpath is shadier, but unless it's very hot, you may want to take the road back to Seguin here; it's easier and just as nice in its own way.) Cross the lower of the two lots, taking the footpath that leads out the far end of it into the woods, with the Aiguebrun below you on your left.

When path forks at a stone building in a minute, bear left. Follow the path along the stream, until a few minutes later it crosses the stream. Cross over and bear right on the other side, again paralleling the stream (now on your right).

Soon the path forks at a boulder with a steep right downhill to the stream, but you continue straight, passing around to the left of the boulder. You're now walking some way above the stream, still paralleling it, and always in a generally eastern direction. Keep generally forward and level (don't take trails leading uphill to the left) and parallel the stream.

About five minutes later, you'll catch a glimpse of a bridge below you and some buildings beyond that on the other side of the stream, and 5–10 minutes later you pass horse stalls on your left and arrive at Seguin just after.

Seguin to Bonnieux

Note: Since the section between ⓕ and ⓖ is new, and not on the IGN map, our mapping of it is necessarily approximate. We haven't shown any of the intersections, but it's a short section and the written directions will suffice.

The letters are in reverse going in this direction.

Leaving the Auberge des Seguins, go out their driveway and bear right on the gravel road that is also the car road (red and yellow blaze on the right).

About 10 minutes out of Seguin, you'll come to a way mark, "Moulin Clos," and the turnoff to the Fort du Buoux, both on your left. Stay on the road here, ignoring the yellow and red "X" on the telephone pole ahead.

In five minutes or so, watch for a parking area below you on the right. When you pass the entranceway to this parking area, watch in another 10 meters/yards for a path on the left, just before the road bends right and crosses the river. Take this path on the left **K** (with a little white Colonie de Vacances sign on the left of its entrance).

Follow this path with the Aiguebrun to your right, staying on the main path and not taking any of the smaller paths down to the river (remember this is private property; please be considerate and respect the owners' privacy).

In about 10 minutes you'll pass an oak with a light-blue blaze and a dark-blue "+" blaze, and about five minutes later note a wide grassy right turn down to the *colonie de vacances*. Carry on straight, and in a minute or less the path forks, with a bigger branch downhill right and a narrower path on the left (these two paths meet, but we want to give as much clearance as possible to the *colonie*); take the narrower left path. Stay forward-bound on this, ignoring a left-hand turn off it in less than a minute.

A few minutes past the narrow fork, the path comes to a T junction with a similar-size path **J**: Turn right here.

The path first bends left and then makes a hairpin right: Leave the track here, taking a smaller path on the left, with a little blue One Way sign nailed high up the trunk of an oak tree at this path's entrance.

Follow this path as it winds downhill and comes to a rustic wooden bridge over the Aiguebrun in about 100 meters.

Cross the bridge and follow the path uphill for another minute or two, when it comes out on a T junction with a gravel road with a stone entranceway on your left. Turn left here, immediately leave the gravel road, and take the uphill path to the right **I**, with a multicenturian oak on your right, and signed to Lourmarin and Bonnieux and with a yellow blaze on a rock.

In a couple of minutes, you'll come to an intersection with a small footpath to the right (signed to Bonnieux), a double-rutted track ahead, and the continuation of the path you're on to the left: Take this left.

Follow this path for about five minutes, and just past a field you'll come to a T junction with another little path (but just before reaching the T junction you can see the tower of the Prieuré St-Symphorien). Turn right at the T junction **H**.

Follow this path for about five minutes more, when you'll arrive at the Auberge de l'Aiguebrun.

Just past the entrance to the restaurant the road forks at a way mark, "La Tour." Take the right uphill branch, signed to Bonnieux. Continue uphill, reaching the asphalt road (D943) in 4–5 minutes.

Turn left and walk down the road about 40 meters; you'll see the way mark "Le Pas de la Truie" across the road **G**. Cross over and take the footpath uphill, signed to Bonnieux.

Follow this footpath (well blazed in yellow). After 5–10 minutes it levels out as it travels along between two old stone walls.

About 10–15 minutes past **G** the path comes out of the woods and bends right, paralleling a gravel road (on your left after you make the right bend). All is well blazed.

In another minute or two the path crosses over that gravel road, continuing on the other side (yellow blaze).

In another minute or two the footpath comes out at a wider dirt track: Turn left on it.

In under a minute this track ends at a big rock outcrop at ground level. Turn right and then immediately left on another narrow dirt footpath (yellow blaze on a tree at the entrance).

Follow the footpath, well-blazed. In about three minutes the path ends at a T junction with a wider dirt track; turn right on this **F**.

Be very alert now: In less than two minutes there's a narrow footpath going off the trail on your right. Just before it is a yellow blaze on a tree (also on your right). Take this footpath **E**.

The path is well blazed with yellow along here. About five minutes' climbing leads you out onto a wide gravel road **D**. Go straight ahead here.

Follow this road, ignoring all turnoffs (blazed yellow all along), for about 650 meters (6–8 minutes), when the road becomes asphalt and forks. Take the left fork and walk down to the asphalt road **C** (about 25 meters); turn left on the asphalt road and immediately pass an asphalt driveway on your left, and on the other side of the driveway is a dirt track; take this, and stay on it, crossing over another track about 15 meters after it starts.

In another minute or two this narrow dirt footpath comes out at a house. Take the dirt track ahead, which in another minute or two becomes asphalt just before it meets a larger asphalt road **B**. There's a way mark here, "Les Cabanes."

Cross over the larger asphalt road and take the gravel road ahead (there was a yellow blaze on a signpost at the entrance to the road). In another few minutes you'll come to a T junction with a little asphalt road with a way mark on the left, "Les Blayons." Turn left on this asphalt road, signed to Bonnieux.

In 150 meters or so, you'll come to a T junction with another asphalt road; turn right on that.

About 350 meters farther, near a way mark, "Aire des Croix," the road forks **Ⓐ**; bear right uphill, passing an iron cross in a stone base on your right. In another 125 meters or so, as you approach the edge of town, the road forks again (you'll see a big iron cross up on the right above a very tall stone wall); bear left through the stone arch and follow the cobbled road steadily downhill for a couple of minutes, when the road will become steps and make a hairpin left, leading down to the asphalt road, on which you turn right, arriving at the Hôtel-Restaurant Cesar in another minute or two.

3 Seguin–Buoux Ring Walk

3 Hours

After a strenuous, dramatic, but brief climb along the *lacets* (laces) zigzagging up the cliff face above the inn, this levels out into a pleasantly varied walk which, combined with a stop at one of the two restaurants in Buoux, makes a perfect day's outing.

After some vertiginous moments along the cliff path (be sure to keep on the path itself) you pass through the high lavender fields and pasturage of Les Ramades, coming soon into the scattered little village of Buoux set above the very charming Loube valley. There's a drinking water tap in the village. From here you circle the mountain on an easy track with fine views over rugged gorges, passing the gloomy, half-ruined Chateau of Buoux (now an Environmental center), climbing to the touching little country chapel and graveyard of Ste-Marie (you can go inside but be sure to close the gate and door), and arriving back in Buoux in time for an excellent lunch at either the Étape du Promeneur Buvette-Restaurant or the somewhat fancier Auberge de la Loube. A shorter route takes you back to the cliff path for a steep, swift descent home. Part of this route now goes along a road, skirting property that has been privatized since the IGN routes were

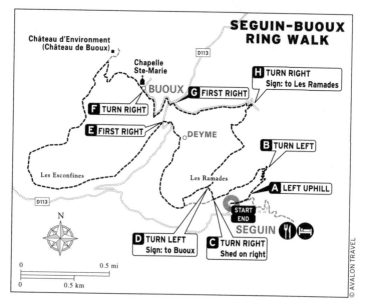

drawn, but it's a very quiet road (not a single car passed us) with a good view over the Loube valley as you climb, and it's soon behind you.

FOOD

There are two choices in the tiny village of Buoux, both interesting. The fancier is the **Auberge de la Loube,** a popular haunt among the better-off locals and expats alike, full of rather stagily homey odds and ends of furniture, trinkets, photos, and dried flowers that give it the feel of a slightly surreal living room, a quality that extends to the atmosphere in general. There's a €30 *menu,* but you can order from it à la carte, with main courses running around €16. The highlight is without a doubt the hors d'oeuvres provençale, a selection of local dishes. We ordered it for three and were brought a vast array that included tapenade, lentil salad, roasted peppers, two eggplant dishes, chicken liver pâté, a sweet onion confit, barley salad, and numerous other things. Almost all were delicious, and it certainly would have made a meal in itself for the four of us (two adults and two children). The main courses tended toward the gratuitous creaminess of *cuisine touristique*—a piece of fish aswim in white paint, a duckling breast in an equally bland sauce of acacia honey and balsamic vinegar, both accompanied by ravioli in yet more

cheesy cream. The roast lamb, on the hand, mercifully sauceless, is excellent: tender and aromatic. The desserts are nothing special. Cash only.

And then there is the tiny but excellent little place up the road, **L'Étape du Promeneur Buvette-Restaurant.** This is everything that most Provençal restaurants no longer are: honest, unpretentious, and inexpensive. The menu looks more like that of a snack bar than a fully fledged restaurant (thus the *"buvette"* in its name), with salads, charcuterie plates, and omelettes occupying most of it, all around €6 or €7. But everything is so well prepared, so generously abundant, that you come away feeling as if you have eaten at a gourmet restaurant. The omelettes, in particular, are stunning, whether the *fine herbes* bursting with tarragon and parsley, the perfectly golden and velvety emmenthal, or the vegetable, with its delicious eggplant and zucchini filling. They're all around €6. You can order them with *frites frais,* a mountain of rustic fries cooked with sprigs of wild savory (our daughter declared these the best she'd ever had), and then if you have room, follow it all with a superb homemade *tarte aux myrtilles* (wild blueberries) or some lavender ice cream, which, as our son said, "tastes of soap but really delicious," and it *was.* Though simple, Promeneur was one of our favorite meals of the trip.

If all this sounds too insubstantial for a hiker's lunch, you can assure yourself of a full-scale meal by calling a day ahead, and it'll prepare you a large meat course such as lemon chicken, stuffed lamb, or roast guinea hen (€16). Judging from what we saw on the table of others who had had the foresight to do this, these are hearty, at the very least.

LOGISTICS
IGN Map Number and Name
#3243 OT—Pertuis/Lourmarin

Restaurants
For Seguin listings see Walk 2.
  Name: L'Étape du Promeneur Buvette-Restaurant
  Address: Buoux village; see Walk Directions for exact location.
  Phone: 0490/ 04 60 21
  Closing Day: Wed., but call ahead to avoid possible disappointment.

Name: Auberge de la Loube
Address: Buoux village; see Walk Directions.
Phone: 0490/ 74 19 58
Closing Day: Sun. eve, Mon. and Thurs. except holidays

Accommodations

For Seguin listings see Walk 2.
Name: La Sparagoule
Address: Buoux village
Phone: 0490/ 74 47 82
Website or Email: http://perso.orange.fr/lasparagoule
Type of Lodging: *Gîte d'étape* and *chambres d'hôte*
Price: Room with breakfast: one person €33, two people €45, three people €55; *dortoir:* €12 per person per night, breakfast €5, evening meal *(le repas de soir)* €14; picnics available for your onward journey the next day for €6; children under 10 receive a reduced rate

Transportation

There's no public transport in Seguin or Buoux.

WALK DIRECTIONS

Facing the Auberge des Seguins from the parking lot, go to your right, passing its pool on your right. There's a sign at the pool reading Sentier Pedestre Vallon de l'Aiguebrun; the path bends left here, behind the back of the stone building—*buvette* (bar)—and begins to climb.

In a minute you'll come to a way mark (no name, but signed to Sivergues and Aiguebrun) and a fork. Take the left uphill fork **Ⓐ**.

Follow the path, a stone-paved, steady climb with switchbacks, ignoring deviations. (Watch for the "X"es that tell you where *not* to go.)

In 10–15 minutes be aware that you turn left where the path also continues straight ahead **Ⓑ**. Blazes (both red and white and red and yellow) on the rock outcrop show that you turn left. Climb up the rock; there's also a blue-painted "Buoux" on it.

About 5–10 minutes along the path (flat now), *watch* for a fork **Ⓒ** to the right (blazed) where the path also continues straight, and take the right turn, passing a shed on your right in about 15 meters, from which you can see a way mark ahead. When you reach this way mark, "Les Ramades" **❶**, turn left, signed to Buoux.

About 15–20 minutes later the road turns to dilapidated tarmac at a little house and winds gently downhill to an intersection with the road (D113), just below Buoux. Cross a stone bridge and take the stony uphill path on your right between the bridge and the Auberge de la Loube.

If you're eating now: There's an entrance to the Auberge de la Loube off this path. To get to the smaller restaurant, L'Étape du Promeneur Buvette-Restaurant, go to the top of the path, bear right onto the road, passing the *gîte d'étape* La Sparagoule on your right. At the intersection in front of the *mairie* (town hall), keep to the lower road, arriving in another minute or two at the restaurant.

If you're continuing your walk: At the top of the stony uphill path, turn left on the asphalt road and pass the "Esconfines" way mark on your left. Just past the way mark take your first right off the asphalt road onto the gravel road **❷** across from Auberge de la Loube.

Follow the road for about 45 minutes, until you reach an intersection with a way mark, "Bosquet," and see the Château de Buoux, now the Château d'Environment, in front of you. Turn right, signed to Buoux, on a little footpath.

Once you're on the footpath, you have a fairly steady climb of 10–15 minutes, and then you reach the chapel, Chapelle Ste-Marie, and the path levels out. You'll be walking along the back wall of the chapel, and when the path turns left you'll see the way mark "Chapelle Ste-Marie" at a T junction.

Turn right at the T junction at the way mark **❸**, signed to Buoux. Follow the road back down toward Buoux, and about 10 minutes later, after it makes a hairpin left-hand turn (just above Buoux), bear right off the road onto the cobbled downhill ramp, and then your first cobbled left turn, passing a drinking-water faucet on your left.

Continue down the steps and turn left on the road to the *mairie* (town hall).

If you're eating now: To get to L'Étape du Promeneur, continue straight along the road past the Mairie. If you're going to Auberge de la Loube, turn right downhill and the auberge is on your left.

If you're continuing your walk: From the *mairie* continue straight along the road, taking the first right **G** (signed toward Visitor Parking, which is just a little patch of bare ground) and cross the concrete bridge.

Stay on this road, in about 10 minutes passing a *gîte* where the path—as marked on the IGN—used to turn right. (You have to keep on the road a little longer now.)

About 10 minutes later, after the road bends around to the right near a house, you'll come to a way mark, "Chante Duc." Turn right onto the gravel road **H**, signed to Les Ramades.

Climb the road and after five minutes or so, ignore a turnoff to the right downhill, signed Le Haut Deyme *gîte,* and follow the gravel track (there's a GR 9 sign here on a tree to the right) as it climbs uphill and makes a sharp left-hand turn.

Pass the gate of Mas Augusta on your right and then follow the road as it turns right at the end of the (fenced) Augusta property.

The path follows to the left of a stone wall, which ends at the way mark "Les Ramades" **D**. Turn left, signed Chemin de Frau.

Retracing your steps here, pass the shed on your left and then turn left when you reach the T junction just beyond **C**.

The path is easy to follow down, well blazed and familiar now. At the bottom (20–25 minutes past **C**), where you come to the T junction at the unnamed way mark **A**, turn right, signed to Buoux, which leads back to the Auberge des Seguins in a minute.

4 Seguin–Sivergues Ring Walk
2 Hours

This is undoubtedly the more spectacular of the two ring walks up in the Buoux area—a half-day excursion into the gorge country above the Aiguebrun, going along hidden valleys, past fortress-farmhouses, up to the remote hamlet of Sivergues, and offering a spur to the even more remote farm/auberge of le Castelas.

A short way up the Ravin d'Enfer (Ravine of Hell), you turn off along the top of a deep, secluded valley with caves in the cliffs opposite and the ancient farmstead of Chantebelle built partly into the rocks above. Passing under the farm itself you turn along another valley, with views across the Aiguebrun gorge to the farms of Marrenon and la Bremonde, before crossing an

THE LUBÉRON MOUNTAINS

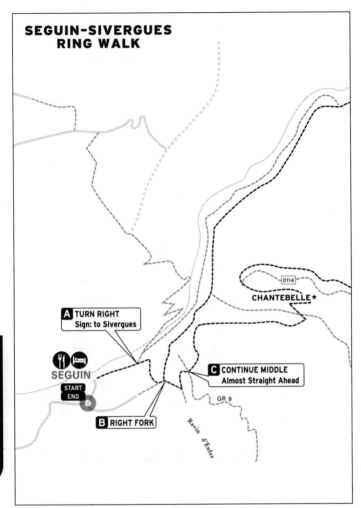

SEGUIN-SIVERGUES
RING WALK

A TURN RIGHT
Sign: to Sivergues

SEGUIN

START
END

B RIGHT FORK

C CONTINUE MIDDLE
Almost Straight Ahead

GR 9

Ravin d'Enfer

D114

CHANTEBELLE ★

overgrown bridge that brings you out to the trail leading into
Sivergues, a remarkably pretty mountain hamlet whose difficult access by road seems likely to ensure its deep tranquility for
many years to come. There are *gîtes* to rent here, and a small *gîte
d'étape,* but no shops or restaurants.

From here you can take the spur there and back to le Castelas,
a magnificently situated farm with goats, pigs, and olive trees (the
owners are rebuilding the old olive terraces sweeping down from
their property, and the results promise to be stunning). You can stay
here or, from late March, just stop in for a meal (make reservations).

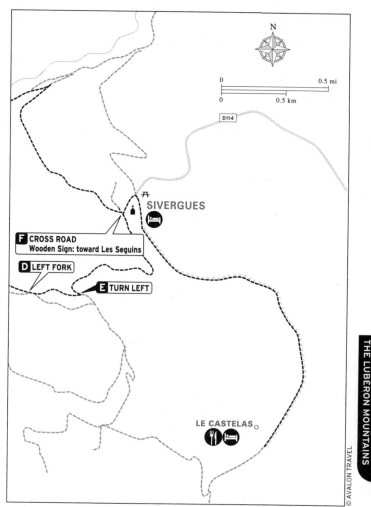

The last part of the walk takes you from Sivergues down a valley with monumental stone terracing to the wooded banks of the Aiguebrun itself. It's yet another world down here: a shaded, level walk along the stream, with small waterfalls and beguiling green pools on the way. In spring the path is bordered with primroses, violets, and hepatica (the purple flowers with dotted white circles at the center). Birdsong fills the air, accompanied by the sound of the stream itself, living up to its name, which means "murmuring water" in old Provençal.

LE CASTELAS FOOD

This remote, gorgeous farm/auberge has a primeval air about it, with stone buildings looking out over olive groves and vast, tilting mountainsides. On cold days you eat around a blazing fire, on warm days outside at great farm tables, with goats and pigs wandering around you and occasionally jumping up onto the tables themselves.

The food is simple, homegrown, and splendid. Dinner (reserve) is €30 a head (including children), which includes generous quantities of sangria and wine. After an enormous green salad with a fantastic dressing that included whole cloves of crushed garlic (one of few really decent salads we had anywhere), platters of home-cured ham were served along with a basil and garlic–creamed goat cheese as well as some delicious zucchini fritters. After this a massive cauldron of pork stew with carrots and celery was brought out, followed by a plate of yet more goat cheeses, arranged by age from tender newborns to rock-hard oldsters.

Depending on the season you might get goat or chicken instead of pork. There isn't much choice, so if you're concerned you should ask what's on the menu when you make your reservations. Lunch, a little cheaper, consists of the above without the main meat course and is abundantly satisfying.

LOGISTICS
IGN Map Number and Name

#3243 OT—Pertuis/Lourmarin

Restaurants

For Seguin listings see Walk 2.
Name: Le Castelas
Address: 20 minutes' walk beyond Sivergues; see Walk Directions.
Phone: 0490/ 74 60 89
Closing Day: Make reservations.

Accommodations

For Seguin listings see Walk 2.
Sivergues:
Name: Le Fort de l'Archidiacre
Address: Hamlet center
Phone: 0490/ 74 14 87 and 0490/ 74 49 23

Type of Lodging: *Gîte d'étape*
Price: Half pension €34, or you can pay €14 just for a bed and use the kitchen to cook for yourself.
Notes: It has rooms for two, four, six, and 12 people.
Castelas:
Name: Le Castelas
Address: 20 minutes' walk past Sivergues; see Walk Directions.
Phone: 0490/ 74 60 89
Website or Email: le.castelas@yahoo.com
Type of Lodging: *Chambres d'hôte* and *gîte d'étape*
Price: Demipension €59 per person if you're in a room and €39 if you're in the *dortoir*
Notes: It has rooms for two, three, and four people and a *dortoir*.

Transportation

There is no public transportation in either place.

WALK DIRECTIONS

Facing the Auberge des Seguins from the parking lot, go to your right, passing its pool on your right. There's a sign at the pool reading Sentier Pedestre Vallon de l'Aiguebrun; the path bends left here, behind the back of the stone building—*buvette* (bar)—and begins to climb.

In a minute you'll come to a way mark (no name, but signed to Sivergues and Aiguebrun) and a fork Ⓐ. Take the right downhill fork, signed to Sivergues. The path is blazed with red and white and yellow and red.

In another minute the path bends right and crosses a bridge (though you'd hardly know it's a bridge it's so overgrown) over the Aiguebrun stream.

The path climbs for another minute or two and then you reach a way mark, "Aiguebrun," at a T junction; turn left, signed to Sivergues.

Just beyond here (20 meters/yards) you come to another fork; take the right fork Ⓑ, signed Críte du Lubéron.

After a short climb (2–5 minutes) you'll reach a T junction at a wider path; turn left.

Almost immediately you'll reach a short (15 meters) stretch of concrete slab that bends right and comes out on an open area

C with three paths: a path bending right uphill (the GR 9), a smaller path on the other side of the open area, more or less straight ahead but bending left, and a small footpath downhill to the left. Take the middle, almost straight-ahead path. There's a blue arrow on a tree to the right and a red and white "X."

Stay on the path, ignoring deviations. There are some blue blazes and some yellow blazes and a spectacular view of the cliffs.

When the path curves around the end of the valley you've been paralleling, ignore paths to the right, but just beyond here, when you've reached the other side of the valley, the path narrows considerably, bends sharply right, and takes a couple of quick hairpin turns, ending at a little T junction. Turn right here (left is west and leads back toward the valley), where you can see a stone house (Chantebelle) just above you.

In another minute you come to another T junction, still below the house (there is a sign here for Auberge des Seguins, pointing right). Turn left here.

Climb to where there's a stone outbuilding built into the rock (there's also a blue blaze on a rock to your right just before). Bear left on the path here (passing the outbuilding on your right).

It's a nice wide path along here. In a couple of minutes, there's a fork between two huge boulders (both forks bend right); take either fork, as they're basically parallel and reconnect shortly. There are blue blazes and a yellow one on the boulder to your right.

In 5–10 minutes the track meets a similar-size, slightly better-quality gravel track at a flat open dirt area. Turn left on this and you'll see a smaller track going downhill to the left, where the main track goes very slightly uphill and bends right. Take the left fork **D**.

This path immediately crosses a grass-covered bridge over a gorge. At the end of the bridge bear right uphill. A few minutes later the path comes out on a gravel road; turn left **E**.

Follow this road into Sivergues.

Spur to le Castelas

Climb to the center of the hamlet, passing the *gîte d'étape* Le Fort de l'Archidiacre on your right, at a T junction. Turn right here.

Climb to the top of this cobbled road, to a T junction with a tiny asphalt road. Turn right on this. Stay on this road until you arrive at le Castelas, 20–25 minutes later.

Leaving Sivergues

On the road coming into Sivergues from le Castelas, as you reach the outskirts of the hamlet (southeast edge of town), just past the first house on the right, there's a cobbled road on the left downhill. Take that, soon passing under an arch (with stairs on top of it) and coming to a little intersection by the *gîte d'étape* Le Fort de l'Archidiacre. Bear left here, passing in front of the *gîte d'étape,* and continue downhill on the cobbled road.

At the bottom of the cobbled road, cross the little asphalt road (you came into Sivergues on) and follow the small footpath (by a wooden way mark, signed toward Les Seguins) that leads downhill just across this road **F**.

Follow this lovely footpath, ignoring in 10–15 minutes—just after a hairpin left turn—the first fork of any comparable size, which drops downhill right, and just stay on the main path. From here the path will basically follow the stream, mostly above it, but with a bit of up and down, for 20–25 minutes. It then heads away from the stream and comes to a way mark, "Ravin d'Enfer" **B**. Keep on the path as it bends right and in about 20 meters, at the "Aiguebrun" way mark, turn right.

Pass the unnamed way mark **A**, keep straight on (not signed in this direction), and in another minute reach the Auberge des Seguins.

5 Vaugines Two-Day Ring Walk
5 Hours

This overnight walk will take you from Vaugines to Seguin on the first day and includes a stop at **Fort de Buoux.** The return trip from Seguin to Vaugines on the second day includes **Sivergues** and **le Castelas;** allow three hours. Note that there are other walks you can take from Seguin, including our Walks 3 and 4; another option would be to walk to Bonnieux from Seguin.

VAUGINES TO SEGUIN
VIA THE FORT DE BUOUX– 5 Hours

This day walk across the Lubéron mountains is one of the most satisfyingly adventurous in this book, with its great variety of landscapes and the extraordinary ruins of the ancient cliff-top fort of Buoux, which it passes toward the end.

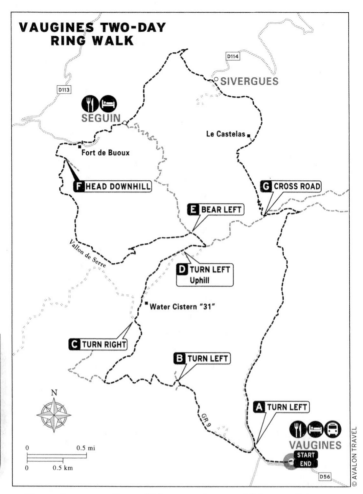

VAUGINES TWO-DAY
RING WALK

D114

SIVERGUES

D113

SEGUIN

Le Castelas

Fort de Buoux

F HEAD DOWNHILL

G CROSS ROAD

E BEAR LEFT

Vallon de Serre

D TURN LEFT
Uphill

Water Cistern "31"

C TURN RIGHT

B TURN LEFT

A TURN LEFT

N

VAUGINES
START
END

GR 9

0   0.5 mi
0   0.5 km

D56

THE LUBÉRON MOUNTAINS

© AVALON TRAVEL

From the stone alleys of Vaugines (parts of *Manon of the Spring* were filmed here), the walk climbs to a mountainside section with splendid views down over the Durance valley and then crests at the high, rolling plains above the wonderfully named Grand Vallon de Roumagoua before descending through the Vallon de Serre, where the dramatic cliffs and gorges of the area around Fort de Buoux come into view. (If you're planning on picnicking, the area on top of the mountains, around the way mark "L'Ourillon," has a spectacular view.)

The fort is perched on a kind of island cliff above a house where your path comes out. To visit it—very strongly recommended— knock at the door and buy tickets and a map for €3. With its successive defense systems—a deep stone trench, walls within walls, ramparts with arrow slits, a moat and drawbridge, secret stairways, and a final redoubt at the edge of the highest part of the precipice surrounding it—the place gives off a powerful sense of the hunted, persecuted lives of the various groups of people who have taken refuge there over the ages. Primarily these were religious dissenters: members of the Waldensian sect during the religious wars of the Middle Ages, Protestants during the renewed intolerance of the 17th century. You'll see a partially restored chapel, impressive stone cisterns, and amazing cylindrical grain silos cut six feet deep into solid rock. The site takes about an hour to visit and has no protection around its vertical falls, so watch children carefully.

From here it's a short walk along the wooded banks of the Aiguebrun river to the magnificently situated Auberge des Seguins, couched below gigantic cliffs, where you can spend the night.

SEGUIN TO VAUGINES VIA SIVERGUES AND LE CASTELAS– 3 Hours

A secluded mountain hamlet and a remote farm/auberge serving excellent food form the high points of the route back across the Lubéron mountains from Seguin.

Sivergues, once a refuge for the persecuted Waldensian Protestants, still feels very far away from the world. It's hard to get there by car, and with luck this will help preserve its charm and tranquility. Le Castelas, a little deeper into the mountains, is an old farmstead with fine buildings, lots of pigs and goats wandering around it, and lovely views from its outdoor tables. From here there's a 40-minute climb to the ridge, after which it's an easy descent to Vaugines. This last part, on a dirt road leading straight down the valley, isn't especially beautiful, but it gets you back fast, which might be an advantage after the two or three days' hard walking you're likely to have done if you came up here in the first place.

VAUGINES FOOD

The friendly, bustling **L'Origan** restaurant/pizzeria in the small square at the center of Vaugines is a good place to go for a relaxed, inexpensive meal. The pizzas, made in a wood oven, are excellent, many of them with a distinctly French twist (*lardons* and crème fraîche featured alongside the usual tomatoes and olives). There are substantial salads, including an excellent "Lubéron" salad with goat cheese and pine nuts, filling pasta dishes, and a *grillade* section with andouillettes, tripes à la provençale, and—if you're in the mood for fish—a gratin of *coquilles St-Jacques,* scallops. As always in such places, the main focus of the kitchen (pizzas) is generally the best choice, but the other dishes are fine. A rather salty plate of ham braised in mustard sauce was redeemed by deliciously creamy potatoes *dauphinoise,* and there are several homemade desserts to choose from, including a very good chocolate mousse.

Pizzas are around €10, the other main courses €11 to €15. No credit cards or travelers checks are accepted. And as always, be sure to check your bill—we were given someone else's.

LOGISTICS
IGN Map Number and Name
#3243 OT—Pertuis/Lourmarin

Tourist Information
There's a physical tourist office in the neighboring town of Cucuron serving both Cucuron and Vaugines. But for online help, there's a very useful Vaugines tourist office website: www.vaugines-Luberon.com.

Restaurants
For Seguin listings, see Walk 2.
For le Castelas listings, see Walk 4.
Vaugines:
 Name: L'Origan
 Address: Place de la Mairie (the main village square, with the fountain)
 Phone: 0490/ 77 11 08
 Closing Day: Open evenings only; closed Wed.

Accommodations
For more Vaugines accommodations, see the Vaugines tourist office website.
For Seguin listings, see Walk 2.
For Sivergues and le Castelas listings, see Walk 4.

Vaugines:

Name: La Cigale

Address: Place de la Mairie (the main village square, with the fountain)

Phone: 0490/ 77 17 90 or 0612/ 27 45 36

Website or Email: annickkrumenacher@hotmail.com (You can see a photo on the Vaugines tourist office website under "Hébergement.")

Type of Lodging: *Chambres d'hôte*

Price: €50 for two people, including breakfast

Notes: She will prepare a picnic for your onward journey if you reserve the day ahead (as is always the case, there will be a modest additional charge for this).

Name: Hostellerie du Lubéron

Address: Vaugines

Phone: 0490/ 77 27 19

Website or Email: www.hostellerieduLuberon.com

Type of Lodging: Logis de France hotel

Price: Double rooms starting at €90 in low season and €109 in high season, including breakfast

Transportation

There's a bus between Vaugines and Lourmarin on Fridays, for market day in Lourmarin (five minutes away). It leaves Vaugines early in the morning and returns to Vaugines from Lourmarin at noon.

You can get to Vaugines from Pertuis (which has an SNCF train station) Mon.–Fri. (except during school holidays) on the Cabriéeres d'Aigues–Marseille bus, at the time of this writing leaving Pertuis 17:50, arriving Vaugines 18:20; phone: Autocars Sumian (Marseille) 0491/ 49 44 25.

For a taxi, call the tourist office, either for Vaugines or Lourmarin.

WALK DIRECTIONS

From the Vaugines village center, with your back to the fountain and the cafés to your left, go straight ahead (west) up the little asphalt road between houses, blazed GR 9. At the end of this exceptionally pretty street (about five minutes), bear right on the asphalt road, ignoring the first fork downhill left, and continue to the T junction at the end **Ⓐ**. There's a way mark here, "Vaugines." Turn left.

Follow this asphalt road, ignoring deviations. In 5–10 minutes the road turns to gravel, and a few minutes later narrows a bit as it enters a more wooded area.

In another 15–20 minutes (always stay on the main path), the path bends right where another path goes off to the left, and 1–2 minutes later you reach the first fork of comparable size and material **Ⓑ**. It's an actual *fork* and you can't miss it. The right branch is more uphill than the left, which is also uphill. Take the left branch.

Note: The section of the official trail (GR 9) that goes north shortly after **Ⓑ** as marked on the IGN map has been rerouted. We describe it here, and it's easy to follow "on the ground." Perhaps new editions of the IGN will be corrected to conform to the new routing. Basically, the path follows the mountain contour westward for about a half hour before climbing steeply northeast.

About an hour past **Ⓑ**, the path comes out on a stony dirt road **Ⓒ**. Turn right on this.

In about five minutes you reach a little blacktopped area at a water cistern with a "31" painted on it. Immediately past the cistern bear left off the road onto a wide stony uphill path, where there's a red and white blaze on a tree on the right side of the path.

Soon the path narrows and begins to climb. When you reach a wide-open area of grass and white stones about 10 minutes later (with a cairn), carry on straight across, continuing uphill. There's a red and white blaze on a rock flush with ground level in the middle of this area, and shortly beyond that one, another one on a tree trunk to your right (but still in this big open area). Keep heading up toward the top of the hill. As you approach the last hump, there's another red and white blaze on a tree to your left, and you can see a vague path of stones marking a path up this last hill face. (Crossing the whole of this open area takes only a matter of 5–10 minutes.)

From the top, head down the other side (you can see your "destination path" curving up a hill in front of you). There are two paths leading down this side of the hill, both coming down to the road you left at **Ⓒ**. You can aim toward the white iron cross toward your right, and you'll meet a track that brings you down to the road. Take this road, and as it's bending right there's a wide but lesser-quality path off it (which you could see as you came down the hill) left uphill; take this **D**. There's a red and white blaze on a rock at ground level here.

There are red and white blazes on the ground as you climb this next hill; watch for one pointing out a left bend. You can see a way mark at the top of the hill; head for that.

Reaching the way mark "Pelat de Buoux," follow the direction pointed to Buoux (north). A series of cairns marks the route, one with a red and yellow blaze, and a minute beyond the way mark "Pelat de Buoux," you'll reach the way mark "L'Ourillon" **E** at a spectacular view, a great place to picnic if it's not too windy.

Bear left from this way mark (west northwest) in the direction of Fort de Buoux (*not* the direction of Buoux, which is the stony path cresting the hill ahead), across a grassy area (again marked by a series of cairns), where in about 30 meters you can see some yellow and red blazes on two trees on the left side of the grassy open area. Between these two trees is the beginning of a foot-path: Take this, soon passing another yellow and red blaze on a tree to the right.

Stay on this path, following the red and yellow blazes.

About 45 minutes past **E**, you'll pass a way mark, "Serre," on the left of the track. Continue straight.

After the fort comes into view high above you (you'll see a left-hand-turn blaze on a tree on the left side of the path), the path comes to a T junction with another similar path **F**. The left branch leads downhill, and you'll take this either now, or if you're going to visit the fort, later. For the fort, turn right uphill and immediately the road bends left up to the fort. The fort is open daily, sunrise to sunset.

After visiting the fort, return to **F** and turn right on the road, which you follow downhill, reaching the fort's official entrance gate in about 10 minutes. Pass through the gate and bear left downhill.

In less than two minutes you'll come to an intersection with another road, at the way mark "Moulin Clos." You can turn right here and follow the road to Seguin, or cross the road and take the footpath there that leads down toward the stream (and cliffs). There's a 30 speed-limit sign marking the entrance to it.

Just past the entrance the path goes over some tree roots and then steeply down for 10 meters or so and turns right: Stay straight on the path here (don't drop to the stream on the left downhill path). There are blue blazes along the way. Soon you'll pass a waterfall and pool downhill on your left (in spring), and then the path goes up some rock steps (this is all just a minute or two). Beyond here the path is well worn and soon drops to the stream and comes to a little concrete bridge across it. Cross the bridge and the path climbs about 10 meters on the other side to a T junction; turn right.

From here the path is easily followed to Auberge des Seguins (ignore downhill deviations to the stream) just beyond the horse stalls on your left about five minutes past the concrete bridge.

From the Auberge des Seguins take the path between the *buvette* and the pool, following the path uphill and in a minute coming to the unnamed way mark where the path forks; take the right. It's blazed red and white and red and yellow.

The path bends right and crosses a bridge (which you hardly notice is a bridge, it's so overgrown with vegetation) over the Aiguebrun. Follow the path straight ahead, ignoring a smaller deviation to the left.

In another minute or two you will come to a T junction at the way mark "Aiguebrun." Turn left here, signed to Sivergues. In another 25 meters/yards you'll reach another way mark, "Ravin d'Enfer," where you bear left, again signed to Sivergues.

The path leads first along the bank of the Aiguebrun and then climbs to the hamlet of Sivergues, which you reach less than an hour after leaving Seguin.

Climb to the center of the hamlet, passing the *gîte d'étape* Le Fort de l'Archidiacre on your right, at a T junction. Turn right here.

Climb to the top of this cobbled road to a T junction with a tiny asphalt road. Turn right on this. Stay on this road until you arrive at le Castelas, 20–25 minutes later.

Leaving le Castelas, turn right from its entrance, continuing along the road you came on, which is now less of a road.

In about 20 minutes, the path begins to zigzag uphill. As these "laces" (*lacets* in French) begin, you come to a fork, plus another path to the left of the fork. The right prong of the fork you ignore. Take the left prong of the fork. The path to the left of the path you take does meet up with your path a little higher up and is a little longer and less steep.

It is perhaps comforting to know that the rest of the laces are not as steep.

Follow the laces to the top; at the time of this writing, there's a tree down on the path about 10 minutes after the laces begin, where there's a yellow and red blaze on a rock on the ground. Turn left off the main path and take a smaller path uphill, in 30 meters reaching a big concrete water cistern. Follow the path to the left of the cistern and come to a T junction with a big gravel road ❻.

Cross the road and head downhill on the track ahead. (About five minutes later stay on the main track as it hairpins to the right where a lesser path comes in from the left.)

Stay on this track, which is easy to follow, for just under an hour, when the road surface turns to asphalt. Five minutes later you'll reach the intersection at the way mark "Vaugines" ❶. Bear left on the asphalt road.

In another five minutes bear left up through the village, reaching the square five minutes later.

6 Gordes–Abbaye de Sénanque Ring Walk
3.5 Hours

The perched village of Gordes is one of the most popular destinations in the Lubéron area. Its highly photogenic charms are best appreciated from afar: Up close it has the eviscerated atmosphere of a place given over entirely to tourism. It has a lot of bad art to see, a nice castle, and a restored "village" of bories, a little outside. The latter is worth visiting, though it seems to have given rise to a kind of *borie*-kitsch aesthetic in much of the hotel and villa development around Gordes itself.

But the surrounding countryside—much of it abandoned farmland—is very pleasant, with dramatic views of the Regagnades, the valley to the east as you leave town.

And then of course, there is the goal of this walk: the magnificent Abbaye de Sénanque, arguably the most impressive—if only for its setting amid lavender fields and olive groves—of the three great 12th-century Cistercian monasteries of Provence. You can drive there, naturally, and spend a pleasant hour on a guided tour of its cloisters and church. But there's nothing like approaching

THE LUBÉRON MOUNTAINS

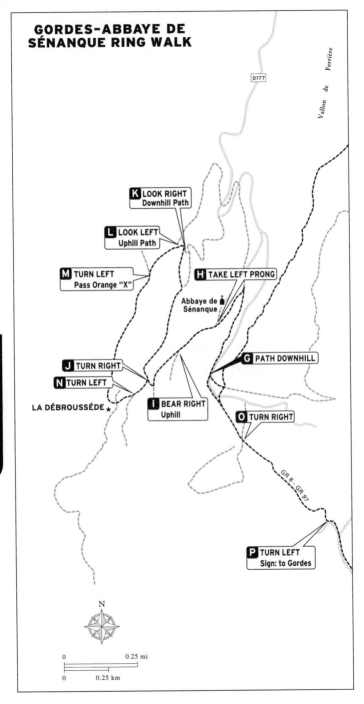

GORDES-ABBAYE DE SÉNANQUE RING WALK

K LOOK RIGHT
Downhill Path

L LOOK LEFT
Uphill Path

M TURN LEFT
Pass Orange "X"

H TAKE LEFT PRONG

Abbaye de Sénanque

G PATH DOWNHILL

J TURN RIGHT

N TURN LEFT

LA DÉBROUSSÉDE ★

I BEAR RIGHT
Uphill

O TURN RIGHT

GR 6 - GR 97

P TURN LEFT
Sign: to Gordes

D177

Vallon de Ferrière

N

0   0.25 mi
0   0.25 km

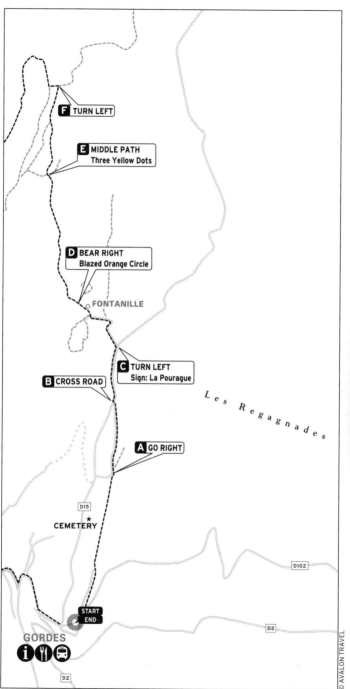

F TURN LEFT

E MIDDLE PATH
Three Yellow Dots

D BEAR RIGHT
Blazed Orange Circle

○ FONTANILLE

C TURN LEFT
Sign: La Pourague

B CROSS ROAD

L e s   R e g a g n a d e s

A GO RIGHT

D15

★
CEMETERY

D102

START
END

D2

GORDES

D2

THE LUBÉRON MOUNTAINS

© AVALON TRAVEL

these great ecclesiastical buildings on foot, at least when the landscape around them is still relatively wild, as it is here (readers of our Tuscany book will recall the approach to Sant Antimo). Your first sight of it, about an hour outside Gordes as you walk along the cliffs above the Vallon de Ferriére, is little different than it would have been for pilgrims of the early Middle Ages: an image of reposeful order rising in splendid isolation out of pure wilderness. Even when the car-parks become visible, the place retains a sublimely tranquil charm, monumental in scale, but full of intimate touches, such as the rough, rustic-looking stone tiles on the curving roofs, that seem to marry the international Romanesque style with the local vernacular, bringing *bories* to mind again.

Our walk continues around the back of the abbey, climbing to the very pretty terraced land opposite. This is mostly private, but we found a path that brings you to a perfect picnic and viewing spot without trespassing. Avoid going any farther down toward the abbey from this side, or the monks will surely close off the path.

The way back to Gordes follows a much shorter trail leading straight back across country from the top of the road above the abbey. Allow 2.5 hours from Gordes to Sénanque, one hour from Sénanque to Gordes.

FOOD

As in many places where tourism has completely ousted any other form of life, it's hard to find a restaurant here that we can wholeheartedly recommend. Frankly, our advice would be to bring a picnic on this walk. There's a good **Tuesday market** with plenty of cheeses, breads, salads, and roast meats to choose from (try the succulent duck thigh—*cuisse de canard*—if it's on offer at one of the rotisserie stalls). Failing that, you can get a decent, not-too-expensive sandwich at Canelle, just down from the *place* behind the castle. If you're dead set on having a sit-down meal, there's an okay place called **le Bouquet de Basilic** on the route de Murs, just up from the castle, specializing in giant bruschettas. Otherwise you can take your chances in either the very flossy or the slightly less flossy of the two restaurants in the *place*.

LOGISTICS
IGN Map Number and Name
#3142 OT—Cavaillon

Tourist Information

Address: Le Château (main square in Gordes)
Phone: 0490/ 72 02 75
Website or Email: www.gordes-village.com
Hours: 10:00–12:00 and 14:00–18:00

Transportation

Bus
Name: Durance Voyages
Phone: 0490/ 71 03 00
Frequency and Duration: There are two buses a day each way between Cavaillon and Gordes. It's a 35-minute ride. Check with the tourist office for further information.

Miscellaneous Notes

The Tuesday market in Gordes is a good one. Along with the food, there are plenty of stalls selling all manner of tempting merchandise.

WALK DIRECTIONS

Note: The hairpins near **H** aren't represented on the map, because the map isn't of a detailed enough scale to be able to show them.

Leaving Gordes, with Le Château on your right, walk past the front of it and then fork left in front of the post office. Follow this road, staying on the right-hand side by the low wall, and stay on the road as it leads out of town.

There's a beautiful view along here, out over the Regagnades, the valley to the east. Watch your step while looking, though; dog owners don't seem to clean up after their animals.

Pass the cemetery on your left (about 10 minutes from the start); along the cemetery wall the road gives out and becomes a stony dirt path.

About 10 minutes past the cemetery you'll come to an asphalt road and go right **A**. Less than a minute later the road forks; take the left uphill.

In another few minutes the path comes to a bigger asphalt road **B**. Cross over and walk about 300 meters/yards (3–5 minutes; it's not a very busy road) until you come to an asphalt road on the left **C**, signed des Sources and with a way mark signed

"La Pouraque." Turn left on this and climb uphill, passing a house on your right, Fontanille, and ignoring the right just beyond that, and a minute or two later bear right at a fork whose left prong leads to a campground.

In another minute the asphalt ends at another fork; bear right here **D**. It's blazed with an orange circle and blue.

In 15 meters take either prong of the fork; they meet up. Continue slightly uphill on this dirt path.

Past **D** 10–15 minutes you'll come to a three-way fork **E**. Take the middle path, which drops slightly, signed with three yellow dots on a rock.

In about 10 minutes you'll come to a T junction. Go left here **F**, and then in about 60 paces, at a T junction, go right.

The path from here soon curves round on to the edge of the cliff that leads along the Vallon de Ferriére. We had no difficulty following the path here, except about 50 minutes in, there's a fork in the path near a ledge; go either way, as they meet up.

About an hour past **F**, you'll come to a T junction with a left, middle, and right; take the right fork, which leads to the road (D177) in less than a minute, coming out near a sign saying Côte de Sénanque. (Note a way mark across the road to your left for future reference, as the route passes that way on the return trip.) Turn right on the road.

Cross the road and walk down the left side of it, and in about 50 meters you'll see a path off the road leading downhill **G**. Take that. In five minutes or so the path forks right flat and left downhill; the right is blazed red and white, but turn down left here.

When you get to a fork **H** just above the asphalt road next to the abbey, where the left goes straight on and the right drops downhill about seven meters to a T junction, take the left prong straight ahead. In about a minute, at the next fork behind the abbey, make the hairpin right, coming out at the Notre Dame statue and the abbey.

Picnic Spur– 1–1.5 Hour

Note: Please be discreet about using this picnic spot so as not to attract attention. It's a delicate little jewel that indiscretion will destroy. Please respect the privacy of the monks and the vulnerability of this little path you follow after **K**.

Facing the statue of Notre Dame, with the abbey on your right, there's a fork where the right side is a concrete downhill path, and the left one is gravel and leads to the statue. Take the right fork (heading toward the back of the abbey and with a stone wall on both sides of it).

The concrete gives out and the path becomes gravelly. Follow it as it curves right at the back of the abbey (there's a high stone wall to your right) and then bends left along a green metal fence. In a minute or two the path forks **I**; bear right uphill.

In 10 minutes or so (a minute after the path makes a hairpin right turn), you'll come out at a dirt road. Turn right **J**.

In less than five minutes the road suddenly becomes smooth dirt instead of stony and comes to a lavender field on your right. Staying on this wide dirt track, in 2–3 minutes more you'll reach a second, bigger field, this time on your left. (Toward the end of the field, there will also be a derelict orchard on your right.) When you come to the end of the field, look on your right for a very tiny path downhill (*before* the main path bends left), about five steps beyond the corner of the field; take this **K**.

About 30 meters downhill the path comes to a T junction, where the right turn is an old, hardly usable path. Turn left here.

Follow this path downhill for 3–5 minutes until the path ends at a T junction with a cart track. Please stop here. If you go right, it's too near the monastery; the path is gated off, and the monks will certainly close off this access as well.

To Return to the Abbey

Climb back to **K**. From here you can either retrace your steps (for a shorter walk), or to do a loop, turn right here, where the road is making a left turn. About 55–60 paces farther, just before the road makes a right-hand turn, watch on your left for a little uphill path **L**. Take this.

Climb to the top of this path (about 3–5 minutes), where it comes to a T junction; turn left here **M**, passing an orange "X." (You can see a little view of the abbey from here.)

Stay on the path, until 10–15 minutes later you come to a ruined house, La Débrousséde. The path skirts the side of the house and then wraps left in front of it. Keep straight along the front of the house (ignore a bigger right-hand turn in front of the arch).

The path widens beyond the house. Keep on it for two

minutes or so, when it meets a bigger dirt track **N**. Turn left on this, and in less than a minute you'll come to **J** (just as the path you're on becomes a kind of rough stony concrete surface and bottoms out), where you rejoin the path you came in on, and take it right downhill. Ignore forks off it when the path makes a hairpin left in less than a minute. Catch another glimpse on the way down here.

Leaving Sénanque you'll be retracing your steps up to the main road (D177) **G**, about 20 minutes' climb. When the path comes out at the asphalt road, turn right on it and walk about 75–100 meters (a minute or two) to the way mark ahead, which you noticed earlier. Turn right on the path here, signed to Gordes. (It's the GR 6–GR 97, marked on the IGN map.)

About five minutes later the path comes out on a bigger path **O** coming from uphill left. Turn right on this, which almost immediately (less than 10 meters) forks three ways. Ignore both the tiny leftmost path (not indicated on our map) and the right-most path (which is actually straight ahead), and take the middle one, which bends left.

About 15 minutes later the path comes to a little asphalt road **P**, at a way mark, "La Rouguiére." Turn left, signed to Gordes.

In 100 meters (1–2 minutes) you'll come to an asphalt road and turn right. Walk about 200 meters (3–4 minutes) and watch on your left (across the road from the Hôtel Domaine de l'Enclos) for a wide gravel turn off the asphalt: there's an old-style lamppost here with a red and white blaze on it. Take this.

Follow this downhill between stone walls and stone houses for a minute or so, coming to the asphalt road again, where you turn left.

Cross at the crosswalk at the bridge, and continue along the sidewalk into Gordes about five minutes from the bridge.

7 Oppède-le-Vieux Ring Walk
4 Hours

Tucked tight against the northern side of the Lubéron mountains, in the stretch known as the "Petit Lubéron," Oppède-le-Vieux hasn't been able to expand like most of the other villages here, which makes it a great place to embark on a hike. Steadily abandoned after the violence of the late Middle Ages, it was

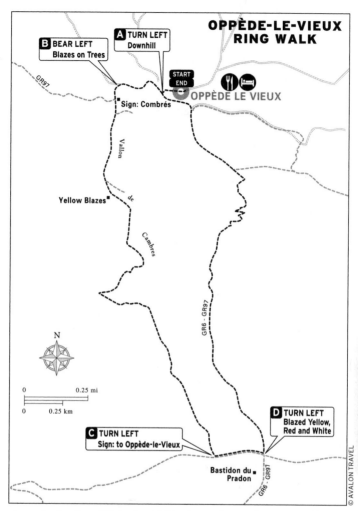

OPPÈDE-LE-VIEUX RING WALK

A TURN LEFT
Downhill

B BEAR LEFT
Blazes on Trees

START END

OPPÈDE LE VIEUX

GR97

Sign: Combrés

Vallon

de

Yellow Blazes

Cambres

GR6 - GR97

N

0   0.25 mi

0   0.25 km

C TURN LEFT
Sign: to Oppède-le-Vieux

D TURN LEFT
Blazed Yellow,
Red and White

Bastidon du
Pradon

GR6 - GR97

THE LUBÉRON MOUNTAINS

brought back to life in the 1960s, but it has so far managed to avoid the chichi aesthetic that so often accompanies that kind of resurrection. There are some fine buildings around its square, a ruined castle above it, and a very pleasant, informative botanical garden spreading down to the car park below.

The walk, much of it shaded, is a great way to explore this side of the Lubéron. It climbs fairly steeply up the Vallon de Combres, with good views opening as you come to the tall cliffs halfway along. Before that you might notice some massive evergreen trees among the lesser pines and oaks. These are Atlas cedars, outcroppings from the Massif des Cedres near Bonnieux, a cedar forest propagated from seeds brought over from Morocco in the 19th century. The trees, which were actually indigenous to the Lubéron in prehistoric times, have thrived here since their reintroduction.

At the top of the slope you'll come out on one of the main tracks running east–west along the Lubéron—a popular walking trail (no cars allowed, mercifully), leaving it to return soon after down the GR 6, which passes in and out of woods, allowing intermittently magnificent views over the village and the dramatic cliff formations jutting off to the west.

FOOD

There are two places to eat in the congenial square here. **Le Petit Café,** probably the better, serves substantial salads for around €10 and daily set *menus* for €17, featuring, when we went, succulent lamb brochettes and a passable crème brûlée. It was in the process of opening a larger, full-scale restaurant that looked promising (it also offers accommodation).

Across the square is an even more modestly priced restaurant/ snack bar, **L'Echauguette,** where you can eat well for under €11. Main dishes included a generous, tomatoey daube provençale served with a very good ratatouille; chicken cooked with local herbs; pasta with homemade *pistou* and emmenthal; as well as crepes and other desserts.

LOGISTICS
IGN Map Number and Name
#3142 OT—Cavaillon

Tourist Information
There's no tourist office in Oppède-le-Vieux, but you can get online information at www.tourisme.fr/tourist-office/bonnieux. htm or www.holidays-in-Lubéron.com.

Restaurants
Name: Le Petit Café; see listing under Accommodations.
Name: L'Echauguette
Address: Village center
Phone: 0490/ 76 83 68
Notes: closed out of season

Accommodations

Name: Le Petit Café
Address: Village center
Phone: 0490/ 76 74 01
Type of Lodging: *Chambres d'hôte* attached to restaurant
Price: 3 rooms for 2 persons, €55, €65, and €75. One very large room €100, plus €5 extra for kids.
Name: Belle de Nuit
Address: village center
Phone: 0490/ 76 93 52 or 0683/ 00 30 32
Website or Email: belle2nuit@free.fr
Type of Lodging: *Chambres d'hote, table d'hote,* restaurant
Price: €65 includes breakfast. Extra bed €20. Also 3-course meal available every evening, €25-30
Notes: One of the proprietors is an English-speaking Canadian.

Transportation

Bus service goes only as far as Oppède proper (not Oppède-le-Vieux) on the Cavaillon–Bonnieux line.

WALK DIRECTIONS

Standing in the main square (Place de la Croix) with your back to both the iron cross and the arch, go down into the road in front of you (passing the drinking fountain on your left—good water) and turn left on it. Go downhill about 40 meters/yards, first passing a little dirt road on your left and then, about 20–25 paces farther along, where there are blazes on a telephone pole on the right of the road and on the stone wall on the left of the road, take the steps off the left side of the road **Ⓐ**, leading downhill.

At the fork at the bottom of the steps, bear right downhill. Watch in five minutes or so for a fork (if you come to the asphalt road you've gone about 15 meters too far); bear left here **Ⓑ** (many colored blazes on the trees here).

In another minute you come to a way mark, "Combrés." Continue straight (leaving the GR 6 here; blazes will now be yellow and blue).

Ignore the next left turn (in a minute or two), and just beyond you'll see two big Atlas cedars. (About 20 minutes past **Ⓑ**, at a little fork after a sharp right-hand bend, stay on the right, lower path. Look for the yellow blaze beyond.)

About an hour past **B**, just around the time you're getting your first views of the valley, the path bears right uphill. There are some blazes on stones along here, but not immediately. If you lose the path along the top, it doesn't really matter; the path braids around with other paths. Just keep going in the same general direction (basically paralleling the next ridge over to your right), up toward the crest. You'll see yellow blazes from time to time. You'll also see cairns from time to time, including one especially tall one (about 4.5 feet tall). About 15 minutes beyond this tall one, you'll come to the road **C**.

At the road there's a way mark, "La Jassine." Turn left on the road **C**, signed to Oppède-le-Vieux.

In five minutes or so, you'll come to another way mark on the left, "Le Pradon" **D**. If you want to visit the Bastidon du Pradon, turn right here. The trail is red and white–blazed, and you'll reach this little mountain refuge in less than 10 minutes. Otherwise, turn left off the road here, following the trail back to Oppède. It's blazed yellow and red and white.

In about an hour you'll reach a wide fork, right uphill and left downhill; take the left.

In 15–20 minutes the path ends at a dirt road and a way mark, "Le Vieil-Oppède." Turn left on the road. In less than a minute, watch on the left for an old stone drainage leading uphill between two stone walls. Climb this, bearing either right or left at the top of the steps; both directions lead back into the village.

Wine and Lace: Gigondas and the Dentelles

A few miles south of Vaison-la-Romaine lies a range of mountains, the Dentelles de Montmirail, named for the bizarre-looking crests of limestone running in gigantic lacelike fringes along their crests (*dentelles* means "lace"). The prosaic explanation for their appearance has to do with folds in the earth's crust forcing up layers of Jurassic limestone that were then eroded by millennia of wind and rain, but they give an impression of having been created by nature in a mood of pure antic delight, and there is something irresistibly buoyant about the whole region. Prettier and less tourist-infested than the Alpilles (the next range down), it offers fabulous walking in a landscape ideally poised between wildness and cultivation, with the bright green of its vineyards set off by the white limestone and the amazing gold of the broom that flowers over the mountains throughout the spring into early summer.

It also happens to be one of the great wine-growing areas of

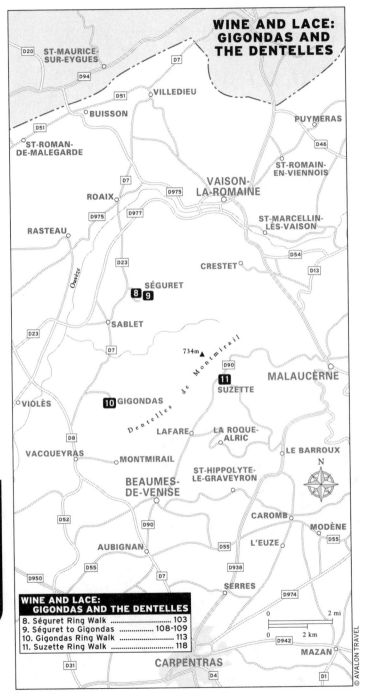

WINE AND LACE:
GIGONDAS AND
THE DENTELLES

GIGONDAS / DENTELLES

© AVALON TRAVEL

Provence, its well-favored terroir shared by Beaumes-de-Venise, Rasteau, Vacqueyras, Sablet, Séguret, and the incomparable Gigondas. This of course adds considerably to the charm, as does the presence of several good restaurants and the scattering of ancient, unspoiled villages. Our walks connect two of the prettiest of these—Séguret and Gigondas—with additional ring walks from each and a third from Suzette, a pleasant village in stunning scenery.

If you've been battling the crowds in Avignon, Les Baux, St. Remy, or other major tourist spots of western Provence, and you want a change of pace (and enjoy some great wine), this would make the perfect, easy escape. The Romans named Gigondas "Jocunditas," meaning Joy, and—as every guidebook rightly says—it seems as applicable today as it did 2,000 years ago.

WINE NOTES

Gigondas. Vacqueyras. Rasteau. The villages all within a stone's throw: Why go anywhere else?

The delight of being in such close proximity to so much great wine (that we could actually afford) lent a lightness to every step, an overarching jollity—*jocunditas*—to every moment spent in these parts. But: to walk or to shop? That is the question. Here is the place, now is the time, to cull those souvenirs...and for that you must *shop*. Out to the domaines—La Soumade in Rasteau, Sang des Cailloux and Montirius in Vacqueyras, Santa-Duc, St-Cosme and La Bouissière in Gigondas...the list could go on.

On the other hand, you could take it easy and do your shopping at the *caveau des vignerons* in the main square of Gigondas. The *caveau* is run by the Syndicat des Vins and sells the wines of all the Gigondas producers for the same price you'd get them if you went to the trouble of driving out to the domaines themselves. The only drawback is that it doesn't sell the full range of any producer. When you find a winemaker you like, or are interested in, it's lovely to taste your way through his or her range, and the lesser-known (and usually the more expensive) of those will be available only at the domaine. To make visiting easier, both the *caveau* and the tourist office have a map with every Gigondas domaine marked on it.

The restaurants too have their part in all this fun, for there you will still find the local wines, but in earlier vintages than those now on sale; a vertical tasting becomes possible, especially if you're traveling in a group.

All three of these villages produce stong, full-bodied, grenache-based wines. Gigondas is the best known, but that may work to your advantage. Vacqueyras has a finer structure; it comes from slightly lower-lying plots, ripens two weeks earlier, and quite often has a lower price tag (for *now*). Rasteau, unlike the other two, doesn't have its own AOC yet, except for its sweet wines. Again, the wines are robust and delicious, entirely competitive with those of its neighbors.

So much wine, so little time....

8 Séguret Ring Walk

1.5–2 Hours

Positioned between the rich vineyards of the Ouveze plain and the fantastical shapes of the Dentelles mountains, the unspoiled village of Séguret stands like a portal between two worlds. This short ring walk offers lovely views of each, with the wine-producing village of Sablet to the west giving way to the strange crests and tilting vineyards of the mountains as the path curves east into the Dentelles themselves. A moderately easy climb then gives you splendid aerial views over both before returning down a steep hunter's trail into Séguret.

It's well worth taking the time to wander around the village—officially one of France's "Most Beautiful" (the French are very fond of these designations). Its lovingly restored medieval buildings and covered stone alleys make it a delightful place to explore.

FOOD

The pleasant **Le Mesclun** at the heart of the village is well worth trying if you're in the mood for something more elaborate than the inexpensive salads available at the café next door. There's a €19 three-course lunch *menu* (not available on the weekend) and fancier *menus* at €32 and €45. The food is fresh and well prepared, though it has to be said that both the appetizers and the desserts were disappointing (expensive too—around €14—if you eat à la carte). A tempting-sounding dish with lemon-marinaded prawns

GIGONDAS / DENTELLES

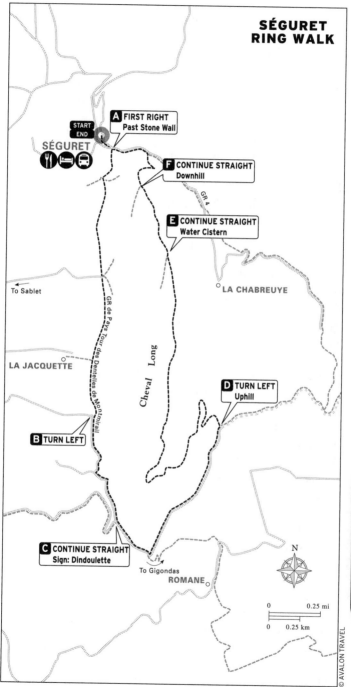

SÉGURET RING WALK

START END

SÉGURET

A FIRST RIGHT
Past Stone Wall

F CONTINUE STRAIGHT
Downhill

GR 4

E CONTINUE STRAIGHT
Water Cistern

To Sablet

○ LA CHABREUYE

GR de Pays Tour des Dentelles de Montmirail

LA JACQUETTE ○

Cheval Long

D TURN LEFT
Uphill

B TURN LEFT

C CONTINUE STRAIGHT
Sign: Dindoulette

To Gigondas
ROMANE ○

N

0   0.25 mi

0   0.25 km

and rillettes of fresh salmon was almost all fuss and decoration. A cherry *tatin* at the other end of the meal wasn't much better. On the other hand, the main courses were excellent, roasted meats especially, and of these the roast pigeon in particular, cooked to succulent, gamey perfection, cut up and served very simply on a bed of peas in broth. So our advice here would be to cut straight to the chase, and then, if dessert is a necessity, head down the street to the **salon de thé** opposite the *lavoir* (on the other end of town from the *lavoir* noted in the walk directions).

LOGISTICS
IGN Map Number and Name
#3040 ET—Carpentras/Vaison-la-Romaine/Dentelles de Montmirail

Tourist Information
Séguret doesn't have its own tourist office. The Vaison-la-Romaine office has information for Séguret:
  Address: Place du Chanoine Sautel, Vaison
  Phone: 0490/ 36 02 11
  Website or Email: www.vaison-la-romaine.com
  Hours: 9:00–12:00 and 14:00–17:45 Mon.–Sat.; open 9:00–12:30 and 14:00–18:45 every day in summer

Restaurants
  Name: Le Mesclun
  Address: Rue des Poternes
  Phone: 0490/ 46 93 43
  Closing Day: All day Mon., lunch Tues., closed in Jan.

Accommodations
See the Vaison tourist office website for more listings.
  Name: Auberge-Restaurant la Bastide Bleue
  Address: Route de Sablet (500 meters outside the village)
  Phone: 0490/ 46 83 43
  Website or Email: http://perso.wanadoo.fr/labastidebleue
  Type of Lodging: Hotel/restaurant
  Price: €53–62 double rooms with shower and bathroom, breakfast included
  Notes: It's a pretty Provençal house, rustic and tidy, with a good

price/quality relationship. In addition to double rooms there are some larger rooms for families, and a pool, nice dining room, and terrace. The restaurant is closed out of season.

Transportation
Bus
Name: Cars Lieutaud
Phone: 0490/ 36 05 22 or 0490/ 86 36 75 (usually has a person who speaks English)
Notes: Séguret is accessible from Avignon, Orange, or Vaison-la-Romaine on the Avignon–Vaison line (to look up schedule information, see the Vaucluse bus information in the introduction to the *Classic Provence: The Lubéron Mountains* chapter). For taxis, see Walk 9.

WALK DIRECTIONS

Standing in front of the restaurant Le Mesclun and with your back to it, turn right (rue de Poternes) and follow the road out through the arch (Portail Neuf), passing a *lavoir* on your left just outside the arch. Turn right and follow the road downhill, ignoring the first left but taking the hairpin left shortly beyond it, leading away from the village center.

Follow this road, with a stone wall on your right (blazed yellow and red) and views out to the Dentelles and surrounding countryside.

Take the first right past this stone wall ❶ (about five minutes past the arch).

In a couple of minutes you'll come to a three-way fork; take the middle option (actually a left turn, but not the left hairpin turn).

In about 10 minutes the path comes out at an intersection with four options, two of which are straight ahead: Of these two, take the one on the right (actually straight ahead).

In five minutes or so you'll pass the way mark "La Jacquette." Continue straight here, signed La Font di Fades, and a few minutes later the path comes out on an asphalt road ❷; turn left.

In another five minutes you'll come to a T junction (signed D.M. 210, which points left). Turn left.

In less than 10 minutes, you'll pass the way mark "La Font di Fades" ❸. Continue straight, signed Dindoulette.

In about five minutes, as the road bends left, you'll pass the turnoff on the right for Gigondas. Ignore it, continuing for another 10 minutes or so, until the asphalt ends at a fork with two gravel roads ahead and a vineyard on your right. Of the two gravel roads ahead, one is on the right and slightly downhill, the other left and uphill. Take the left uphill one **D**, a stony track, signed D.M. 210 and with a yellow "#1" arrow pointing to the right-hand fork.

After about a half hour at a leisurely pace, you'll reach some asphalt and a water cistern for firefighting **E**. The big path makes a hairpin left, but instead contiunue straight here, on the little path ahead, passing the cistern on your right.

After about 15 minutes of quite steep downhill track, you'll come to a triangular intersection **F**. Continue straight downhill on a steep and narrow track. About five minutes later the path emerges into a little vineyard and you'll see the asphalt road about 15 meters ahead. Go to that and turn left on it.

When the road forks 2–3 minutes later, bear right uphill. In another minute or so again bear right, and passing the old *lavoir,* go through the arch (Portail Neuf) and onto the rue de Poternes, and so into town.

9 Séguret to Gigondas
3–3.5 Hours

This gorgeous walk not only connects two of the prettiest villages in Provence (one of which, Gigondas, produces some of the area's most delectable wine), but also happens to meander through some of the region's loveliest countryside. Vineyards, quirkily shaped to follow the twisting contours of the mountains, accompany you most of the way, interspersed with flowering woods and hedgerows, while up on the heights the brocades of white limestone "lace" gleam against the sky. We were there in May: The light was extraordinarily clear, giving the broom that runs along every fold and crevice a glitter like gold leaf and turning an already stunning landscape into something downright celestial in appearance. The last part of the walk, along the valley that leads into Gigondas, is especially beautiful, with the Ravin du Pourra cutting through the meadows below you and the rock formations known as Les Trois Yeux ("the three eyes") gazing down from above.

FOOD

For Séguret and Gigondas listings see Walks 8 and 10.

LOGISTICS
IGN Map Number and Name

#3040 ET—Carpentras/Vaison-la-Romaine/Dentelles de Montmirail

Tourist Information

For Gigondas listings see Walk 10.

Restaurants

For Séguret and Gigondas listings see Walks 8 and 10.

Accommodations

For Séguret and Gigondas listings see Walks 8 and 10.

Transportation

The distance between Séguret and Gigondas is minimal but not well-served by the bus system. To get back to Séguret after your walk (or to get to Séguret to start the walk if you're staying in Gigondas) you can either walk back (though don't try this unless you've first walked following the directions from Séguret to Gigondas), take a taxi, take a bus, hitchhike, or, if you're traveling with friends and have two cars, leave one at each end. Séguret and Gigondas are on different bus lines (see Walks 8 and 10 for more information), with the village of Sablet in between, which can serve as a connection point as it's on both.

During school time (see *Transportation* in the *Introduction* chapter for a rough idea of these dates), the bus line Transdev Comtadins runs at least one bus in each direction between Séguret and Gigondas Mon.–Sat., with the additional possibility of doing the Séguret–Sablet and then Sablet–Gigondas connection (or in reverse), which would give you at least one further option per day.

Outside of school time, the bus between Gigondas and Sablet operates by reservation only, which must be made at least 48 hours in advance (not counting weekends and holidays) by calling Comtadins (0490/ 67 20 25). The Gigondas tourist office can help with these arrangements—and bus information

GIGONDAS / DENTELLES

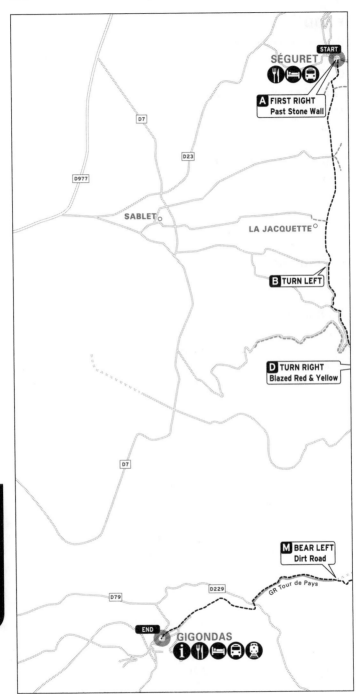

SÉGURET

START

A FIRST RIGHT
Past Stone Wall

D7

D23

D977

SABLET

LA JACQUETTE

B TURN LEFT

D TURN RIGHT
Blazed Red & Yellow

D7

M BEAR LEFT
Dirt Road

GR Tour de Pays

D79

D229

END

GIGONDAS

GIGONDAS / DENTELLES

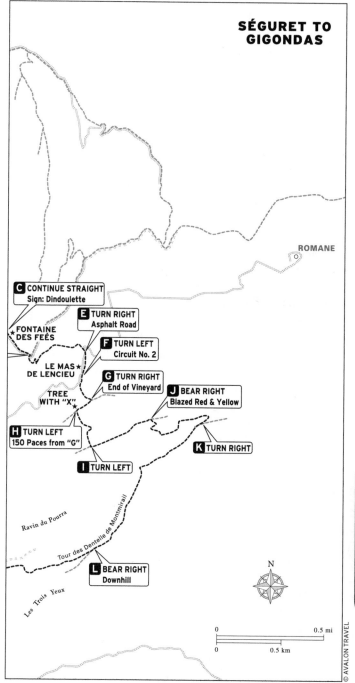

SÉGURET TO GIGONDAS

ROMANE

C CONTINUE STRAIGHT
Sign: Dindoulette

E TURN RIGHT
Asphalt Road

★ FONTAINE
DES FEÉS

F TURN LEFT
Circuit No. 2

LE MAS ★
DE LENCIEU

G TURN RIGHT
End of Vineyard

J BEAR RIGHT
Blazed Red & Yellow

TREE
WITH "X"

H TURN LEFT
150 Paces from "G"

K TURN RIGHT

I TURN LEFT

Ravin du Pourra

Tour des Dentelle de Monmirail

L BEAR RIGHT
Downhill

Les Trois Yeux

N

0   0.5 mi

0   0.5 km

GIGONDAS / DENTELLES

© AVALON TRAVEL

in general—but if it comes to using the "connecting" buses, if you can afford the taxi it will make your life easier. (Also see the introduction of the *Classic Provence: The Lubéron Mountains* chapter for finding bus schedules, and also Walks 8 and 10 for specific listings.)

Taxi
 Name: Taxi de Dentelles
 Phone: 0490/ 46 89 42
 Notes: The price (which is regulated throughout the Vaucluse, and which changes once a year, in Oct.) between Séguret and Gigondas is about €15 weekdays and €30 nights and weekends (i.e., 19:00 Sat.–07:00 Mon.). If you call during opening hours Mon.–Fri., you can make a reservation in English.
 Name: Taxi Séguret
 Phone: 0490/ 46 81 36
 Notes: See Taxi de Dentelles for pricing information.

WALK DIRECTIONS

Standing in front of the restaurant Le Mesclun in Séguret, and with your back to it, turn right (rue de Poternes) and follow the road out through the arch (Portail Neuf), passing a *lavoir* on your left just outside the arch. Turn right and follow the road downhill, ignoring the first left but taking the hairpin left shortly beyond it, leading away from the village center.

Follow this road, with a stone wall on your right (blazed yellow and red) and views out to the Dentelles and surrounding countryside.

Take the first right past this stone wall ❶ (about five minutes past the arch).

In a couple of minutes you'll come to a three-way fork; take the middle option (actually a left turn, but not the left hairpin turn).

In about 10 minutes the path comes out at an intersection with four options, two of which are straight ahead: Of these two, take the one on the right (actually straight ahead).

In five minutes or so you'll pass the way mark "La Jacquette." Continue straight here, signed La Font di Fades, and a few minutes later the path comes out on an asphalt road ❷; turn left.

In another five minutes you'll come to a T junction (signed D.M. 210, which points left). Turn left.

In less than 10 minutes, you'll pass the way mark "La Font di Fades" **C**. Continue straight, signed Dindoulette.

About five minutes later watch for a little fountain on the left, Fontaine des Feés. About 30 meters farther on, as the road bends left, leave it for a track on the right **D**, blazed red and yellow. Take this path downhill (ignoring the first path off it to the right, blazed with a yellow and red "X").

After 5–8 minutes of downhill, the path comes out at a streambed. You can see the trail across the streambed a bit to the left, heading uphill. Continue on that.

About five minutes later bear left at a fork (the slightly larger downhill fork), blazed with an "X."

A minute later the path comes out at a wider dirt farm track at the corner of a vineyard. Turn left here, and shortly you'll come to an asphalt road **E**. Turn right.

In a few minutes you pass a big stone house on your right, Le Mas de Lencieu, (called Romane on the IGN map) and about 10 meters beyond, leave the road for the dirt track on the left **F**, marked with a way mark, "Circuit No. 2."

In 3–5 minutes, at the end of the vineyard on your right, take the right-hand turn **G** and *start pacing off* because the next turnoff (**H**) is easy to miss. From **G**, count off 150 paces (regular walking steps), noticing at about 100 paces a red and yellow blaze on a tree to the left of the path. Just as the farm track you're on is bending right (and beyond there, bending left), if you look to your left you'll see there's a big vineyard there. Leave the farm track you're on, turning left **H** and walking up a few steps into the corner of the vineyard, and then continue walking uphill along the right side of the vineyard. (If you miss your turnoff at **H**, there's a yellow and red "X" on a tree to the left of the farm track you're walking on, just beyond the point where you've missed the turnoff.)

When you reach the top of that edge of the vineyard (a minute or two), turn left and in a few feet you'll see a farm track just above you on your right: Climb to it and turn right, whereupon the track bends left.

In about five minutes, you'll come to a T junction after climbing up the farm track between two vineyards. Turn left here **I**.

About 7–10 minutes later the path forks **J**; bear right uphill (the left fork is basically straight and slightly downhill), blazed red and yellow.

Keep climbing on this for another 20–25 minutes, until the path ends at a T junction with a gravel road. Turn right on this **K**.

In about 25 minutes, after you've walked quite a way above a vineyard, the path forks **L**, with a straight or a right option: Take the right downhill, blazed.

Follow this track downhill, ignoring a left fork in less than a minute.

In about 10 minutes the path meets another dirt road; bear left onto this **M**.

Continue downhill on this road for 10–15 minutes until it comes to a main asphalt road (D229). Cross over and take the path on the left of the road (way mark there), downhill.

Cross a bridge on a little stream, bear right, and come in about 20 meters to a way mark, passing it on your left and continuing straight, signed to Gigondas.

Keep on this path, ignoring deviations, until it turns to asphalt and comes to a fork, right downhill, left uphill, both asphalt (and with a way mark to your left): Take the right downhill fork.

Come to the bottom of this at the edge of town; turn left and so into the town square in another minute.

10 Gigondas Ring Walk
2.5 Hours

This is a bracing, splendid walk that forms the perfect preamble to a tasting session in the **Syndicat des Vins** of this wine lover's paradise, where you can go to sample some of the 40-odd domaines permitted to bear the famed Gigondas appellation.

The walk climbs above the village (a handsome, surprisingly low-key place), offering larger and larger views of the very pretty vineyards below. The high point—in all senses—is the stretch along the crest known as the Dentelles Sarrasines, where the path threads its way between the rock formations of the Dentelles themselves—contorted plates of limestone that are every bit as bizarrely beautiful up close as they are from a distance. You can see northeast to Mont Ventoux from here, its outline perfectly illustrating the great

GIGONDAS / DENTELLES

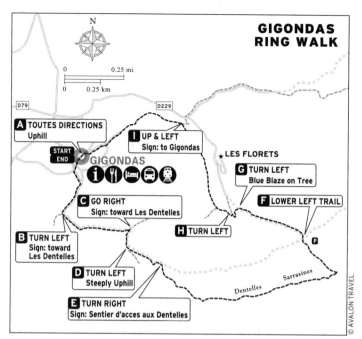

Provençal poet Frederic Mistral's image of it as a cloaked shepherd leading his flock of sheep. Winds up on the crest can be extremely strong.

After a steep descent you pass back through very pleasant farmland and vineyards, with the option of a brief detour to an excellent restaurant, before returning to Gigondas.

FOOD

There are two or three pleasant-looking restaurants in Gigondas itself, but our choice here, **Les Florets,** a kilometer outside the village, not only has a well-deserved Michelin "Bib" recommendation for good value but also happens to be very conveniently placed near the itinerary of our walk.

It's a hotel as well as a restaurant, with a slightly gloomy atmosphere inside, so eat out on the ample terrace if you can. And once the food starts arriving, things liven up. The cooking and presentation are elaborate, even a little over the top, but in an appealingly festive spirit rather than one of fussiness. There's the usual bewildering array of set *menus*—from €20–40—to study, and a surprisingly fabulous children's *menu* too, for much less. There were a large number of us when we ate here,

GIGONDAS / DENTELLES

and enough good Gigondas wine—a Domaine La Bouissière 2000—for it to be impossible to say for sure which dish belonged to which *menu* (if we even knew at the time). Suffice it to say that everything looked great and tasted pretty good too: the velvety *amuse-bouche* of shellfish *veloute* and crème fraîche, a *millefeuille* of eggplant, tomato, feta, and pesto that seemed to jump us a few months forward into deep summer, a ridiculously rich but very good roulade of shrimp and smoked salmon with a mousseline of asparagus and scallion, an excellent *duo* of lamb (a confit and a cutlet) served in a thick garlic sauce with a lovely light artichoke flan on the side. Vegetables were in unusually good supply—mounds of barley, pureed sweet potato, excellent courgette *tians*. And the desserts were real show-stoppers—sensational platters containing various combinations of coffee *pot de crème*, mango ice cream, almond *sablet* with white chocolate mousse, caramelized pineapple, cape gooseberries in chocolate…all of it glistening with great golden scribbles of caramelized sugar that thrilled the kids and seemed entirely in keeping with the dazzling light and fantastical rock formations that give this walk its singular character.

LOGISTICS
IGN Map Number and Name
#3040ET—Carpentras/Vaison-la-Romaine/Dentelles de Montmirail

Tourist Information
Address: Rue du Portail
Phone: 0490/ 65 85 46
Website or Email: www.gigondas-dm.fr
Hours: 10:00–12:00 and 14:00–18:00 Mon.–Sat. (closes at 17:00 Nov.–Mar. and at 19:00 in July and Aug.).
Notes: Its website has lots of useful information, including the weather report. The office can give you a list of the local wine producers, with a handy locator map to find the individual domaines should you wish to buy a wider range of any single producer's wares than are sold at the Syndicat des Vins (which also has the locator map). It also sells the local hiking map (€3) and walking guidebooks (in French).

Restaurants

Name: Les Florets
Closing Day: Wed., also Tues. out of season
See listing under Accommodations.

Accommodations

Name: Gîte d'Étape des Dentelles
Address: At the entrance of town
Phone: 0490/ 65 80 85
Website or Email: www.gite-dentelles.com
Type of Lodging: *Gîte d'étape*
Price: €12.50–14.40 per person
Notes: Closed Jan. and Feb. Handsome modern building, impeccably clean. Equipped kitchen area. Ten rooms for two people, one room for three people, and two *dortoirs* for 12 people each. Four bath/shower rooms, eight w.c. English spoken. Owners are very knowledgeable about walks in the area.

Name: Les Florets
Address: Two km from the village, on the walk route
Phone: 0490/ 65 85 01
Website or Email: www.hotel-lesflorets.com
Type of Lodging: Logis de France hotel
Price: Double room €95; half pension for two people €188
Notes: Charming hotel with restaurant reviewed above.

Transportation

Bus

Name: Transdev Comtadins
Phone: 0490/ 67 20 25
Notes: Gigondas is accessible from Carpentras on the Carpentras–Sablet line, #13 (for specific schedule information, see the introduction to the *Classic Provence: The Lubéron Mountains* chapter, or check with the Gigondas tourist office). For taxi listings see Walk 9.

Miscellaneous Notes

Syndicat des Vins, place de la Mairie (main square), open 10:00–12:00 and 14:00–17:30 daily, sells the local wares at the same price as the vineyards themselves, but without the entire range of any single producer.

GIGONDAS / DENTELLES

WALK DIRECTIONS

Standing on the main square, looking out on the valley below, take the road that leads out to the left (south)—not the one leading up to the tourist office, but the larger one with the Toutes Directions sign on it **Ⓐ**. Take this road uphill and to the left (i.e., the opposite direction of the way the Toutes Directions sign is pointing). It's blazed red and yellow.

Keep on the road as it curves right, past the Domaine La Bouissière shop. In 10–15 minutes you'll come to a T junction with a way mark **Ⓑ**; go left toward Les Dentelles (blue blazes).

The path goes uphill, turning to the left (ignore a yellow-blazed trail off to the right in a few minutes). In 15 minutes or so you'll come to a T junction with a way mark **Ⓒ**; go right, signed toward Les Dentelles.

Be alert: In two minutes take a much smaller blue-blazed path off to the left of the main track, cutting steeply uphill **Ⓓ**.

In five minutes you'll come to a picnic and parking area, with a belvedere up steps to the left. Ignoring the steps, continue forward and in about 50 meters/yards you'll see a way mark pointing to the right, a small uphill path: Take this **Ⓔ** (signed Sentier d'acces aux Dentelles).

Pay attention to the blue blazes on this small path (there's a right fork a minute or so after you begin, which you take). The path gets a bit ribboned near the top (i.e., it splits and meanders) but look for blue; generally the clearest path is the correct path.

In 15–20 minutes the path brings you to the crest. Here the valley to the south becomes visible, but your path sticks to the north side of the crest.

In 20–25 minutes the path begins descending fairly steeply and then *very* steeply. Keep following the blue blazes along here. You'll pass a way mark, "Col de Cayron" (easy to miss, but it doesn't matter).

When you reach the parking lot at the bottom (10–15 minutes), cross it, taking the lower left trail (with a way mark signing you to Village de Gigondas), a wide dirt road blazed yellow as well as blue **Ⓕ**. (If you look back up to the Dentelles across the vineyard just after the parking lot, the big blade of rock you see is the Rocher du Turc.)

Be alert: About 10 minutes past the parking lot, just where the road changes from dirt to concrete, the path goes left, down a narrow trail (look for the blue left-hand-turn blaze on a tree) **G**.

After going down some steps the path turns right, passing a little fountain, then a little concrete shed (a water cistern), before coming to a T junction **H** (about two minutes from **G**), where you go left for Gigondas or right (ignoring a blue "X") for the restaurant Les Florets.

To take the optional spur to Les Florets from **H**, turn right at **H** (ignoring the blue "X" blaze), and in two minutes you'll come to a road; go left (i.e., forward), passing the Domaine des Florets winery. The restaurant is a sharp right uphill in two more minutes.

To return to Gigondas, go back to **H** and turn right. (*Note:* This is where you would have turned left originally, if you had not been going to Les Florets.)

To continue to Gigondas without doing the spur off to Les Florets, turn left at **H**. Take your first right (less than a minute past **H**, and with a yellow triangle blaze "3–4" pointing right), following along to the right of a vineyard for about 50 meters, when the path becomes a narrow footpath (blue blazes are on the path as it goes through some woods).

In 10 minutes or so, ignore a fork uphill right, just above a view over a vineyard. Another minute later the path drops to the right, to the vineyard.

Continue straight ahead to the other end of the vineyard, and take the small trail leading up and left out of the vineyard. You'll see a way mark ("345") **I** directing you to Gigondas.

Ignoring all deviations, you'll come to a three-way fork in about 10 minutes. Keep right. A minute later, at an iron cross, keep straight, bearing around to the left, with the cross directly on your right. This takes you into the village center.

11 Suzette Ring Walk
2.5–3 Hours

For sheer magnificence of scenery, this walk would be hard to beat. The little village of Suzette, though not especially ancient and not noted for its wines, is a pleasant, remote-feeling spot, set in the midst of unspoiled countryside, with superb, panoramic views all around. There's a hotel/restaurant where you can

GIGONDAS / DENTELLES

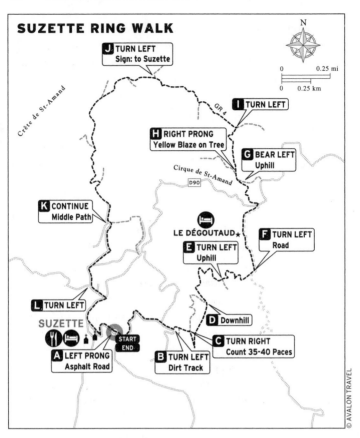

SUZETTE RING WALK

N

0   0.25 mi
0   0.25 km

Crête de St-Amand

J TURN LEFT
Sign: to Suzette

GR 4

I TURN LEFT

H RIGHT PRONG
Yellow Blaze on Tree

G BEAR LEFT
Uphill

Cirque de St-Amand
D90

K CONTINUE
Middle Path

LE DÉGOUTAUD★

E TURN LEFT
Uphill

F TURN LEFT
Road

L TURN LEFT

SUZETTE

START
END

D Downhill

A LEFT PRONG
Asphalt Road

B TURN LEFT
Dirt Track

C TURN RIGHT
Count 35–40 Paces

© AVALON TRAVEL

stay—a great place if you're looking for somewhere peaceful and absolutely rural. The walk itself, much of it following the crests of the Cirque de St-Amand, has a bit of everything: vineyards, pine-scented woods, *garrigue*, small streams, and dreamy views of the Dentelles and several ranges beyond.

FOOD

Restaurant Les Coquelicots is a friendly, relaxed place to eat. Its pizzas (which include one with snails) are served only in July and August, but there's a good year-round menu. Fresh fish dishes and standard treatments of lamb and beef for €18–21 are supplemented by rather more adventurous appetizers at around €10. These include a tasty confection of roasted eggplant, peppers, and quinoa, a salad composed of both fresh and oven-dried tomatoes, with the different sweetnesses of each—one tart, one caramelly—mingling deliciously. Vegetarians could easily fill up on a couple of these appetizers or move on to one of the pasta dishes: tiny ravioli served with a choice of black olive tapenade, *anchoiade* (olives, garlic, and anchovies), or a *pistou*. All are good, if slightly overburdened with cream and butter. Crepes feature prominently on the dessert *menu,* and given the name of the village, there of course has to be a crêpe suzette (€7). This arrived in a conflagration of Marc, an *eau-de-vie* distilled from Beaumes-de-Venise, which burned for an alarmingly long time, leaving behind the fuming wreckage of what might have been a decent crepe: It's best to stick with the simpler offerings for this course.

LOGISTICS
IGN Map Number and Name
#3040ET—Carpentras/Vaison-la-Romaine/Dentelles de Montmirail

Restaurants
Name: Restaurant Les Coquelicots
Address: At the village entrance
Phone: 0490/ 65 06 94
Closing Day: Lunch Mon. and Tues., all day Wed.
Notes: Panoramic terrace; reservations recommended.

Accommodations
Name: Le Dégoutaud
Address: Two km outside the village on the walk route
Phone: 0490/ 62 99 29
Website or Email: www.degoutaud.fr
Type of Lodging: *Chambres d'hôte*
Price: €52 single, €63–68 double, €73–78 triple, €83–88 for four
Notes: It also sells farm products and serves meals. See the website for more details.

Transportation
There is no public transport to Suzette. You could use one of the taxi services mentioned in Walk 9, or take public transport to well-connected Malaucéne and get a taxi from there—which would be less expensive, as it's closer.

Miscellaneous Notes

There are two organic farms in Suzette:

Guy Jullien: Domaine ferme St-Martin, 0490/62 96 40 and 0620/ 68 00 20, www.fermesaintmartin.com; it sells AOC Beaumes-de-Venise and AOC Côtes du Ventoux.

Bernard Mendez: Domaine Beauvalcinte, 0490/ 65 08 37 and 0688/ 57 73 69, www.domainebeauvalcinte.com; 10:00–12:00 and 14:00–18:00 Mon.–Sat. and by appointment; it sells AOC Côtes du Rhone, AOC Beaumes-de-Venise, and fruit juices.

WALK DIRECTIONS

Leaving the main parking lot below town, turn left (southeast) on the asphalt road.

In five minutes or so you'll come to an asphalted fork to the left: Take this **Ⓐ**.

In 7–10 minutes another asphalt road comes in from the left, joining ours. Continue downhill.

A minute later, as the asphalt road makes a right hairpin turn, leave it, instead taking the dirt track to the left **Ⓑ**, immediately bending right, and following along the bottom of a terraced vineyard to your left. (Ignore the right fork about 25 meters/yards along, keeping straight uphill, now between two vineyards.)

Pay attention here: As you climb straight uphill between these two vineyards, the one on the left ends. As you get to the top of this little hill you're climbing, the path begins to bend left. Keep your eye on the vineyard to your right: When you get to the end of it, the path you're on is bending left, but you want to leave it **Ⓒ**, dropping to the right and following along the left side of the vineyard. *Count your paces* after you make this right turn at **Ⓒ**, starting to count at the point where the vineyard begins. Use normal walking-size paces, and watch on the left for a little footpath at 35–40 paces. It's marked with a blue left-turn blaze on a small rock cairn, but in case that disappears, you can find it by pacing it. Turn left (northeast) onto it. You'll see blue blazes along here.

In 5–10 minutes this little well-blazed footpath ends at a bigger dirt farm track **Ⓓ**, which is in the process of making a hairpin turn. Take this bigger track downhill.

Continue all the way downhill on this track, ignoring tracks off it.

The path bottoms out over a streambed, where it begins to climb the other side as a grassy path. In two minutes or so, as you're walking above a ravine (to your right), and you come to the corner of a field, watch on your right for a right-hand turn blaze on a tree. (Here is a description to use if, for some reason, the blaze has disappeared: At the corner of the field, as you're still walking parallel to the ravine, there's a little track straight ahead where you'd otherwise be turning left to follow around the field.) Go straight up this path about three meters and turn right, again blazed blue on several trees.

Two minutes later, watch for a fork uphill left, and take this ❺, ignoring the blue "X" on a tree. *Note:* If this shortcut, which cuts out some road walking, gets closed off, simply follow the blue blazes from ❺ to the road, turn left on the road, and pick up directions at ❻.

In a minute or two, when you come to an orchard, turn right, walking above it, and almost immediately (10 meters) as you reach a higher orchard turn right again (so you're walking *away* from the higher orchard). In another 10 meters turn left and walk up along the edge of a vineyard (to your left), toward some pine trees in a forest scrub ahead. Wrap around the vineyard to the forest scrub and take the dirt track (a hard-baked, whitish color) off to the right through some big pines.

Cross through the pines and then immediately bend left uphill, following the line of scrub (just to your left now). In about 10 meters, at the end of the scrub and on the edge of a field, turn right, again heading for a line of pine trees ahead and to the left. Reaching the corner of the field (30 meters or so) turn left, following the track parallel to the pine trees. Follow this line of scrub woods (another minute) out to the road ❻ and turn left.

(If you're staying at le Dégoutaud, watch for it on the left in less than five minutes.)

In 5–10 minutes (from ❻) you'll come to a T junction with a larger asphalt road (D90). There's a great view back to Suzette here. Cross over and take the path uphill toward the left (yellow blaze).

After about five minutes' climb, you'll meet another path coming in from the right ❼; bear left uphill, in another minute coming to a fork ⓗ with a yellow blaze on a tree and a yellow "X" on a stone. Take the right fork.

Another 7–10 minutes' fairly ambitious climbing brings you to a T junction with the GR 4 (which is also just a narrow path at this point) ⓘ. There are red and white blazes on the GR side of the trees at this intersection. Turn left here.

In 5–10 minutes remember to turn around for views of Mont Ventoux to the east and of the valley to the southeast. Keep straight on the GR 4; don't take paths off it. (About 5–8 minutes past ⓘ ignore a blue left-hand-turn blaze with a "10" on a rock near the summit and the blue "X" on the tree just beyond.)

About 20 minutes or so past ⓘ, you'll come to a fork ⓙ at a way mark, "Combe Fréu." Leave the GR 4 here, turning left, signed to Suzette.

In another three minutes you'll pass a second way mark, "Le Partifiage." Continue straight, signed to Suzette.

(In a few minutes a path comes in from the right to join ours, and another five minutes beyond that, we join a path coming in from the right. Keep on downhill.)

Continuing to descend, after skirting some vineyards the path turns to asphalt 15–20 minutes past ⓙ.

Stay on this asphalt road, in 5–10 minutes coming to an intersection of three paths, all paved. Take the middle one ⓚ, and then bear left (less than a minute) when you intersect the next asphalt road.

In another 10 minutes or so, when the road forks ⓛ, turn left. At the T junction 100 meters or so beyond, turn right, and so into town.

Banon and the Lure

Between the eastern end of the Lubéron and the next range of mountains to the north, the Lure, lies a relatively unknown region of quiet farming villages set in a largely unspoiled landscape of lavender fields, sheep pastures, rolling hills, wooded valleys, and an occasional spectacular gorge, making it an ideal area for walking.

Banon, famous for its goat and sheep cheeses wrapped in chestnut leaves, is the liveliest of these villages, and would make a good base for any of these walks, but there are many other options, varying from the nearby bustling town of Apt to what must be some of the quietest little *chambres d'hôtes* to be found anywhere in Provence. In the latter category would be the ring of tiny, low-key villages that we've linked together into a three- or four-day walking tour (the Bistrots de Pays Walk), which can be done either in its entirety or in sections of your choice, using the bus or a taxi (see *Transportation* in the *Logistics* section of the walk) to get you back to your starting point if you choose not to walk all the way.

BANON AND THE LURE

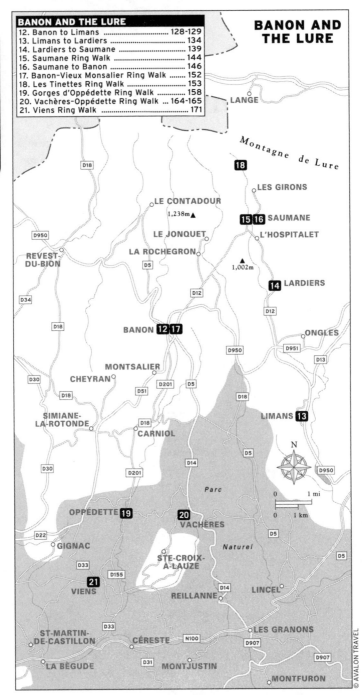

BANON AND THE LURE

BANON AND THE LURE

LANGE

Montagne de Lure

18

LES GIRONS

LE CONTADOUR
1,238m ▲

15 16 SAUMANE

L'HOSPITALET

LE JONQUET
LA ROCHEGRON

D950

▲ 1,002m

14 LARDIERS

REVEST-
DU-BION

D5

D12

D34

D12

D18

ONGLES

BANON 12 17

D950

D951

D13

MONTSALIER

D30

CHEYRAN

D201   D5

D51

D18

LIMANS **13**

D18

SIMIANE-
LA-ROTONDE

D18

CARNIOL

D5

N

D30

D201

D14

D950

Parc

0   1 mi

0   1 km

OPPÉDETTE **19**

20

VACHÈRES

D22

GIGNAC

STE-CROIX-
A-LAUZE

Naturel

D5

D5

21

VIENS

D155

D33

D14

LINCEL

REILLANNE

ST-MARTIN-
DE-CASTILLON

D33

CÉRESTE

N100

LES GRANONS

D907

LA BÈGUDE

D31

MONTJUSTIN

D907

MONTFURON

© AVALON TRAVEL

Aside from Banon itself, each of these villages boasts an official Bistrot de Pays. Like the Slow Food phenomenon, the Bistrot de Pays movement is an attempt to preserve or revive authentic local cuisines, using locally grown food and employing the best traditions of home cooking. Restaurants wanting to hang the distinctive Bistrot de Pays placard over their doors make a pledge to deliver a warm family atmosphere, serve local dishes, even to sell local products. It isn't an absolute guarantee of quality, but they do tend to be pleasant places, and often the food is very good indeed. In addition to the walks from village to village we've also included some short ring walks from a couple of the villages themselves.

From Banon it's a short drive north to the Lure mountains—higher and more remote feeling than the Lubéron—where we have a walk that passes some monumental old stone sheepcotes, stunning examples of the ancient vernacular architecture of this part of the world.

Heading south you come to the village of Oppédette, one of our favorite in all of Provence; a perfect fusion of stone mountain into stone habitations, perched above a vast gorge, which—if you have a head for heights—offers some very rewarding walking. We've also connected Oppédette to the sleepy village of Vachères (which has a great Bistrot de Pays) in a long ring walk through exceptionally pretty countryside.

There's a well-known area known as the "Colorado" of Provence, a little to the west of here. Its name comes from the extraordinarily vivid reds and oranges of the rubble left behind by various ochre-quarrying enterprises that once flourished near the village of Rustrel. There are trails running through them if you're interested, but you'll be joined by large numbers of people arriving by bus/coach in the parking lot outside Rustrel. We did think of including a walk here but decided it belonged in our "drive-by" category of places you might just as well see from a car. Not far from here, however, is the village of Viens, a medieval gem surrounded by gorgeous farmland, where we have a short ring walk. We've also included in the Viens walk some listings of high points in nearby Apt.

WINE NOTES

Midway along the Bistrots de Pays Walk comes the wine lover's mecca of Le Bistrot de la Lavande. When we were in Provence for this book, la Lavande was the first time we had a *really* good bottle of wine, a Rasteau from Domaine La Soumade. It was not particularly expensive, but on a completely different level from what we'd been drinking the first month in the Lubéron. The owner of la Lavande is passionate about wine, and that makes so much difference when it comes to a restaurant's wine list. Crowded on the shelves to your right as you walk in the door are all the bottles comprising the *bistrot*'s "wine list" (with their prices on them), and you can look through, pick them up and fondle them, and decide what you want, a very pleasurable experience in itself. We took notes on some of the bottles we weren't going to be able to drink that night, to guide us in future purchases, and asked the owner where to find them. It was he who pointed us in the direction of the excellent La Cave du Septier in Apt, for which we are eternally grateful as that address served us well during the next four months.

ALPES-DE-HAUTE-PROVENCE BUS SCHEDULES

The Conseuil Général for the Département of Alpes-de-Haute-Provence (which, as they go by alphabetical order, is 04) has a website, on which you can find the map of bus routes for the region, as well as all the current schedules at www.cg04.fr/politique/missions/equipement/equipement.html. Scroll down the page to the "Guide Horaire des Transports," and click on whichever is your geographical area of interest.

When reading bus schedules, remember to look at the top and bottom of the column of bus times, to see *which* days of the week the bus operates (it might be one day a week only!), whether it's during school time, school vacation, or *annuel,* which is all through the year.

BISTROTS DE PAYS MULTIDAY WALK

A restaurant bearing the Bistrot de Pays logo is part of a movement that seeks to express the French concept of terroir. Of course one most often connects terroir with wine, but the Bistrots de Pays, too, aim to be expressions of what is local. Established in rural "villages of character," they focus on recipes and dishes in the traditional regional cooking styles, prepared with local products. They are often the last, or one of the last, businesses in their village, and fulfill a variety of central functions, particularly as purveyor of local products and information. Often they serve as the village's only grocery store, newsagent, and bakery.

In practice the *bistrots* are all unique and subscribe to the official Bistrot de Pays manifesto in varying degrees. As a movement and in practice, while casting a look at the past, the concept is interesting, positive, and unquestionably modern (although they often don't accept credit cards).

Logistical Overview

The Banon tourist office has listings of *chambres d'hôtes* throughout the area covered by the Bistrots de Pays tour: Banon, Lardiers, Rochegiron, L'Hospitalet, and Saumane. Only Limans is not covered, as it is under a different jurisdiction (Forcalquier). These villages are small, and accommodation—and other amenities—are not abundant, so it's even more important than usual to make sure to book ahead, not just for lodging but for the restaurant as well. It's a good idea to call the *bistrot* yet again the day of your planned arrival: Remember these are tiny operations with just one chef; if something comes up, they don't have a staff to fall back on and have to close instead. For Limans, try the Forcalquier tourist office for additional lodging options that may have come into operation since this book was published (see *Logistics* for *Walk 12, Banon to Limans*). If worse comes to worst, you can always call a taxi. Carry its number with you, or ask one of the Bistrots de Pays to call for you. For that matter, if you get stuck without a room, you might ask the proprietor of the village Bistrot de Pays to help you out. He or she is likely to know who might be willing to rent you a room for the night; part of the Bistrot de Pays mission is to provide tourist information and help people organize their holiday and leisure activities.

For this multisegment walk we've put the logistics for the *arrival* village in each walk.

12 Banon to Limans
4 Hours

This half-day (at least) village-to-village walk goes high over hill trails and on through beautiful, unspoiled farmland. It begins

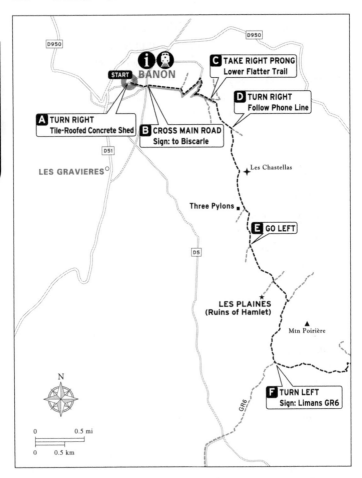

D950

D950

ⓘ 🚉 **BANON**

START

C TAKE RIGHT PRONG
Lower Flatter Trail

D TURN RIGHT
Follow Phone Line

A TURN RIGHT
Tile-Roofed Concrete Shed

B CROSS MAIN ROAD
Sign: to Biscarle

D51

LES GRAVIERES ○

◆ Les Chastellas

Three Pylons ▪

E GO LEFT

D5

LES PLAINES
(Ruins of Hamlet) ★

▲ Mtn Poirière

N

F TURN LEFT
Sign: Limans GR6

GR6

0   0.5 mi

0   0.5 km

with a long and rather sharp ascent to the crests opposite Banon, but from there on it's almost all a gentle descent. Crossing the peaks of Les Chastellas, the trail comes down past a forlornly lovely ruined hamlet, where you can look for the stone marking the spot where a World War II resistance fighter was killed by a Nazi collaborator (it's opposite the third set of ruins). From there you pass goat and sheep farms (we watched a lamb being born in a grassy meadow when we passed one of them), and then climb again through an arid, parched landscape before coming back into the lavender fields and pastures of Limans, a very pleasant village famous for its 16th-century *pigeonniers* (pigeon houses) as well as a Gothic church with remains of an extremely ancient chancel (where the choir sat)—possibly as old as the 6th century.

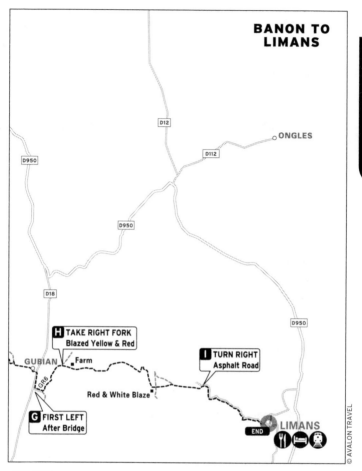

**BANON TO
LIMANS**

ONGLES

D12

D112

D950

D950

D18

D950

H TAKE RIGHT FORK
Blazed Yellow & Red

I TURN RIGHT
Asphalt Road

GUBIAN   ■ Farm

GR6

Red & White Blaze

G FIRST LEFT
After Bridge

END   LIMANS

© AVALON TRAVEL

FOOD

Eating outside the unpretentious little **Bistrot du Nord** in the pretty village of Limans is a very pleasant way of relaxing after the longish walk from Banon. The cooking isn't stellar, but it's acceptable and very inexpensive. There are *menus* at €12, €16, and €22 (the latter coming with three appetizers, a main course, three desserts, and wine). Appetizers included an excellent homemade terrine of pork, some rather-too-lemony marinated artichokes, a decent *pissaladiere* (a sort of pizza with slow-cooked onion and anchovy). Duck with green olives, an oily but very tasty sauté of lamb with confit of tomato, and a hearty if not very subtle *niçoise* treatment of salt cod—with tomatoes, eggplant, and peppers—comprised the main courses. Excellent raspberry cake and chocolate fondant followed, along with a very nice pear stewed with what appeared to be—of all things—red peppercorns.

LOGISTICS
IGN Map Number and Name
#3341 OT—Montagne de Lure
Note that the actual village of Banon is just off the periphery of this map. You don't need the IGN map with the village on it (which is #3240 OT—Banon/Sault) for this walk, but it also covers the other walks in this series.

Tourist Information
Address: 13, place du Bourguet, Forcalquier
Phone: 0492/ 75 10 02
Website or Email: www.forcalquier.com
Notes: Use this office (as well as the Bistrot de Pays in Limans, listed below) if you need further help securing lodging in Limans.

Restaurants
Name: Bistrot du Nord (sometimes called Café du Nord)
Address: Center of village
Phone: 0492/ 74 53 31
Website or Email: cafedunord@orange.fr
Closing Day: Thurs. in season, Wed. and Thurs. outside season

Accommodations
Accommodation in Limans is very thin. The owner of L'Aguilas knows another woman who will rent a room overnight, so if L'Aguilas is booked, ask the proprietor to refer you. You can also check the Forcalquier tourist office for new listings, and ask the owners of the Bistrot de Pays.
Name: L'Aguilas
Address: Near the *bistrot*—call for directions
Phone: 0492/ 73 15 44
Website or Email: http://gîte.aguilas.free.fr
Type of Lodging: *Gîte,* available by the night or week, one bedroom with double bed, plus double sofa bed in living room, and single bed on a mezzanine level
Price: €40, plus additional €10 per person, including breakfast

Notes: English spoken. The owner will make you a picnic for the onward journey, but make sure to ask for this at the time you make the reservation. There aren't any shops in Limans.

Transportation

Bus
Name: Autocars Sumian
Phone: 0491/ 49 00 49
Website or Email: autocars@sumian.fr
Frequency and Duration: One early-morning bus from Banon to Limans (at the time of this writing, leaves Banon 7:40 Mon.–Sat.). Three buses per day from Limans to Banon (at the time of this writing, 11:35 Mon.–Sat., and 16:45 Mon.–Fri. during school vacation, or 18:10 during school periods). It's a 25-minute ride.

Taxi
If you get stuck, you can always call a taxi. You can ask the owners of the Bistrot de Pays to call for you.
Name: Taxi les Cigales
Phone: 0492/ 73 35 66
Price: About €15 between Limans and Banon
Taxi Services from Forcalquier
Name: Taxi des Garriques
Phone: 0607/ 47 26 97
Name: Taxi Forcalquierens
Phone: 0492/ 75 34 34

Miscellaneous Notes
Visit the Bistrot de Pays website at www.bistrotdepays.com. While Limans has no shops, it does have some visiting merchants: at 9:00 daily (except Mon. and Thurs.) the baker van; 5:00 Fri. the grocery van; afternoon Tues. the wine van.

WALK DIRECTIONS
Standing at the fountain in the Banon village square, facing away from both the fountain and the post office, walk to the intersection at the end of the square (about 20 meters/yards) and turn right downhill. Pass Le Bleuet bookstore on your right and then come to the first cross street and cross over it. There's a way mark on your left, "Chemin de l'Orge," and the same is signed on the wall to your right.

Walk down this road about 250 meters (about three minutes) until you come to the first asphalted right turn, by a tile-roofed concrete shed and an electric pylon. Turn right here **A**.

Follow this road downhill for another 250–300 meters (3–4 minutes) to the main road (D12). There's a way mark here; follow the direction of Biscarle by crossing the main road and continuing on the gravel road directly across **B**.

This track takes you immediately into pretty farm country. After half a kilometer (5–7 minutes) the road turns right at an intersection. Follow the main road, ignoring deviations. It's blazed red and yellow.

Follow your progress on the map; when you reach the third hairpin turn (left) in another 10 minutes or so, watch 3–5 minutes later for a significant path off to the right (ignore it), and just beyond that, the road forks, with two similar-size options: Take the right, lower, flat trail **C**.

About 5–7 minutes later you'll reach a wide intersection **D**; turn right here (following the phone line).

Big views down to Banon as you walk close to the crests of La Chastellas; 15 minutes past **D**, under the lines of three pylons, there's a way mark with a turnoff for Banon par le Puy. Continue straight here.

In another five minutes or so the road forks; go left **E**. In 10 minutes or so, there's a big intersection of four paths, where you continue straight.

Soon you'll come to the ruined hamlet of Les Plaines. Opposite the third group of ruins is a plaque marking the place where a certain Elie Mille was assassinated by French collaborators during World War II.

Continue past Les Plaines through beautiful countryside. About 15 minutes past Les Plaines, you'll reach an intersection with two way marks, one on each side of the path **F**. Turn left here (ignoring a fork up left immediately after the turn), signed Limans GR 6.

You'll reach a house 20 minutes later. Bear left around the house, ignoring a path off to the left when the path you're on curves right and back toward the rear of the house. The path continues downhill, soon reaching the hamlet of Gubian. Two minutes past Gubian, turn right on the little asphalt road.

About 3–5 minutes later cross a little bridge and take the first left after the bridge **G**. In two minutes the path bends left and crosses a beautiful stone bridge.

In 5–10 minutes watch for a lesser fork off to the left at a sheep meadow **H** (blazed yellow and red). There's a way mark here on your right, somewhat hidden by the electric pylon. Take the right fork here, passing the farm on your left.

After a half hour's rather strenuous uphill climb, through a parched, arid landscape, you'll reach an intersection at a pylon with a red and white blaze. Continue straight, beginning the gradual descent into Limans.

In another 10–15 minutes, at a T junction with a little asphalt road, go right **I**. Follow this road into Limans, reached in another half hour.

13 **Limans to Lardiers**
4–5 Hours

This is a long day's march, taking you up through goat farms and lavender fields, across quiet pine woods, and along the hunting and logging trails of the high hills above Ongles and Lardiers. *Note:* Our itinerary is not the same as the blazed GR trail marked in red on the map (IGN #3341 OT). Though quite a bit shorter, the GR takes the valley route, passing through some built-up areas. We think it's worth the climb to go along the crests—better views, cooler breezes—but if you want a shorter walk, stay on the GR where we depart from it at **E** (this will be noted in the walk directions). It looks straightforward on the map, but we didn't do it, so we can't vouch for it.

Another option is to leave our route at **D** and detour into the village of Ongles, where there's another extremely friendly Bistrot de Pays, the Café de la Tonnelle (see *Logistics*); again, we mention the departure point for this version below. We didn't include Ongles because we thought it would be one night too many for this circuit. The path to Ongles is an official path and should be signed all the way.

Finally, you could stay on the GR after we deviate from it, and take it to Rocher d'Ongles, which has two restaurants. If you're doing any of these alternatives, make sure you have the IGN map.

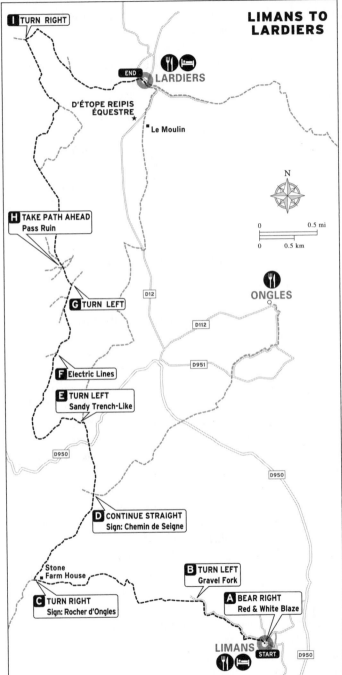

LIMANS TO LARDIERS

I TURN RIGHT

END
LARDIERS

D'ÉTOPE REIPIS ÉQUESTRE
★
■ Le Moulin

N

0   0.5 mi
0   0.5 km

H TAKE PATH AHEAD
Pass Ruin

ONGLES

D12

G TURN LEFT

D112

F Electric Lines

D951

E TURN LEFT
Sandy Trench-Like

D950

D950

D CONTINUE STRAIGHT
Sign: Chemin de Seigne

■ Stone
Farm House

B TURN LEFT
Gravel Fork

A BEAR RIGHT
Red & White Blaze

C TURN RIGHT
Sign: Rocher d'Ongles

LIMANS
START
D950

© AVALON TRAVEL

Lardiers is a tranquil country village, with a tiny but excellent Bistrot de Pays, Le Bistrot de la Lavande.

FOOD

Le Bistrot de la Lavande is the real thing: a place where the aspiration to preserve the simplicity of home cooking is matched by a skill and attentiveness to detail that makes everything memorably delicious without being in the least bit fussy or pretentious.

The tiny space, with its touches of chrome and glass and its impressive display of wines, manages to be both intimate and elegant: You sense immediately that food is taken seriously here, and it is.

A spectacular *brandade de morue* (salt cod pureed with potatoes, garlic, and olive oil) formed the centerpiece of a generous selection of appetizers that showed off local seasonal produce very handsomely in the form of an aspargus tart, cold roasted fennel, and the best marinated artichokes we had in this region. To follow there was a choice of an elemental daube of beef with a hint of juniper over the usual black-olive base, served with polenta, or a *navarin* of lamb—a light casserole (preferable to the starchy *blanquette* style more commonly favored in these parts), cooked with potatoes, turnips, carrots, and beans. Dessert lovers will be more than satisfied by the array of sweet things arriving at the end of the meal: a cake of chocolate and coffee, another of lemon, both excellent, and an enormous bowl of pears in wine. The wine choices here are much broader and better than usual. We had an organic red: a Rasteau, Domaine de Soumade 2003, Cuvee Prestige. Rasteaus are considered one of the last "undiscovered" (i.e., affordable) first-rate Côtes du Rhône wines. This was by far the best bottle we'd drunk after several weeks in Provence.

The three-course dinner *menu* here is €22; there are usually a couple of options for the main course. Reservations are essential, and vegetarians should give as much notice as possible.

LOGISTICS
IGN Map Number and Name

#3341 OT—Montagne de Lure

Tourist Information
Use the Banon tourist office listing; see Walk 16.

Restaurants
Ongles:
  Name: Café de la Tonnelle
  Address: Ongles village center
  Phone: 0492/ 73 19 89
  Closing Day: Open every day
  Notes: Barbecue grill Fri. nights in season; Sat. night is pizza
  night. It also offers a vegetarian menu.
Lardiers:
  Name: Le Bistrot de la Lavande
  Address: Lardiers village center
  Phone: 0492/ 73 31 52
  Closing Day: Evenings Tues. and Wed. out of season, open
  evenings Wed. in season, also closed for a period in Feb. and
  mid-Nov.–Dec. 10
  Notes: Make your reservation as far in advance as possible.
  The place is small and can be booked out way ahead of time.
  No credit cards.

Accommodations
  Name: Les Deux Vignes
  Address: Lardiers
  Phone: 0492/ 73 24 88
  Website or Email: www.deuxvignes.com
  Type of Lodging: *Chambres d'hôte*
  Price: €70 per night includes aperitif on arrival and breakfast; it
  also has *table d'hôte* or does a half-pension deal in conjunction
  with le Bistrot de la Lavande (which is only 50 meters away).
  Name: Le Moulin
  Address: Outside Lardiers village (see walk map)
  Phone: 0492/ 73 38 54
  Website or Email: gitelemoulin@orange.fr
  Type of Lodging: *Gîte d'étape*
  Price: Three rooms for 2–5 people, one person €24, two people
  €43, half pension €45. Dinner is available (made with local
  products) €25, picnic for onward journey €10. The hosts don't really
  speak English; you can send them an email to reserve, or call them.

Transportation

No public transport.

Miscellaneous Notes

Point **B** on the Limans to Lardiers map is the same place as point **G** on the Banon to Limans map. All of **A**–**C** is retracing your tracks from Banon into Limans.

WALK DIRECTIONS

With the Bistrot du Nord on your left, head out of town on the asphalt road. In about 100 meters/yards, at the edge of town, the road forks at a war memorial; bear right and then immediately left, where a stone wall will be on your left. Follow this road uphill (ignoring the right leading to an industrial-looking shed) to the fork 50 meters beyond, and bear right **A** (there's a red and white blaze on a speed limit sign).

Keep on this little road, ignoring all forks off it. It's blazed red and white. About 15–20 minutes past the *bistrot,* watch for a blaze on a telephone pole on the left side of the road directing you left. The turn itself **B** (which you'll take) is on the left, a little farther beyond the blaze. There's another blaze on a telephone pole *beyond* the entrance to this track.

If the blaze goes missing for any reason, you can find the left turn like this: There's a telephone line that's been paralleling the road, and then you pass under one that's crossing the road. About 15 meters beyond the lines crossing the road (the asphalt paving ends here), there's a gravel fork off to the left **B**; take that.

In another 7–10 minutes, ignore a fork off to the right. There's a left-turn blaze on a telephone pole on the left side of the path.

In another five minutes or so you'll cross over a track next to an electric pylon.

In about a half hour, you'll pass a sheep and goat farm, with a big stone farmhouse on your right. Past the house is another fenced sheep meadow on your right. At the end of this fence you'll come to a way mark on the left, and a fork off to the right **C**. Take this fork to the right, signed (on the way mark) Rocher d'Ongles. As you enter the path there's a yellow and red blaze on the left.

Be alert here: The path descends for a minute and then bottoms out by a streambed and forks; take the right fork.

After about 25–30 minutes on this path, you reach a crossroads with a way mark **D**. This is the turnoff for Ongles (see the introduction to this walk). Otherwise, carry on straight ahead here, signed Chemin de Seigne.

In about 10 minutes the path meets an asphalt road (D950). Cross over the road to the way mark and continue on the wide dirt track, signed Chemin de Seigne.

Be alert here: In a few minutes you'll pass a relay tower on your right. A minute or two past the tower, watch for a sandy trenchlike left turn (there's a rock on the ground with an orange sprayed mark). Take this **E**, leaving the GR, unless you have decided to take the shorter walk by staying on the GR.

This is a steady, but for the most part not too steep, climb. The path is obvious and unchallenged by competing forks. It's easy to follow.

In about 10 minutes the path crosses under a power line. In another 10 minutes you pass some areas of whiter and grayer stone than the sandy orange dirt which has comprised the path so far; you're still going uphill but more gently so.

A few minutes later, you reach the top and begin to level out.

In another 5–10 minutes the path passes under some electric lines. In another 5–10 minutes it passes under electric lines again, with a path coming in from the left **F**.

About 10 minutes past **F** you pass below a house uphill to your left, and a little shed on your right, and the driveway from the house comes into our path from the left.

About 15–20 minutes past **F** you come to a fork off to the left (similar in size and color to the path you're on); take this **G**. In about 15 meters this comes to a T junction; go left.

In another five minutes or so, you come to a big confluence of paths **H**, where an old ruined *bergerie* is ahead. Take the path ahead that passes next to the ruin.

In a minute the path forks again; take the right uphill fork.

Stay on the path now, ignoring forks off it (including a slightly lesser one forking off to the right in another 15–20 minutes, and another one 15–20 minutes after that, a lesser path coming in from the sharp right), until nearly an hour later the path ends at a T junction **I**; turn right (east).

Stay on this path, going rather steeply downhill. About 15 minutes later it comes out at a T junction with another path; turn right.

Five minutes later the path leads into a little asphalt road bending gently right; take this, which leads into town in another 5–10 minutes.

14 Lardiers to Saumane

1.5 Hour

This is the shortest leg of the Bistrots de Pays walk, a pleasant stroll taking you past lavender fields and on through a quiet woodland valley to L'Hospitalet, which, as its name suggests, was once home to a religious order devoted to the care of the

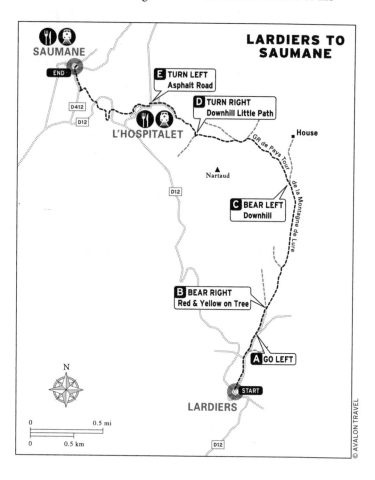

infirm. From there it's a short walk to Saumane, an attractive village tucked into the foothills of the Lure, where there are places to stay as well as two restaurants.

FOOD

There are two restaurants in Saumane. Both are good, and both are pleasantly low key, in keeping with the general tenor of this set of walks.

Le Bistrot de la Mini Auberge, the Bistrot de Pays, serves simple but tasty home cooking, with a €12 lunch menu and a €15 *menu* for weekends and dinner. A salad with an excellent goat cheese tart and tapenade on olive bread was followed by a lightly *piquante* casserole of pork with green olives served with rice: plain but satisfying. Desserts included a fabulous lemon pound cake with chantilly cream, and a goat crème fraîche served with honey. The menu changes constantly, featuring couscous, roast lamb, chili, along with whatever produce comes into season locally.

La Bergerie, just down the road, an old stone sheepcote refurbished with a pleasant arbor for outdoor eating, is a tad more expensive and ambitious, but not by any stretch fancy. Its €16 set *menu* features main courses of goat cheese lasagna (a rare vegetarian option) and *Pieds et Paquets*. Grilled lamb, with mushrooms or herbs or peppers, is available à la carte at around €15. There are simple *assiettes* of charcuterie or cheese, and every Friday it does an aioli for €20. This is delicious, and if you do arrive on a Friday and you're in the mood for this quintessentially Provençal specialty, you should try it. The garlicky, velvety mayonnaise is accompanied by steamed vegetables, tiny but intensely flavorful clams, meaty cockles, marinated baby octopus, and the freshest piece of fish (cod) we ate inland, sautéed in a light dusting of flour. We had an excellent Gigondas, and it also has the Domaine Mayol white and rosé: We never had these Mayol offerings, but we found its red quite acceptable. An apple and strawberry crumble stood out among the homemade desserts.

LOGISTICS
IGN Map Number and Name
#3341 OT—Montagne de Lure and #3240 OT—Banon/Sault

Tourist Information

Use the Banon tourist office listing; see Walk 16.

Restaurants

Name: La Bergerie
Address: Village center
Phone: 0492/ 74 22 17
Closing Day: Opens for the year around Easter
Name: Le Bistrot de la Mini Auberge
Address: Village center
Phone: 0492/ 73 20 71
Closing Day: Afternoon Wed. and all day Thurs., open every day in season, Sat. evening themed dinners

Accommodations

If you can't get a room in Saumane, there's a *gîte d'étape* in nearby L'Hospitalet.

Saumane:
Name: Maison la Farigoule
Address: Village center
Phone: 0492/ 73 31 48 or 0688/ 08 25 59
Website or Email: gporteous@orange.fr
Type of Lodging: One-bedroom apartment with kitchen
Price: €90 per night; the owner will furnish croissants and yogurt in your refrigerator, as well as all supplies needed to make your own coffee or tea. There's a small shop in Saumane if you decide to cook.
Notes: The proprietor is English and very knowledgeable about walks in the area.

L'Hospitalet:
Name: Evasion Equestre
Address: 4, route de Banon
Phone: 0492/ 73 23 62 or 0669/ 44 07 58
Website or Email: See it on the Forcalquier tourist office website, www.forcalquier.com; click on "Hébergement," then "Gîtes d'étape."
Type of Lodging: *Gîte d'étape*
Price: €15 per person per night
Notes: Basic accommodation, six-bed *dortoir* with some separation, kitchenette, pool. *Table d'hôte* available by reservation. English spoken.

Transportation

Bus

Name: Autocars Sumian

Phone: 0491/ 49 00 49

Website or Email: autocars@sumian.fr

Notes: There's a free bus on Tuesday mornings from L'Hospitalet, Saumane, and Rochegiron to Banon (because of the Banon market on Tuesday mornings), and also returning to these villages from Banon at 11:00. From L'Hospitalet at the place du Village (in front of the *lavoir*) 8:40, from Saumane by the phone booth in the place de l'Église at 8:45, and from Rochegiron at 8:53. The trip is about 15 minutes between Saumane and Banon.

Miscellaneous Notes

Saumane has a little grocery store (alimentary). It is very small and very basic, but you could provision a picnic. It has some very nice fresh local sheep cheeses.

WALK DIRECTIONS

Standing with your back to the front door of le Bistrot de la Lavande, cross the road and bear right up the narrow road to the right of the phone booth and stone shelter with seats (the old *lavoir,* or laundry). You can see the street sign once you're on the street: Montée de la Garouyére. Follow this street out of town.

About 5–7 minutes past the *bistrot,* when the road forks, bear right (basically straight) uphill, immediately passing a way mark on your right signed Sentier du Contras.

Ignore a turnoff to the right in another 100 meters/yards or so, staying on your road, signed again Montée de la Garouyére.

Beyond this right turnoff 200 meters (about three minutes), the road forks again **A**; go left, where a very low stone wall will be to your right. It's blazed red and yellow on a tree. Almost immediately the road turns to gravel.

About 3–5 minutes past **A**, the road forks again **B**; bear right, signed red and yellow on a tree.

In another 5–10 minutes ignore a fork off to the left as the main path bends right. In another 50 meters ignore a fork to the right.

In another 10–15 minutes ignore a fork off to the right where a house is straight in front of you (up a hill at some distance). Instead bear left **ⓒ**.

In another 5–10 minutes you come to a T junction below a stone house; bear left.

In another minute you reach another fork; take the left downhill.

Go rather steeply downhill for another 5–10 minutes. *Be alert:* Watch for a right-turn blaze on a telephone pole on the left side of the track. Just beyond this blaze, as the track bends around to the left, you'll see a little path going off to the right downhill **ⓓ**; take this, finding a blaze on a tree to the left just beyond the entrance to this footpath.

In another few minutes the footpath ends at the beginning of a little asphalt road. Follow this road, ignoring a right-hand turn in about 250 meters (three minutes). About 50 meters beyond that right-hand turn, you come to a T junction with another asphalt road; turn left **ⓔ**.

The road immediatley bends right. In another minute you reach another fork (you'll see the old laundry—*lavoir*—on your right here); go straight here, ignoring the left turn.

In another 30 meters, bear left again at a fork, entering the old village of L'Hospitalet, passing downhill through the place des Écoliers and bearing left, after which the road comes out into an open area (the place du Village) in front of the war memorial. Turn right here, passing the war memorial and phone booth on your right and entering the rue du Defends (yellow and red blaze on house at left of entrance).

In about 15 meters bear left downhill at a fork. In 20 meters enter the downhill stone path straight ahead, where the asphalt ends.

In a minute or two you'll come out at the road (D12). Cross over to enter the small footpath just to the left, downhill and blazed.

In 50 meters, at an intersection, continue sharp right, downhill. In 2–3 minutes, after passing a water-treatment plant, you'll come out at the road again. Cross it, taking the path that leads from the large stony turnoff on the other side, straight ahead.

In a few minutes this takes you up into Saumane. Turn left on the asphalt and then immediately left again for the Mini Auberge. From here La Bergerie and Le Bistrot de la Mini Auberge are around the corner on the right.

15 Saumane Ring Walk

1.5 Hour

If you just want to stop in Saumane for a few hours and try out one of the restaurants, this is the perfect preprandial two-hour walk: very pretty, easy to follow, strenuous enough to work up a good appetite, but not so much as to knock you out for the rest of the day.

Following the first part of the Saumane to Banon walk, the route follows along one of the hunting trails that flank the Pimerle (the hill to the west of the village) and returns along another, with excellent views down onto the quiet farmland below—a soft palette of lavender, sage, and silvery-green wheat, liberally sprinkled with poppies and buttercups.

LOGISTICS

For Logistics and Food, see Walk 14.

WALK DIRECTIONS

From the center of Saumane, standing with your back to the clock tower and looking toward the war memorial, turn right and follow the little asphalt road away from town.

Stay on this road, passing a right turn in about two minutes

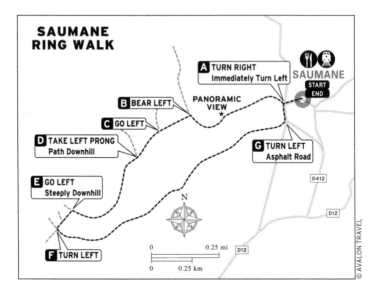

or so and then bearing left at the fork less than 10 meters/yards later. There's a red fire hydrant on your left here.

Stay on this road, passing between old houses and high stone walls. Follow it to the end, where it comes to a T junction with another little asphalt road.

Turn right at the T junction and then immediately left (west-northwest) on a gravel track **Ⓐ**. This track turns to grass; follow it as it bears left, with a stone wall to your right.

Climb for about 15 minutes, when you'll come to a panoramic view on a rock, and then the path bends right into the woods again. About two minutes past the panoramic view there's a little fork; bear left **Ⓑ**. (The path isn't blazed.)

Five minutes later come to a T junction with a bigger path **Ⓒ**; go left.

In another 4–5 minutes you'll reach another T junction with a similar-size path **Ⓓ**. To the right (north) as it goes uphill, the character of the stones is different—lighter colored. Instead take the left (southwest).

Follow this downhill path. About 10 minutes past **Ⓓ**, the village of le Jonquet comes into view ahead and below. A minute or two after le Jonquet comes into view, the path forks again **Ⓔ**. Go left, rather steeply downhill, but before you do, read on: You can also take the right option here, which is slightly less steep and bends back to join the steep downhill (i.e., left) path in 2–3 minutes. While still here at **Ⓔ**, look down and see where they join below; **Ⓕ** will be about 20 meters farther downhill from that point.

About two minutes' steep downhill from **Ⓔ**, pass the aforementioned point where the less steep path rejoins the steep downhill path. Continue about 20 meters farther downhill, where two much smaller paths cross your path, one going right, one going left **Ⓕ**. Turn left.

Stay on this path (it's always evident which is the main path) for about 20–25 minutes, when you'll see Saumane come into view.

The path meets a farm track just on the edge of town. Keep going straight until you come out on a little asphalt road **Ⓖ**. Turn left on that and then immediately right (at the iron cross). This road leads back to the village center in another two minutes.

16 Saumane to Banon

2.5–3 Hours

A pleasant climb along a hunting trail leads you high above the quiet farming valley of Saumane, passing through oak woods and rocky scrub full of pungent wild thyme. Rounding the southern end of a large hill, la Pimerle, you drop steeply into the lavender and sage fields above La Rochegiron (an extremely quiet village—no shops). From here a track leads past farmland with the occasional lavender distillery still in business (the sheds with the tall chimneys) and on into the ancient and extremely appealing village of Banon.

Famous for its goat cheeses wrapped in chestnut leaves, Banon

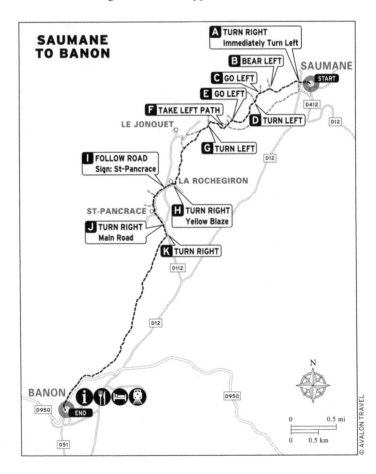

SAUMANE
TO BANON

A TURN RIGHT
Immediately Turn Left

B BEAR LEFT

C GO LEFT

E GO LEFT

F TAKE LEFT PATH

LE JONQUET

D TURN LEFT

SAUMANE
START

D412

D12

G TURN LEFT

D12

I FOLLOW ROAD
Sign: St-Pancrace

LA ROCHEGIRON

ST-PANCRACE

H TURN RIGHT
Yellow Blaze

J TURN RIGHT
Main Road

K TURN RIGHT

D112

D12

BANON

END

D950

D950

D51

N

0   0.5 mi

0   0.5 km

© AVALON TRAVEL

has a bustling little square with several shops (including a video store with Internet access), a lively market on Tuesdays, and a more modest one on Saturdays. With its steep cobbled streets and fortified buildings, it's a handsome place, but not in the least chichi, which is perhaps why it hasn't yet been entirely given over to tourism.

FOOD

For a village with enough interest in food to support two butchers, two grocery stores, and two boulangeries, the eating-out options are surprisingly modest here. There's an okay restaurant in the square, but it's open only for lunch most of the year, two cafés where you can get sandwiches, a *salon de thé* for cakes, and a pizzeria, **La Braserade.**

The latter—understandably crowded at night—isn't bad, though its pizzas (€10–12) are less good than its other dishes, which include a garlicky *côtes d'agneau* for €11 and a very good salad with *tourtons:* little hot pastries filled with potato and goat cheese.

If you time your arrival in the village for the Tuesday market you'd do better to buy something there—there's usually a rotisserie stall with excellent roast chicken or pork, and often a stall serving paella or *zarzuela* (a rice-based bouillabaisse) from vast cauldrons. And of course, this is the place to sample the famous chestnut leaf-wrapped Banon cheese, which comes in every degree of ripeness, from a firm chalky white to an oozing yellow effluvium.

LOGISTICS
IGN Map Number and Name
#3240 OT—Banon/Sault

Tourist Information
Address: Place de la République, Banon
Phone: 0492/ 72 19 40
Website or Email: www.village-banon.fr
Hours: 9:30–12:00 and 14:00–17:00 Mon.–Sat., 10:00–12:00 Sun. July–Sept., reduced hours out of season
Notes: The Banon tourist office website also has accommodation listings for the surrounding villages.

Restaurants

Name: La Braserade Restaurant—Pizzeria
Address: Village square
Phone: 0492/ 73 32 77
Closing Day: Evening Tues. and all day Wed.

Accommodations

There are many *chambres d'hôtes* in and around Banon. See the Banon tourist office's website for listings.

Name: La Maison du Voisin
Address: Place St. Just
Phone: 0492/ 73 37 66 or 0686/ 26 41 47
Website or Email: www.sud-gîte.com
Type of Lodging: *Gîte d'étape* and *chambres d'hôte*
Price: One single room for €32 per night, three double rooms €37–47 per night, price includes access to dining room and kitchen. You can store food in the fridge and use the equipped kitchen to cook your own meals. Breakfast isn't included in the price, but there are coffee, tea, butter, milk, jam, and honey at your disposal. (Don't forget the bakeries in town!)
Notes: English spoken.

Transportation

Bus

There are two free buses on Tuesday mornings (to bring people to the Banon market), one from L'Hospitalet and Saumane to Banon (place de la Gendarmerie), and one from Vachères to Banon (see Walk 20). There are also the return buses, the Saumane/ L'Hospitalet leaving Banon at 11:00, the Vachères bus at 12:05.

You can also pick up the Banon–Marseille line, which stops at numerous towns along the way, including Apt, Bonnieux, Lourmarin, and Aix-en-Provence. Banon to Marseille takes 2.5 hours. Check with the Banon tourist office for current schedule information.

Taxi

Name: Taxi les Cigales
Phone: 0492/ 73 35 66

WALK DIRECTIONS

From the center of Saumane, standing with your back to the clock tower and looking toward the war memorial, turn right and follow the little asphalt road away from town.

Stay on this road, passing a right turn in about two minutes or so and then bearing left at the fork less than 10 meters/yards later. There's a red fire hydrant on your left here.

Stay on this road, passing between old houses and high stone walls. Follow it to the end, where it comes to a T junction with another little asphalt road.

Turn right at the T junction and then immediately left (west-northwest) on a gravel track **Ⓐ**. This track turns to grass; follow it as it bears left, with a stone wall to your right.

Climb for about 15 minutes, when you'll come to a panoramic view on a rock, and then the path bends right into the woods again. About two minutes past the panoramic view there's a little fork; bear left **Ⓑ**. (The path isn't blazed.)

Five minutes later come to a T junction with a bigger path **Ⓒ**; go left.

In another 4–5 minutes you'll reach another T junction with a similar-size path **Ⓓ**. To the right (north) as it goes uphill, the character of the stones is different—lighter colored. Instead take the left (southwest).

Follow this downhill path. About 10 minutes past **Ⓓ**, the village of le Jonquet comes into view ahead and below. A minute or two after le Jonquet comes into view, the path forks again **Ⓔ**. Go left, rather steeply downhill, but before you do, read on: You can also take the right option here, which is slightly less steep and bends back to join the steep downhill (i.e., left) path in 2–3 minutes. While still here at **Ⓔ**, look down and see where they join below; **Ⓕ** will be about 20 meters farther downhill from that point.

About two minutes' steep downhill from **Ⓔ**, pass the aforementioned point where the less steep path rejoins the steep downhill path. Continue about 20 meters farther downhill, where two much smaller paths cross your path, one going right, one going left **Ⓕ**. (To return to Saumane, via the Saumane Ring Walk, you would take the left path here.)

Continue straight ahead downhill on the wide stony path. In about 50 meters the path levels off and begins to bend left.

Watch for a path off to the right, about equal width, but not as pronounced a path. Take this right, which forks again imme-diately: Take the right fork. (You could take a left too, straight downhill, but the path on the right is easier.)

Follow this track downhill (ignoring a fork off to the right in less than a minute, where your path is bending slightly left).

In a minute or two the path narrows significantly and emerges into an open field. You can see below you, slightly to the left, a winding dirt track, which is where you're ulti-mately heading. For the moment, however, the path you're on (not much of a path at all here) curves right and then ba-sically disappears. Instead, leave the path and head down on the left side of the field, in the general direction of that wind-ing dirt track. At the bottom left-hand corner of the field there's a tiny path leading you out of the field. Take that, which leads you out to connect with the track you saw from above; turn left on this **ⓖ**.

In another minute the path forks, the right uphill path lead-ing to a house. Don't take that; instead bear left here.

In another five minutes or so you'll come to another gravel road (above a big buried drainpipe); bear left onto this.

Stay on this road for 7–10 minutes, until you come to a T junction with an asphalt road **ⓗ** (yellow blaze on a tree to the right here). Turn right.

In another few minutes you'll reach a T junction with another as-phalt road **ⓘ** with a stone wall across from you. Cross the road, tak-ing the road slightly diagonally to the left, signed Saint Pancrace.

Follow this road for about 10–15 minutes, ignoring all turn-offs, until it comes to the main road **ⓙ** (D112).

Turn right on the main road and take your first right **ⓚ**, at a way mark signing you toward Banon. This small lane leads you all the way to Banon, passing farms and lavender fields and a small lavender distillery.

In 3.5 km (about 40 minutes) it comes out on the D112 again, just outside Banon. Turn right, and in a few minutes you'll reach the village itself. Take the street signed D950 to your left: The village center is just around the corner.

17 Banon–Vieux Monsalier Ring Walk

1.5–2 Hours

The hills immediately behind Banon are rather dauntingly steep and gray, but this is actually a very pleasant short walk once you've climbed to the crest, and it takes you to a fascinatingly melancholy spot.

The original village of Monsalier (there's a "new" one right off the road between Banon and Simiane) was up here on the high hill known as la Rouya St. Pierre. It was abandoned after all its men were killed in World War I and the women could no longer keep the place going. The ruins, huddled around the old church, are a moving sight, eloquent testimony to the waste and sadness of war. There are fine views along the way, some ancient windmills, and a forlorn peacefulness about the whole area.

The old village is sometimes called Vieux Monsalier, sometimes Haut Monsalier.

LOGISTICS

For Logistics and Food, see Walk 16.

WALK DIRECTIONS

On the main square, with the post office on your right, go down the steps to the road underneath the square and turn right.

Follow the road 150 meters/yards or so, downhill, passing a garage/gas station on your left and then taking the gravel road 50 meters farther along that goes to the right, just before some recycle bins (yellow and red blaze on pole).

In a couple of minutes, after passing a concrete-block shed on your left, you'll see a stone track off your path, going sharply left uphill. Take this **Ⓐ**.

After a climb, the path enters pleasant oak scrub. In 20 minutes go straight over a crossroad **Ⓑ** (there's an old way mark, but it doesn't point in your direction). In five more minutes the road forks; go right uphill **Ⓒ**.

In another 10 minutes or so you'll reach another junction (actually a crossroads, if you count the grassy path forward and to the left). Go straight, following the sign to La Vieux Monsalier (the sharp right here leads to private property).

BANON AND THE LURE

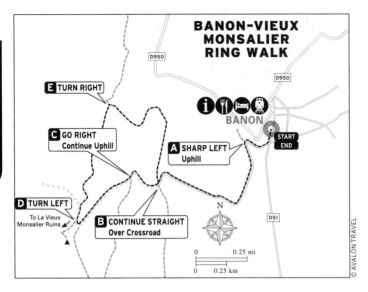

In 50 meters, follow your path as it swings sharply right. In a few meters/yards you'll see the ruins of three old mills ahead of you, and in another 50 meters you'll intersect a stone path the width of yours **D**; go left here. In 100 meters a path zigzags left, up to the ruins.

Keep to the mown path as there are open wells and other hazards in the ruined village.

After seeing it, go back to **D** and turn left, passing to the left of the old mills. At the fork in 50 meters go straight, uphill (north).

Keep on the main path, ignoring a minor left turn in about 10 minutes. About five minutes later you'll see a more major path down to the right; take this **E**.

In about 15 minutes, this path brings you back to **B**. Turn left, retracing your steps to Banon.

18 Les Tinettes Ring Walk

3 Hours

We had two reasons for choosing this particular walk up into the high, remote plateaus of the Lure Mountains: the old stone sheepcotes you pass en route, said to be among the finest of their kind, and the restaurant at the farm of Les Tinettes, which has a reputation for being the best *ferme/auberge* in the area.

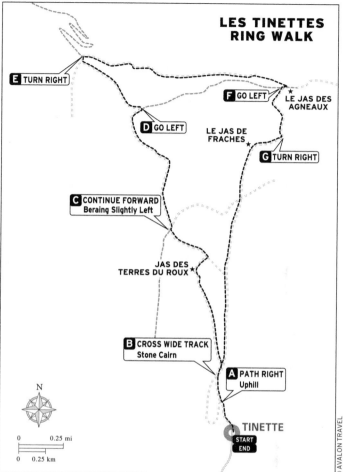

LES TINETTES RING WALK

E TURN RIGHT

F GO LEFT
★
LE JAS DES AGNEAUX

D GO LEFT

LE JAS DE FRACHES ★

G TURN RIGHT

C CONTINUE FORWARD
Beraing Slightly Left

JAS DES TERRES DU ROUX ★

B CROSS WIDE TRACK
Stone Cairn

A PATH RIGHT
Uphill

TINETTE
START
END

N

0   0.25 mi

0   0.25 km

© AVALON TRAVEL

About the latter we had mixed feelings, though it's certainly more than adequate. But the old drystone *bergeries* (or *jas* in old Provençal) are absolutely extraordinary: improvised rustic architecture of a complexity and beauty to rival any of the more commonly visited civic or ecclesiastic buildings in the region.

It's higher and appreciably cooler up here than in the hill country around Banon, or even in the Lubéron, and the air is beautifully fresh. After climbing through pine woods and passing a small ruin of no particular interest, you come to the splendid Jas des Terres du Roux, rightly designated a national historic monument. The long, rectangular structure is the sheep shelter, with four arched, cupola-roofed chambers inside (the corbelled drystone construction of these spaces seems little short of miraculous). The smaller building is the Cabanon du Berger (the shepherd's hut), where you can stay the night (with prior permission from the owners of Les Tinettes) and the circular structure in the entranceway is the cistern, with a channel for collecting water off the roof of the main building.

Rugged trails lead you on up to the Larran crest, with fine views, after which you descend (via another not very interesting ruin, the Jas des Agneaux) to the two ruins of Les Fraches. These aren't as immaculate as the Jas des Terres du Roux, but they are no less impressive: the first for the succession of archways over its sunken rectangular shelter, the second for the heroic scale of its tunnel-like, rather spooky interior.

These particular *bergeries* are believed to have been built in the early 19th century, though the corbelling techniques for constructing them—whereby the outer stones in the immensely thick walls counterbalance the interior stones as they circle inward to form the domed or conical roofs—date back to at least the 13th century. An iron pickax was used to split off *lauzes* of limestone when more evenly shaped pieces were needed, and a saw was employed to cut the timbers occasionally used for lintels and beams. Otherwise these are hand-built.

We went twice to the Jas des Terres du Roux, once on a weekday morning when we seemed to have the entire mountain range to ourselves, but once on a holiday weekend, when the place was full of picnickers who'd arrived in 4x4s and ATVs—not a pleasant sight. So choose your moment.

FOOD

The old-style farm restaurant of **Les Tinettes** up in the hills north of Banon had been recommended to us by several people. It's a pleasant enough place, with a snug fireplace and a welcoming atmosphere. Quantity seems the main virtue of the actual food, or at any rate its guiding principle. We arrived there after a three-hour walk, with what we thought were respectable appetites, but soon realized we were no match for what the kitchen had in mind for us. The food—a €30 set *menu* (wine included)—seems from another era, reminiscent of the kind of thing consumptives were given at

BANON
WALKING A
156 Restaur
Name
A
'D THE LURE
E LURE

sanatoriums 100 years ago to fatten them
of what used to be called Russian salad (cl
etables in mayonnaise) arrived, surrounded
Then came a trencher of very good cured l
tire *fromage de tête* (brawn, or "head cheese
tasty but extremely fatty pickings from the
along with a large loaf of bread to help it down. By the end of
this we were hoping that lunch here, as in some other *ferme/
auberges,* might proceed straight from appetizers to coffee,
but out came a tremendous earthenware dish, heaped high
with a glisteningly creamy *blanquette* of goat. This was pungent, somehow vinegary as well as creamy. It wasn't bad and
might even have been comforting if our hunger hadn't been
blunted, but at this point working through it (and the platter of rice beside it) was more a matter of duty than pleasure. Pride came into it too: The other diners around us,
mostly tiny ancient couples in their Sunday best, were ripping
through their helpings without any trouble at all. A plate of
goat cheeses followed the goat, and just in case we hadn't
had enough dairy yet, a tureen of Provence's unlikely dessert favorite, *île flottante,* was then wheeled out. The whipped
egg-white islands floated buoyantly enough in their ocean of
cream, but they pretty much sank us.

The house wine, a solidly built Lubéron (Domaine de Mayol),
was a great help throughout all this, and perhaps it's churlish
to complain about generous helpings, but the meaty, creamy,
eggy, white-bready copiousness of it all was a little oppressive
(the kitchen did rustle up a quick ratatouille for the vegetarian
among us, but it wasn't good).

Given the enthusiasm with which local people speak of this
place, it seems likely we caught it on a bad day, and certainly our
lunch amounted to a memorable eating experience. So we do,
cautiously, recommend it. But just be sure to fast for a week or
two before going there.

LOGISTICS

For Banon Logistics, see Walk 16.

IGN Map Number and Name

#3240 OT—Banon/Sault

...ants

...: Les Tinettes
...dress: On walk route
Phone: 0492/ 73 27 06
Closing Day: Open from around Easter until end of Aug., closed Sept., open for weekend lunch from Oct. 1 until Easter, reservations essential, set *menu* €25 per person, €15 kids

Miscellaneous Notes

You'll need a car to get to Les Tinettes unless you want to hitch a ride. Les Tinettes is about 12 km from Banon. From Banon, take the D950 northwest, toward Sault. Take a right on the D5 toward Le Contadour. Continue through the hamlet of Le Contadour; from the chapel it's another two km to Les Tinettes.

WALK DIRECTIONS

Pass the auberge Les Tinettes on your right. As the path begins to rise, bear left, passing the tractor shed on your right.

In 3–5 minutes watch for the little path off to the right uphill **A** as the main path swings around left. Take this shortcut, which comes out above in another five minutes or so, crossing over the wide track again **B** and resuming on the other side. There's a stone cairn here.

Follow this shady path, in about 15 minutes passing a ruined building on your right and a couple of minutes later coming to the *bergerie* Jas des Terres du Roux.

The path continues to the right of here (blaze on a rock), in another few minutes coming to a T junction with a dirt track. Turn left here (blazed).

Arriving at a high area in another 5–7 minutes, you come to an intersection **C**. Continue forward, bearing left (but not the extreme left path).

In another 15–20 minutes the path forks again as you approach a T junction **D**. Go left here.

In another 10 minutes the path forks again on approaching a T junction. There's a way mark here pointing in three directions. Go right, signed Montfroc.

Almost immediately you'll reach another way mark **E** signed straight for Les Omergues, but you turn right here, going uphill, not downhill.

After a 25–35-minute climb, you'll come to two large stone cairns. From here, continue along the ridge path, and look ahead of you a little to the right (south) and you'll see a dilapidated shepherd's hut, the Jas des Agneaux. Drop down to this.

Go around the ruin and you'll see a path running parallel with the ruin (and with the crest); go right on this path, almost immediately bending left at a fork ❻, whose other prong continues straight ahead.

Stay on this path (ignoring a path off left made by overexuberant four-wheelers) through pine trees, bearing right at the three forks which follow. Don't worry too much here if the forks are different from how they were when we wrote this; a minute after all these crisscrossing paths you'll come out onto a more open area and come to a fork ❼ (with a small cairn on the right). Turn right here.

In another minute or two you'll see the arched Jas de Fraches just ahead.

Continue along the path. In another 2–3 minutes you'll reach the third of these historic *bergeries*.

Continue, following the main path as it gradually descends. In about 25 minutes, remember to watch on the left for your shortcut at ❷ (just before the path finally bottoms out and would start to climb, and marked by three pine trees on the left of the path as you approach it, but on your right after you turn onto the little path).

At the bottom of the path ❶, turn left and so back to Les Tinettes in another few minutes.

19 Gorges d'Oppédette Ring Walk

3 Hours

If you suffer at all from vertigo your heart will be in your mouth for stretches of this stunningly dramatic walk around the Calavon gorge that plunges below the starkly attractive village of Oppédette. If not, you'll enjoy dizzying vistas of 200-meter cliff faces with enormous "giants' cauldrons" in them—bowls scooped out of the limestone by the stream below. The stream is largely dry these days, except after storms, though water passages beneath the rock are thought to feed into the source of Petrarch's fountain of Vaucluse.

There are a couple of fairly terrifying lookout points along the

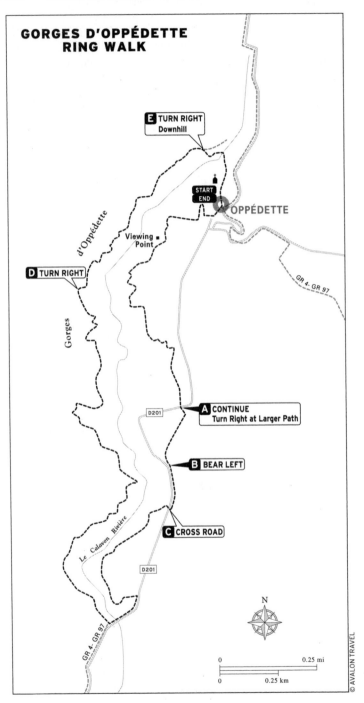

GORGES D'OPPÉDETTE RING WALK

E TURN RIGHT
Downhill

START
END

OPPÉDETTE

d'Oppédette

Viewing
Point

D TURN RIGHT

GR 4 - GR 97

Gorges

D201

A CONTINUE
Turn Right at Larger Path

B BEAR LEFT

Le Calavon Rivière

C CROSS ROAD

D201

GR 4 - GR 97

N

0   0.25 mi

0   0.25 km

© AVALON TRAVEL

way with just a thin iron railing between you and the void, and a somewhat scary passage where you descend partway into the gorge itself (on no account climb down the iron ladders you'll see leading into potholes here). We managed it all with our two children (the youngest was seven at the time), though there were moments when we wished we'd left them behind.

But this is an exhilarating walk. The landscape around Oppédette itself is remarkably free of development: almost no sign of modernity at all other than the road you come in on. Broom, holm oaks, and privet grow along the trail, along with an abundance of wildflowers, including a rare variety of delphinium.

The gorges are difficult to get to without a car, and once you're there, at present there's nowhere to eat (except for very basic sandwiches at the Bistrot de Pays) or stay. The *gîte d'étape* in Oppédette didn't seem to be functioning when we were there, nor is it listed in Gîte-de-France's *gîte d'étape* guide. If you're on foot, the Chaloux *gîte d'étape* is about four km' walk from Oppédette (see *Walk Directions* for Walk 20 and the note at point ❸ of that walk).

If you have a car, La Fontaine is a more luxurious *gîte d'étape,* actually an auberge, and still not far—a 10-minute drive or so, near Simiane-la-Rotonde (see Walk 20 for listings).

If you haven't got a car (or even if you do), you could make a multiday walk by taking public transport to Simiane-la-Rotonde, walking to nearby (about a km) La Fontaine for your first night, then on to Chaloux (about four km away, connected by a path). From there you can do the Gorges d'Oppédette and Vachères–Oppédette walks.

FOOD

There used to be a Bistrot de Pays here. The sign is still up but alas the elderly proprietor serves only sandwiches and drinks now. The sandwiches—ham, camembert, *saucisson,* or pâté—€3.80—are fine for a picnic, but if you want dinner or a full-scale lunch you'll have to get to Vachères (see Walk 20), a few kilometers east, where there's a good Bistrot de Pays.

LOGISTICS
IGN Map Number and Name
#3242 OT—Apt/PNR du Lubéron

Restaurants

For listings, see Walk 20.

Accommodations

For listings, see Walk 20.

Transportation

There is no public transport to the gorges.

WALK DIRECTIONS

From the fountain in the middle of Oppédette (*la lavoir,* which is the old village laundry), take the stairs next to it, and at the top turn right. Follow the path uphill, the road giving way almost immediately to stone path.

At the top of the hill bear to the left of the cemetery on a dirt track. A minute later at a big open dirt area (which looks like a parking area), check out the belvedere (viewing point) on the right, signed with a GR 6 marker.

Continue across the parking lot and take the path that leads off the far end of it on the right (nearest the gorge), not the path you got here on.

Bear right, walking near the edge of the gorge. The path soon narrows as it passes between some scrub bushes. There are blazes on the rocks along here.

The path is well worn and well marked. But you do have to pay attention, especially if there's a fork. We encountered only one fork that tempted us the wrong way (about 15 minutes past the parking lot), but were rescued by an "X" marking "wrong way."

About 25 minutes from the belvedere you'll meet a tiny asphalt road (D201) **A**. The path continues on the other side and soon meets a larger path, where you turn right.

Five minutes later you reencounter the tiny asphalt road (D201) **B**, but the path bears left just before meeting it. *Be alert now,* as you must look for landmarks here in order not to miss an upcoming path.

The path parallels the road for about 50 meters/yards and then bears off left and comes alongside a field. The path is narrow, hard-packed dirt and passes between broom bushes, with the big field to your left.

About 80 paces after you enter this field area, which is actually *two* fields, you'll reach the dividing line between them, marked by a line of trees and a small stone wall. There's a little step-down where the tiny stone wall crosses the path. About another 50 paces from this step-down, you turn off to the right— *not* at the wide grassy area (at about 40 paces rather than 50), but just beyond that, on a very small path, marked with a red and white blaze. (If you miss it, you'll reach a little ruined stone hut on the right of the path. If that happens, go back 50 paces to the correct path, now on your left.)

Take this little path, cross the road ❸, and continue on the other side.

A minute later you come to the gorge edge and the path forks; go left. There are blazes on rocks along here.

In another five minutes or so you'll come again to the little asphalt road (D201). Turn right here, over a little bridge, then cross the bigger bridge ahead, and just beyond it turn off the road onto the path going down to the right.

The path is blazed yellow now. Follow the path, as blazed, for about an hour, at which time, after a lot of rocky path, you come out at a field. Go right along the bottom of the field and then bear right at its corner ❹ (yellow blaze on tree) as the path goes back into the woods.

In another 10 minutes you'll pass a ladder going down on the left of the path; 4–5 minutes later the path seems to go downhill but there's a smaller, quite vague fork up: You can see the blue and yellow blaze on a rock about 15 meters ahead and up.

About 15 minutes later ❺, very near the end of the walk, there's a junction that's easy to miss, rather difficult to describe, and is not, at the time of this writing, blazed. Look across the gorge: There's a huge boulder obscuring your view of Oppédette. Just before you pull up level with the front of it, watch for the path to drop down right. Basically, you're making your way down diagonally toward the gorge bottom here to climb to Oppédette on the other side. (You're going to cross the bottom of the gorge before reaching the road, but fairly near it.)

From here the path winds down and passes an iron railing. Just past the iron railing the path bends right, crosses the bottom of the gorge and starts climbing on the other side, reaching the village about five minutes later.

20 Vachères–Oppédette Ring Walk

5 Hours

This is a long walk for a cool spring day, circling through fine countryside, with magnificent panoramas on the way.

Oppédette and Vachères are both lovely villages and both, in theory, offer something in the way of sustenance. Oppédette's former Bistrot de Pays is at present serving only sandwiches, and only during the daytime, but things may change. Vachères has an up-and-running Bistrot de Pays, but it has unpredictable opening hours, so be sure to call ahead if you want to eat there. Otherwise there are many beautiful spots for a picnic. If you start the walk at Oppédette you'll reach a waterfall with a swimming hole, the Saut du Moine, in about an hour, a good place to stop. The name ("Monk's Leap") refers to a gruesome episode in the 14th century when a monk jumped to his death over the rocks on horseback while being chased from a nearby abbey by the soldiers of a local tyrant, Raymond de Turenne. From here you'll pass a hamlet containing the ruins of the aforementioned abbey along with several farm buildings converted to *gîtes*. There were plans to offer a *table d'hôte* here also, with food for guests as well as travelers passing through. An hour's steady climb begins after this, on a wide gravel track through pine woods. It's not the most scintillating part of the walk, but it brings you up to the high country of the Plan de Brudgiére, where the views become steadily more impressive. At one point (up at the water tower a little before Vachères) you can see the Ventoux, Lure, Lubéron, and pre-Alp mountain ranges, as well as the edge of Mont Ste-Victoire. Lavender fields and mountain pastures lead you down into Vachères, after which a few more miles of relatively gentle ambling through yet more unspoiled, gorge-riven farmland bring you back to Oppédette.

If you've got the flexibility of a car, you can start either at Vachères or Oppédette (or anywhere else), depending on your eating plans, bearing in mind that Oppédette serves only drinks and sandwiches, and the *bistrot* at Vachères is unreliable in its opening times; either way, call ahead.

FOOD

It's well worth trying to organize your w
ing times of the very pleasant **Bistrot de**
heart of Vachères. The owners have evide
nets of the Bistrot de Pays credo to heart
sis on fresh local produce and simple regi
inexpensive food is prepared with quiet skill and flair. The
€17.90 set *menu* changes daily, with a €16 aioli also on offer if
you make a reservation. We asked for some vegetarian meals
along with the regular ones when we made our reservation.
A mixed salad with chickpeas arrived first, followed—for
the vegetarians—by a beautifully prepared dish of courgettes stuffed with herbs and spelt (*epautre,* a delicious ancient grain used by the Romans, and on sale here along with
other local products), served on a griddle cake of potato and
jerusalem artichoke and flanked by fresh asparagus in a velvety red pepper sauce. It is extremely rare to find this kind of
care and imagination applied to vegetables in this part of the
world. Meanwhile, for the carnivores, equal satisfaction was
provided by a tender filet mignon of pork served with wild
mushrooms. Dessert was a lemon tart of celestial lightness
and creaminess.

LOGISTICS
IGN Map Number and Name
#3242 OT—Apt and #3342 OT—Manosque/Forcalquier

Tourist Information
No tourist office in Vachères, but you can try the *mairie* (town
office) at 0492/ 75 62 15

Restaurants
Name: Le Bistrot des Lavandes
Address: Vachères village
Phone: 0492/ 75 62 14
Closing Day: Tues., also closed evenings Mon. out of season, not
open evenings until May or so; also, while the above is the "official" closing days listing, there seem to be many spontaneous
closing days as well, so be sure to call ahead, including on the
day of your reservation.

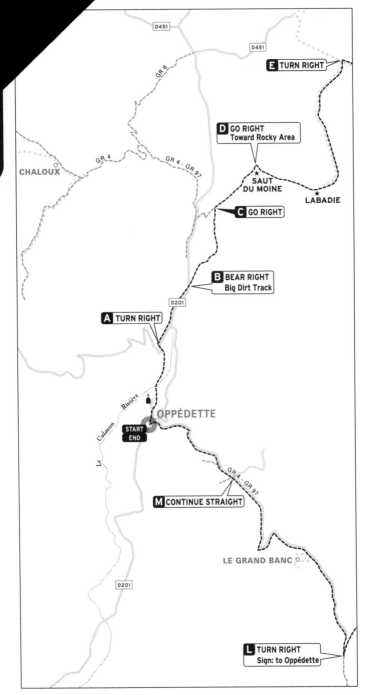

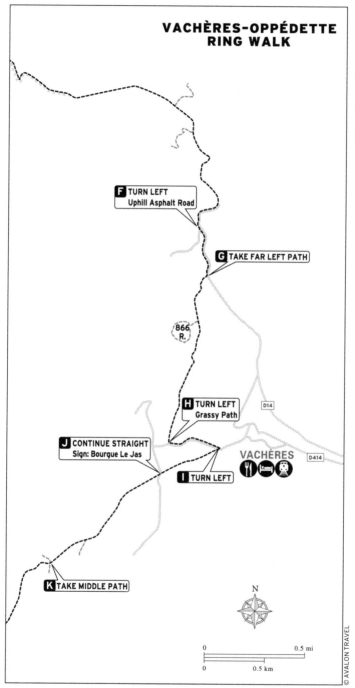

VACHÈRES-OPPÉDETTE
RING WALK

F TURN LEFT
Uphill Asphalt Road

G TAKE FAR LEFT PATH

866 R.

D14

H TURN LEFT
Grassy Path

J CONTINUE STRAIGHT
Sign: Bourgue Le Jas

VACHÈRES

D414

I TURN LEFT

K TAKE MIDDLE PATH

N

0   0.5 mi

0   0.5 km

© AVALON TRAVEL

Accommodations

The *gîte d'étape* in Oppédette didn't seem to be functioning when we were there, nor is it listed in Gîtes-de-France's *gîte d'étape* guide. The Chaloux *gîte d'étape* is about a three-km walk from ❽ (see map and the note at ❽ in the Walk Directions). If you have a car, La Fontaine is a more luxurious *gîte d'étape,* an auberge actually, and still not far—a 10-minute drive or so, near Simiane-la-Rotonde.

Vachères:

Name: No special name, but it is the *chambres d'hôte* of Philippe and Yves

Address: 10 minutes' walk from the Bistrot de Pays; call for directions.

Phone: 0492/ 75 66 71

Website or Email: vyes.monballiu@wanadoo.fr

Type of Lodging: Two *chambres d'hôte* rooms, plus one *gîte* for two people

Price: €50 per night for a room (for two); every room has a shower and small bathroom

Notes: The proprietors, Philippe and Yves, are friends of Ann and Bruno of the Bistrot de Pays in Vachères. English spoken.

Name: Le Château à Vachères

Address: About 0.5 km outside village

Phone: 0492/ 74 62 49

Website or Email: Doesn't have its own website, but you can see photos on the Banon tourist office website's *chambres d'hôte* listings

Type of Lodging: *Chambres d'hôte*

Price: €40–55 in season, extra bed €12–15

Outside Vachères:

Name: Chaloux

Address: On the GR 4, about three km off the walk from point ❽ (see Walk Directions and map)

Phone: 0492/ 75 99 13

Website or Email: www.chaloux.free.fr

Type of Lodging: *Gîte d'étape*

Price: *Dortoirs:* €15 per person per night, half pension €34–51 (children under 12 €24), breakfast €6; individual rooms: room and breakfast €49–73, room and half pension €41–51

Notes: Open Mar. 15–Dec. 31 with three individual rooms

plus two *dortoirs* of 7–8 beds each. English spoken. Many walks right from the *gîte.*
Name: Auberge La Fontaine
Address: Between Oppédette and Simiane-la-Rotonde about a four-km walk from Chaloux, along a path; call for directions or see its website.
Phone: 0492/ 73 13 79
Website or Email: www.gîte-la-fontaine.com
Type of Lodging: Upscale *gîte d'étape*/auberge
Price: €48 per person (less for children), meals €18–23
Notes: Eight rooms for 2–4 people, each with its own bathroom

Transportation
Bus
Name: Autocars Sumian
Phone: 0491/ 49 00 49
Website or Email: autocars@sumian.fr
Notes: Free bus on Tues. mornings to Banon (for the market) at 9:30, leaving Banon at 12:05 to return to Vachères, 35-minute trip

Miscellaneous Notes
Vachères has an interesting Museum of Paleontology and Archaeology, open 10:00–12:00 and 15:00–18:00 May–Sept., 14:00–17:00 Oct.–Apr., closed Dec. 15–Jan. 31 It may sometimes open by appointment as well, either through the *mairie* (0492/ 75 62 15) or the museum (0492/ 75 67 21).

WALK DIRECTIONS
From Oppédette, with your back to the *mairie* at the intersection just outside the village, there are three roads ahead: left into Oppédette, middle, and right, signed to Vachères. Take the middle of the three.

In 15 meters/yards, leave the asphalt road and take the downhill gravel path between buildings, blazed on a corner of the stone shed on your right. Continue straight along the path (north), which soon narrows and heads steeply downhill (ignore the deviation leading back toward the road).

Follow the path to the bottom of the gorge (no more than five minutes from the start of the walk), where it crosses over the stony streambed. There is a brown sign on the far side of this streambed (Commune d'Oppédette: Attention)—head toward the sign, crossing the streambed and bearing right uphill on the path. (If the sign is gone, just cross the streambed and climb up toward the right (north) and continue on the dirt path at the top.)

A minute later follow the trail as it curves left at a big electric pylon.

Five minutes later you'll come to a T junction with a small asphalt road **A**. Turn right.

Coming to the T junction with the asphalt road (D201) next to the bridge, bear left, signed Valsaintes.

In about five minutes, after the road has been straight (northeast) and then makes a curve to the left (north), there's a big dirt track off the road to the right (northeast); take this **B**, following it straight, ignoring a fork to the left 15 meters after leaving the road. (*Note:* If you're going to the *gîte d'étape* Chaloux, rather than taking the dirt track **B**, instead stay on the road as it bends left—the continuation of GR 4–GR 6—and in about 1.5 km, when the GR 4 and GR 6 separate, take the GR 4, arriving at Chaloux in another km or so.)

Follow the path, which soon dips at a little streambed and then curves around to the right and skirts woods on your right.

In another 5–10 minutes you pass a hairpin turn to the right uphill. Then the path bends around to the right, crosses a streambed, and climbs to a T junction with a path on the other side. Go right on this **C**.

When you come to an open rocky area on your right, with rock pools, go toward it **D**. This is Saut du Moine, where the monk was chased over the big cliff to your left.

With this big cliff to your left, you can see the path ahead of you (east-southeast) on the other side of the water (in summer this may dry up and be plain rock). It's very obviously the path.

In about five minutes, in a field with the stream on your right, while the track you've been on stays low, alongside the stream, you leave it for the path bearing left uphill along the edge of the woods on your left. (There's a lone yellow blaze on a tree on your right once you're on the correct path.)

In a minute or two you'll pass on your right Labadie, a *gîte* with remains of the old abbey in it. Stay on the dirt road past here, and follow it until you come to a T junction with another dirt track ❸. Turn right here.

Stay on this road, which begins an hour's climb, the least interesting part of the walk but with payoffs to come.

About an hour past ❸, the road changes to broken asphalt, and 10 minutes later you'll come to a T junction with a bigger asphalt road, which is making a hairpin turn ❻. Take the left uphill fork of this asphalt road.

In about five minutes, as you reach the crest of the road, Vachères comes into view ahead, there's a lavender field to your left, and there's a dirt track off to the left behind you. Just across the road from the entrance to this dirt track is a big open area, with a path leading out from the far left-hand corner of it (southwest). Take this path ❼.

In about 15 minutes the path bends right and comes to a T junction with another path.

The route is left here, but first you may want a small diversion to an excellent lookout point just a minute out of your way. For this, turn right at the T junction and follow it as it curves around to the left and you can see a rectangular stucco building (866 meters on IGN) wedged into the rocks (with a solar panel on top). Walk around to the back of it and climb up on it.

Back at the T-junction, turn left (from the way you approached it originally) and follow the path, with a stone wall to your right. About 15 minutes later (five minutes past a relay tower) the road turns right at a field, and there's a grassy path to your left ❽. Turn left here (east).

This pretty little path has a beautiful view of Vachères. In 5–10 minutes it ends at a little asphalt road ❾. Turn left on this and so into Vachères, noting the pillar dedicated to St. Sebastian at the fork to the right just outside the village.

Leaving Vachères

Backtrack out past the St. Sebastian pillar and down the road you came on, continuing past ❾.

About 10 minutes out of town there's a stone track straight ahead where the road itself bends left before an old stone house (with a plaque memorializing Vincent Arthur, killed here by the Gestapo in World War II). Take the stone path straight ahead ❿, signed Bourgue Le Jas.

In about 15 minutes you'll pass a house on the right with an ugly white pool fence. About 25 meters beyond the house watch for a smaller path forking off to the right, through some little trees. Take this (yellow blaze on a tree).

Stay on this narrow path when it crosses a wider track in another minute. When these tracks meet up again, you come out at an intersection **K**. Of the three paths in front of you, take the middle one, which goes diagonally right. Ignore a similar-size fork down to the right in less than a minute.

Be aware that in about 15 minutes (from **K**) the path makes a hairpin right-hand turn **L** just before a lavender field. You have to be alert because there's also a path that continues straight ahead.

Take this right-hand hairpin turn **L**, signed on a tree to Oppédette in 1 hour and 15 minutes.

In another 15 minutes pass the entrance to a hamlet (now a private residence), listed as Grand Banc on the IGN map.

About 20 minutes later the road, which has been straight for the past 200 meters or so, bends right, while there's also a farm track to the left and a smaller path straight ahead (northwest). Take the path leading straight ahead **M**. There are "X" blazes on the trees on both sides of the road here.

This delightful little path comes out at an open area with grass and rocks in about 10 minutes. Swing around right, toward the electric wires and stone column you can see there by the pylon. Turn left on the path at the pylon.

The path parallels the road, with a beautiful view of Oppédette, and then drops to it, reaching Oppédette in another five minutes.

21 Viens Ring Walk
1.5 Hour

Northeast of Apt 10 miles is a little-known area of idyllic farmland, with some very pleasant villages scattered around it: St-Martin-de-Castillon, Caseneuve, and most notably, Viens—a walled village, largely unvisited despite its ancient intact wall, cobbled alleys, Renaissance château (private), 13th century-houses, and beautiful views. As a friend described it, Viens is "Provence 35 years ago." The rolling countryside all around here

villages in the area, with Apt only about 20 minutes' drive for big-town "action" and conveniences. While far too sprawling for walking purposes, Apt has some good reasons to hang around. The Saturday morning market is one of the best in the region. Lunch at Cabécou et Poivre d'Ane and stocking up at **La Cave du Septier.** One other Apt hot spot, if you lean this way, is the big organic food market **Lubéron Bio,** which had far and away the best organic produce we saw in Provence. In June it had apricots one might feel lucky to experience once in a lifetime, juicy as peaches and with a purity and concentration of flavor impossible to replicate in factory-farmed fruit.

Thus, while we don't usually get into recommending *gîtes,* with their weeklong minimum stays, we thought this was the time to make an exception, for all the reasons above, and also because this one has several independent buildings on the property, which gives you a better chance of finding one available at the time you're planning your stay.

Hautes Courennes is a cluster of old farm buildings lovingly renovated by the proprietor during the course of 20 years or so. The peaceful rural setting comes complete with stunning poppy fields in spring, and if you're lucky, a nightingale to sing you to sleep at night. When the weather gets warm, there's a fabulous pool.

The proprietress, Linda Lorentz, left her home in the United States when she was 19 for a trip to France, and she never went back. She and her French husband renovated the old buildings while raising two children and becoming famous for their goat cheeses, which they sold to all the best restaurants in the Lubéron.

LOGISTICS
IGN Map Number and Name
#3242 OT—Apt/PNR du Lubéron

Tourist Information
There's no tourist office, but the *mairie* has a free local hiking map.

Address: Place Ormeau
Phone: 0490/ 75 20 02
Website or Email: http://viens.mairie.com

Restaurants

Viens:

Name: Café-Restaurant le Petit Jardin

Address: Viens village, rue du Faubourg

Phone: 0490/ 75 20 05

Closing Day: Wed., open every day in July and Aug.

Apt:

Name: Cabécou et Poivre d'Ane

Address: Rue de la Sous-Préfecture

Phone: 0490/ 04 01 78

Closing Day: Open for lunch Wed.–Sat. in spring and summer, Thurs.–Sat. in autumn and winter

Accommodations

Name: La Bergerie

Address: Viens

Phone: 0490/ 75 28 60 or 0687/ 38 47 78

Website or Email: www.labergeriedulubéron.com

Type of Lodging: *Chambres d'hôte* and *table d'hôte*

Price: €58 for two people including breakfast, €14 supplemental for extra person in room

Notes: Dinner is available, €16 per person; make sure to ask for dinner at the time you make your room reservation.

Name: Les Barbiguiers

Address: Viens

Phone: 0490/ 75 24 75

Website or Email: www.gîtes-de-france-vaucluse.com, listing #1225 under *chambres d'hôtes,* or you can email the proprietor at morricone@wanadoo.fr

Type of Lodging: *Chambres d'hôte*

Price: €40 for one person, €45 for two people, including breakfast

Notes: Two rooms, one of which has a kitchenette; no meals served

Name: Hautes Courennes

Address: Hautes Courennes

Phone: 0490/ 75 22 21 or 0677/ 16 73 80

Website or Email: www.gîtesdeshautescourennes.com

Type of Lodging: Independent *gîtes* by the week

Price: From €430 week off-season; it also does an off-season weekend rate

Notes: See the website for photos and prices.

Transportation

Taxi
  Name: Taxi Viens
  Phone: 0684/ 53 69 58
  Name: Taxi St. Martin
  Phone: 0685/ 88 41 04

Miscellaneous Notes

  La Cave du Septier, place du Septier and place Carnot, Apt, 0490/ 04 77 38, www.vcommevin.com; hours are 10:30–12:30 and 14:30–19:00 Mon., 9:30–12:30 and 14:30–19:00 Tues.–Sat. Some of the very knowledgeable and helpful staff speak excellent English; don't hesitate to ask for someone who does.

  Lubéron Bio, 266 avenue de Roumanille (off the N100, on the west end of Apt, near the massive LeClerc grocery store; or email for directions), 0490/ 74 53 75, lubéronbio@wanadoo.fr; open all through the day every day except Sun.

WALK DIRECTIONS

With your back to the phone booth and facing the clock tower, turn right, passing the Restaurant le Jardin on your right. Follow this road, and when you come to the little square with the post office on your left, follow the road as it turns right. Continue down this road, coming to the bigger asphalt road (D33) **A**. Turn left (signed Cereste and Gorges d'Oppédette), passing some recycling bins on your left.

  Take the third right **B** (the second right is only a dirt track), blazed, a small asphalt road that forks immediately: Take the right fork.

  In a minute or two you'll come to a way mark; leave the asphalt road for the track on your left **C**, signed L'Homme Mort.

  In about 20 minutes you'll come to a fork at a way mark **D**. Turn right, signed Ravin du Rossignol (Valley of the Nightingale). The path makes a hairpin right.

  At the next fork (3–5 minutes), bear left, blazed.

  In another 5–10 minutes you'll come to a fork with a way mark, "Ravin du Rossignol" **E**. Turn right here.

  In 2–3 minutes the narrow dirt path ends at a rock outcrop, with a narrow dirt track directly left just where your dirt path ended at the rock. Don't take that, but climb up on this side (left side) of the rock outcrop and at the top you'll see another narrow path off to the left, blazed yellow on a tree; take that (northwest) **F**.

This little path travels between two old moss-covered stone walls, and forks in less than a minute **G**. The right (straight) prong has the yellow blaze, and this is the direction of the walk, but to make a short detour to see two nice *bories,* turn left here, past the yellow "X." The path comes out in about 40 meters/ yards at a *borie.* Turn right on the path here and walk a little farther on to see the second *borie,* and then retrace your steps back to **G**.

Continue along the path, bordered here on both sides by old stone walls, with modern stone "sculptures" presumably the work of various passers-by.

In less than 10 minutes you'll pass a ruined stone house on your right. Less than a minute beyond here, you'll reach a small asphalt road **H**. Turn right here.

In another few minutes you'll pass **C** on your right; retrace your steps back into town from here (by turning left here on the D33, and then turning right into town where the D33 sign points left to Simiane and Banon), arriving back at your starting point about 10 minutes past **C**.

A Dip into Southwest Provence

The brevity of this section—a mere three walks in the large swath of land stretching roughly from Avignon and Arles in the west eastward to Aix-en-Provence and Marseille—will no doubt surprise some readers. No walks around Les Baux? None near St. Rémy? Nothing in Van Gogh's Alpilles? The Pont du Gard? The Camargue?

Well, we did try. But the fact is that the rich and varied attractions of this region—the Roman remains, the stunning medieval towns, elements of the landscape itself—no longer include the kind of extended passages of unspoiled, or even (to lower the threshhold a bit) un*ruined,* countryside that make possible the kind of walks we were looking for. Or if they do, we didn't find them, in which case we apologize and hope to do better in future editions.

The Camargue is of course a special case. Much of this vast saltwater marshland with its flamingos and white horses is now a National Reserve, and all of it is protected. There are trails

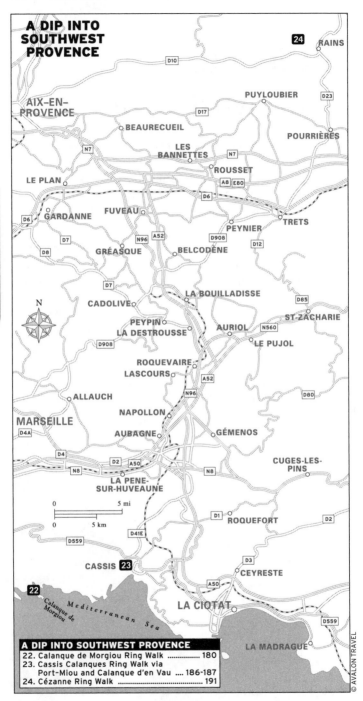

A DIP INTO SOUTHWEST PROVENCE

SOUTHWEST PROVENCE

24

RAINS

D10

AIX–EN–
PROVENCE

PUYLOUBIER

D23

D17

BEAURECUEIL

POURRIÈRES

LES
BANNETTES

N7

N7

ROUSSET

LE PLAN

A8 E80

D6

GARDANNE

FUVEAU

PEYNIER

TRETS

D6

D7

N96 A52

D908

BELCODÈNE

D12

D8

GRÉASQUE

D7

LA BOUILLADISSE

D85

CADOLIVE

ST-ZACHARIE

PEYPIN
LA DESTROUSSE

AURIOL

N560

D908

LE PUJOL

ROQUEVAIRE

LASCOURS

A52

ALLAUCH

N96

D80

NAPOLLON

MARSEILLE

D4A

AUBAGNE

GÉMENOS

D4

CUGES-LES-
PINS

N8

D2 A50

N8

LA PENE-
SUR-HUVEAUNE

0   5 mi

0   5 km

D1

ROQUEFORT

D2

D41E

D559

D3

CASSIS 23

CEYRESTE

22

A50

Mediterranean Sea

LA CIOTAT

Calanque de
Morgiou

D559

LA MADRAGUE

A DIP INTO SOUTHWEST PROVENCE

© AVALON TRAVEL

open to hikers, and if you have a high tolerance for mosquitoes and boiling humidity (both of which can set in as early as March) you'll see some extraordinary wildlife. But try as we did, we couldn't figure out a walk here that would fit our criteria: Aside from there being nowhere to eat along the walks themselves, there's something a bit forbidding about the whole prospect. Even so, we should probably list this among our failures.

We did, however, find what we were looking for in another watery landscape, equally strange and beautiful, and much more accommodatingly simpatico, at least for our purposes. This was the stretch of fjord-like coastal inlets known as the Calanques, running east from Marseille to Cassis. A network of trails runs the whole distance through this protected area, often passing vertiginously close to the edge of the high cliffs plummeting to sparkling turquoise waves. There are some beaches along the way, remarkably uncrowded much of the time because of the fact that you can get to them only on foot or by boat. Of our two ring walks here, one begins just outside the heart of Marseille itself, dipping rapidly out of that bustling city into what seems another universe, the Calanque de Morgiou. The other goes from Cassis, one of the least spoiled, most beguiling of the old Provençal fishing ports. Both offer the possibility not only of great coastal walking but also of wonderful seafood. Because of fire risks, access to both walks is limited between mid-June and early September.

Our third walk is an excursion into Cézanne country: a ring walk near Aix (and accessible from there by bus) through the pine woods and rocky scrub below the master's beloved Montagne Ste-Victoire.

22 Calanque de Morgiou Ring Walk

2.5 Hours

Here's a Calanque walk of exceptional beauty a short drive from the center of Marseille itself. In fact, as we were asking directions for the narrow road that winds down from the forbidding Baumettes prison on the eastern outskirts of the city to the fishing village of Morgiou, we were told that we were going to see the *vrai vieux coeur de Marseille,* "the real old heart of Marseille."

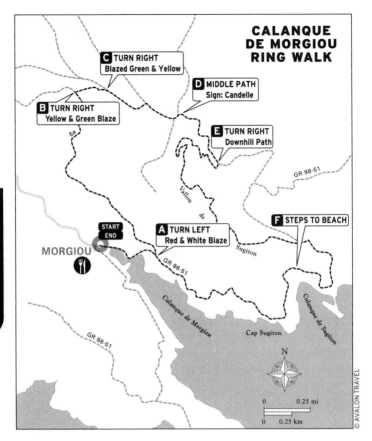

CALANQUE DE MORGIOU RING WALK

C TURN RIGHT
Blazed Green & Yellow

D MIDDLE PATH
Sign: Candelle

B TURN RIGHT
Yellow & Green Blaze

E TURN RIGHT
Downhill Path

GR 98-51

START END

MORGIOU

A TURN LEFT
Red & White Blaze

F STEPS TO BEACH

Vallon de Sugiton

GR 98-51

GR 98-51

Calanque de Morgiou

Cap Sugiton

Calanque de Sugiton

N

0   0.25 mi

0   0.25 km

© AVALON TRAVEL

SOUTHWEST PROVENCE

That was a weekday, and the tiny village was empty except for its few dozen inhabitants, most of whom seemed to be gathered at the Nautic Bar Restaurant, which is itself a reason to seek out this close and yet utterly secluded spot.

The next time we went was a Sunday, and half of the people of Marseille seemed to be there, picking their way along the cliff-side paths leading out of Morgiou to the small beach at Sugiton (the next Calanque along), or thronging the broad trails that lead along the towering cliff tops on the north side of the *calanque* and down the Vallon de Sugiton beyond, with its picture-book views of the sea sparkling around the Le Torpilleur—an island rock that looks like a petrified torpedo boat. So if you want to avoid the crowds, avoid *le Weekend*.

The paths are well marked, but they do involve some fairly strenuous scrambling in places, sometimes over quite slippery

the island ends (if you miss this left you'll come to a dead end), then immediately right, signed Morgiou and Route de Fer. This is Chemin de Morgiou and leads all the way down to the village. There are numerous places to pull off along this road and hike. The restaurant has a 45-minute walk route it recommends.

WALK DIRECTIONS

Walk past the restaurant and along the left side of the marina, and at the end of the marina take the steps cut into the rocks (red and white blaze).

In a minute the path rises and you can see down on a little beach, signed *Baignade non surveillee* (swimming not supervised). Bear left here, beginning to climb, and immediately passing a red-white-red blaze on a rock on your right.

The blazes guide you up this climb. You'll pass a stone pillar on your right in a minute or two. Beyond there watch for a turn-off to the left in about 40 meters/yards (red and white blaze and a yellow-painted "Luminy" on a stone on the ground) **A**. This left goes away from the water and up the hill (and is marked "6a" on the IGN map), while the path you were on continues straight. Take this left.

The path is blazed with yellow dots. In about 3–5 minutes you'll reach a place where a chain is mounted in the rocks to help you pull yourself up.

After crossing a scree outcrop the path begins to descend gently and then climbs again. There are yellow markers along here.

About a half hour past the place where the chain was mounted in the rocks, you'll pass a trail going left downhill by a yellow marker on a rock on the left, signed to Morgiou. Ignore this, but about five minutes later you'll come to a T junction at the saddle (there's an old rusty signpost here, and a rock signed to Col Morgiou to the left) with a yellow and green blaze. Turn right here **B**.

Just beyond here is an open area with paths in many directions. Keep bearing around to the right, on the rightmost path, and then in another 15 meters ignore a smaller path going off to the right.

In another minute this paths ends at a bigger gravel path **C**—almost a road—with a patch of concrete just at the intersection. Turn right (green and yellow blazed).

This wide track, a kind of pedestrian road, with benches here and there along the way, leads in about 10 minutes to a big open blacktopped area **D**. There are three paths here, left, right, and middle. Take the middle path, signed Candelle.

When the path forks ahead of you in 3–5 minutes (equal size paths, left uphill and right downhill), take the right downhill path **E**. This path leads you down the Vallon de Sugiton toward the Calanque de Sugiton.

The path is easy to follow down; stay on the main path rather than shortcuts to help maintain the delicate environment (as always, staying on the main trails helps prevent erosion and maintain the area for the enjoyment of others in the future).

In about 25 minutes you'll come to an open gravel area with a curving concrete wall around the edge, overlooking the water. Cross this and continue on the path, much smaller now, blazed red-white-red on a rock at the entrance to this smaller path.

You can drop to the first beach on the Calanque de Sugiton when you see it (10–15 minutes), or continue along the path to the far side of this inlet, where steps lead all the way down to the beach there **F**.

Return to Morgiou

Leaving the beach, climb up and rejoin the path, continuing the way you were going. The path winds left uphill and comes in less than a minute to a metal ladder: Climb up.

Follow the path up, blazed red-white-red. The route is a bit of cliff scrambling alternating with well-worn path, but just take it slowly and follow the blazes.

About a half hour from the beach you'll pass the point we turned off for Luminy **A**, and you'll reach the restaurant five minutes later.

23 Cassis Calanques Ring Walk via Port-Miou and Calanque d'En Vau

2.5 Hours

A short drive (or half hour's walk along roads) from the very pretty harbor of Cassis brings you to the start of this walk, a not terribly attractive kilometer or so along de Port-Miou (which is essentially an exten But after you cross the neck of land to the n Port-Pin, the harsh beauty of the Calanques jagged white cliffs, green scrub (blossoming and sparkling turquoise waters is something beach at Port-Pin, and there are several beguiling rock shelves for sunbathing as the walk continues along the west side of the *calanque.* At this point the crowds thin out and the walk becomes more strenuous, climbing steeply on rocky (but wellblazed) trails, some of which go close to sheer drops. Small children need to be watched carefully.

As you round the headland of Pointe d'En Vau, the spectacular vertical walls of the Calanque d'En Vau appear like the pinnacled fortifications of some fantasy kingdom. There are viewing points along the way for those who want a closer look at the abyss or at the strange rock tower known as le Doigt de Dieu (finger of God). Those prone to vertigo will be relieved that the path turns away from the cliff edge soon after this, heading back along an easy inland trail to the beach at Port-Pin, from which you return to Port-Miou the way you came.

Strong shoes and plenty of water are essential on this largely unshaded walk. On weekends there tend to be a lot of people about, so if you want solitude, go on a weekday.

FOOD

The picturesque old port in Cassis is lined with restaurants, most with outdoor seating crowded with people tucking into sea urchins and other delicacies. There are some lower-key places up the side streets, and a gourmet restaurant, La Presque'ile, along the coast at Port-Miou (which is where the walk itself begins and ends). But it would seem perverse to come to Cassis and not enjoy a meal right in the midst of its quayside bustle.

It also makes sense to go to an exclusively seafood place, where the concentration on selection and freshness is least likely to be distracted by the need to prepare other kinds of food. Hence our choice: **La Poissonnerie Laurent,** a small, very friendly, and attractive place with daily specials such as bourride or *aioli a l'ancienne.* It's a fishmonger as well as a restaurant, its gleamingly fresh fish laid out on ice inside.

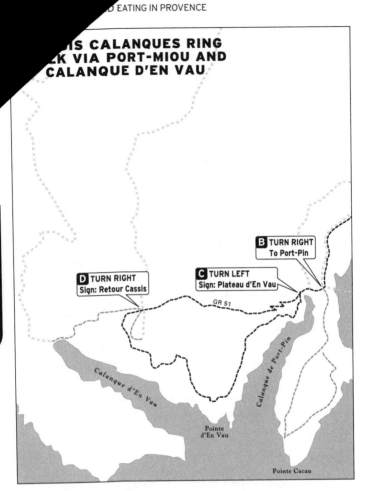

IS CALANQUES RING
K VIA PORT-MIOU AND
CALANQUE D'EN VAU

Appetizers on the all-fish menu include several fish tartars, salads of octopus and *supions* (cuttlefish), and a delicious, lightly battered *friture de poissons*. For main-course grilled fish—*loup de mer* (sea bass), sole, *rouget* (red mullet), and a superb, strongly flavored *dorade royale*—are served with vegetables prepared *à la provençale* (stuffed tomatoes, potatoes cooked with cream and herbs). The fish is sold by the 100 gram, and a decent portion will cost between €20 and €30. If you're in the mood for something more adventurous, this is a good place to try bouillabaisse. Unlike many restaurants that will prepare this dish only for two or more people, this one will accommodate the solitary indulger, for €30.80 (or €38.50 for a bouillabaisse *royale*—with lobster). It's a wonderfully elaborate affair, arriving in solemn stages: first

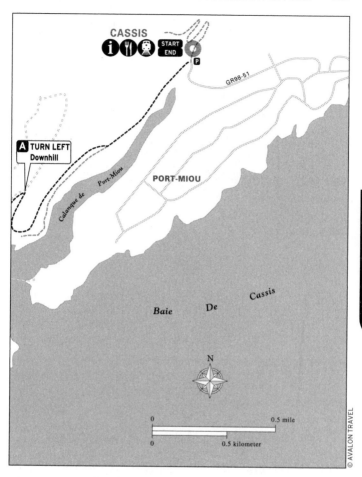

the croutons and a glistening golden *rouille* (the obligatory garlic and red pepper accompaniment), then a large platter with four or five very different species of fish on it—ours included conger eel, *rouget,* and *lotte* (monkfish)—and then a tureen of steaming *bouillon.* You spread the *rouille* on the croutons, put them in a bowl, add some fish, and then ladle the intense, fishy *bouillon* over it. The result is heavenly, and there's a prodigious quantity of it, so share, or at any rate take your time: It's a bit like eating your way through a large rock pool. The wine to drink with this is of course a Cassis, of which there is a small selection on offer by the bottle or half bottle. Otherwise there's a very drinkable *vin de pays*—a Bédoule—available by the glass.

If you have room for anything else, the desserts here are

delicious, especially the *tarte tatin* and a wonderfully creamy lemon tart.

LOGISTICS
IGN Map Number and Name
"Plein-Air" series (1:15,000) #3615—Les Calanques de Marseille à Cassis or regular series (1:25,000) #3245 ET—Aubagne/La Ciotat

Tourist Information
Address: Quai des Moulins
Phone: 0892/ 25 98 92
Website or Email: www.ot-cassis.fr
Hours: 9:30–12:30 and 14:00–17:30 Mon.–Fri., slightly reduced hours Sat., 10:00–12:30 Sun. and holidays Nov.–Feb.; 9:00–12:30 and 14:00–18:00 Mon.–Fri., slightly reduced hours Sat., 10:00–12:30 Sun. and holidays Mar.–Oct.; 9:00–19:00 Mon.–Fri., 9:30–12:30 and 15:00–18:00 Sat., Sun., and holidays July and Aug.

Restaurants
Name: La Poissonnerie Laurent
Address: 5, quai Barthélemy
Phone: 0442/ 01 71 56
Closing Day: Closed Mon. May–Oct., open at lunch and certain evenings Nov.–Apr., depending on the weather, closed Dec. 20–Jan. 10

Accommodations
If staying over in Cassis, see the tourist office's website for accommodations.

Transportation
Cassis is well served by both bus and train transport. The Cassis tourist office's website has great transportation info, and if the English version of the site isn't working (the case at present), here's what to do:

• On the home page scroll down to "Venir" and choose "Accès" from the drop-down menu.

- Choose train or bus info.

- By train: Here you'll find the link to the SNCF website, where you can enter your "from" and "to" information and get all trains, prices, and so forth.

- By bus (from Aix's Gare Routiére/bus station): Click on "Voir les horaires" under "Ligne 68."

- That takes you to the le Pilote website.

- Select line 72 (La Ciotat—Aix-en-Provence par Aubagne) from the drop-down menu.

- Enter your date and time of travel and then click on "Horaires de la ligne." This shows the schedule, but to see it in the other direction click "Autre sens."

- Choose a bus and note its arrival time at "Aubagne Pôle d'Échanges," and then click on "Autre lignes" at the top of the page.

- Select line 68 (Cassis Aubagne par Carnoux) from the drop-down menu, and repeat the process to get your connection from "Aubagne Pôle d'Échanges" to Cassis.

- Buses are frequent, but allow close to two hours, depending on your connection at Aubagne Pôle d'Échanges.

WALK DIRECTIONS

Note: When we were here, the path along Calanque de Port-Miou was under reconstruction. But it's all very well signed and you shouldn't have any difficulty following it.

The route starts out from the Port-Miou parking lot. If you don't have a car you can walk there from Cassis, about half an hour along the GR 98–51, which travels in part along a busy road that leads to the avenue Des Calanques and then to the trailhead.

Opposite the parking lot you'll see a wooden way mark with a sign for GR 51 Calanque d'En Vau. Follow the red and white blazes along the Calanque de Port-Miou (a marina). The path goes straight down a wide gravel avenue. In about five minutes you'll come to a modern but derelict-looking building. Pass to the right of this (blazed), and soon you'll begin to climb steeply.

At the crest the path divides; go left **A** (downhill, following blazes). Your path narrows to a little stony track. In a few minutes you'll come to a sign ❸; go right to Port-Pin (or straight ahead to explore Pointe Cacau).

Two minutes' steep downhill brings you to the Port-Pin beach, at the neck of the Port-Pin Calanque, a nice spot for a picnic or a swim.

From here go left ❹, following the blue sign for Plateau d'En Vau (the GR 51 goes off to the right).

The path here doesn't exactly correspond to the trail marked on the map, but it's well blazed and easy enough to follow. Follow the blue blazes as the path scrambles and zigzags up toward the plateau.

The path rounds Pointe d'En Vau 20 minutes from Port-Pin.

In another 15–20 minutes you'll pass to the right of a little stone cabin, a viewing point for the Finger of God (a tower of stone). Continue past the cabin, ignoring the stone stairway to your right and following the blue blazes. In five minutes you'll come to another lookout, with dizzying views over the Calanque d'En Vau.

Ten minutes from here the path curves back to the east, away from the *calanque.* Watch for the blue blazes, and make sure not to go down paths where there's a blue "X." In a few minutes you'll come to a T junction where you go left for 20 meters and then turn right on the GR path signed Retour Cassis ❹ (a left turn here will take you to a precipitous path down to the beach at Calanque d'En Vau).

Follow the path (blazed), ignoring deviations and watching for the occasional "X" (meaning "don't go here"). In 15 minutes you'll be back at ❹ (Port-Pin). Cross the beach and pick up the path on the other side, turning left at the T junction, and then a few minutes later turning right to reenter the Calanque de Port-Miou.

24 Cézanne Ring Walk
3 Hours

Although this varied walk (based from the village of Le Tholonet) takes you past Roman waterworks, over a dramatic 19th-century dam built by Émile Zola's father, and up to the swift-flowing channel of a working aqueduct, its main point of interest is without any doubt Montagne Ste-Victoire and its association with the master of postimpressionism, Paul Cézanne.

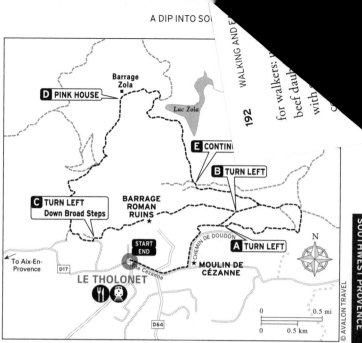

SOUTHWEST PROVENCE

© AVALON TRAVEL

Cézanne made more than 60 paintings of the mountain. "I am trying to get it right," he said.

It was the silhouette seen from this side—like a vast abstraction of a madonna flanked by saints—that haunted Cézanne, and as it comes majestically into view about halfway along this walk, you can see why. Admirers of Cézanne's work may experience curious feelings of déjà vu even before this point. The mixture of red soil, gray boulders, and green pines tilting at odd angles that he made peculiarly his own is so perfectly imitated by nature at odd moments along this path that it's almost as if you're stepping inside a series of his paintings.

This walk makes a good day trip from Aix-en-Provence.

FOOD

It's reassuring to find that lovely modest restaurants such as **Chez Thomé** still exist, untainted by the pretensions of *cuisine touristique*. The village of Le Tholonet is on the Cézanne route around Montagne Ste-Victoire, but aside from its château it isn't much of a place in itself, which supports the growing view that the best eating in France goes on under the radar....

At any rate, this rickety-looking country restaurant with its plain wood paneling and sprawling garden offers perfect food nfussy but well-prepared traditional dishes such as , or coq au vin, or duck with olives, all at around €16, tarters of courgette flan or marinated peppers. The main ourses tend toward the colossal, arriving in their own individual cauldrons. There's a good gnocchi with tomato and *pistou* for vegetarians, and an *assiette tout cochon,* sampling all the more interesting areas of the porcine anatomy, including the *jarret* (knuckle) for ardent carnivores. There's also a crème brûlée with, of all things, lard and *saucisse.*

It was here that we decided to try our first *pieds et paquets,* stuffed tripe and trotter—that least enticing-sounding Provençal standard. It wasn't bad—the little gelatinous lamb trotter surrounded by the matchbox-size *"paquets"* of herbed and tripe-wrapped salt pork, all in a good, strong tomatoey broth. One felt that an ancient tradition had been respectfully and correctly honored. But it would be hard to imagine wanting this on a regular basis in your life, unless perhaps you'd grown up on it. The coq au vin, steaming in its vat of *lardons* and pearl onions, was altogether easier on the palate.

The desserts here are particularly good and unusual: a charlotte of chestnut cream, a gratin of orange and grapefruit, delicious *nems* (logs) filled with molten dark chocolate, all at around €6.

LOGISTICS
IGN Map Number and Name
#3244 ET—Montagne Ste.-Victoire

Tourist Information
Aix-en-Provence:
 Name: Office de Tourisme d'Aix-en-Provence
 Address: 2 place du Général de Gaulle
 Phone: 0442/ 16 11 61
 Website or Email: www.aixenprovencetourism.com/uk

Restaurants
 Name: Chez Thomé
 Address: La Plantation, Le Tholonet
 Phone: 0442/ 66 90 43
 Website or Email: www.chezthome.com
 Closing Day: Mon., open year-round

Transportation

Bus

Buses run frequently between Aix and Le Tholonet.

Phone: 0805/ 71 50 50

Website or Email: Check www.aixenbus.com for current schedule information.

Frequency and Duration: Frequent buses. Allow an hour. Change in Palette.

WALK DIRECTIONS

From the center of the village of Le Tholonet, walk east uphill (away from Aix) on the Route Cézanne, passing the Relais Cézanne on your right. About 150 meters/yards after this, turn left at the Moulin Cézanne (signed) on the Chemin de Doudon. About 100 meters up this you'll see a cemetery; continue on the dirt road immediately to the right of it (the one with the metal barrier, not the blacktopped continuation of the Chemin de Doudon).

Your road climbs left around the cemetery, coming to a vague T junction in 75 meters where you go left (with the cemetery below you to the left) for about 30 meters, and then right (yellow blaze) into the woods, with a green fence soon appearing on your right. *Be alert here:* In another 100 meters or so, just as you come to a pinkish-orange modern house on your right with a pool, a narrow path leads steeply up to your left **A**, blazed yellow. Take this. There's a bit of a scramble up rocks here; follow the yellow-dot blazes.

After winding up the rocks for a few minutes, you cross over the crest and come to a T junction with a larger path, where the yellow blaze gives way to red. Go left here **B**. The path leads you down a little enclosed valley that becomes increasingly gorgelike. In about seven minutes a sign tells you to watch out for falling branches. A minute later another sign warns you of the dangers of flooding streambeds. Here, on your left, are the ruins of a Roman dam/aqueduct over a steep cascade.

The red blazes continue just to the left of the notice, taking you on a log bridge over the stream, passing through some plane trees, and then continuing up the ravine. The path soon goes downhill again, passing some unsightly new development in Le Tholonet below you on the left. *Be alert here:* In a few minutes, as you veer away from the top of the village, the path you've been on swings uphill to the right fairly sharply (you'll see a red "X" on the tree opposite you on the bend). You leave the path here, going *left* instead, down some broad steps **C**. In 30 meters you'll see some information panels about the trails.

With your back to the panels go right on the small tarmac road, where you'll see a way mark pointing uphill to the Roman dam, and right (north) along this road to Zola. Take this right. You'll see infrequent green blazes.

In three minutes you'll come to a T junction with another road that has a barrier across it, just to your right. The green blazes sign you down a narrow path to your sharp right, but we're taking the road with the barrier on it, uphill. Oddly, you'll pick up green blazes here too.

In about 10 minutes you'll come to the top of this road. Just ahead of you, across a clearing with a buried water cistern (it says "citern" on it), you'll see a small stone tower. Follow the main path straight past this, descending. In 50 meters the road divides. Bear left, following green and yellow blazes.

In five minutes you'll come to a secluded pinkish house **D**, a forest shelter, with an information panel outside it. Up to your right is the Barrage Zola, which you'll cross in a couple of minutes (Montagne Ste.-Victoire comes into view here). After crossing it, with Lac Zola down to your left, follow the narrow green-blazed path, which very soon connects, at a clearing, with a wider path that swings around to the southeast.

In two minutes you'll come to a tremendous Ste.-Victoire viewing place, where the path bends right. *Be aware here:* In five minutes you'll come to the end of another straight section; the main path swings left here **E**, but you go straight ahead, up to a small path between rocks (the continuation of a path coming in from your sharp right). You'll see green blazes here.

The rocky path leads downhill, with an immense valley to your right. In five minutes you'll come to a T junction with a red and green–blazed path. Go left here. Keep to the main path, ignoring various blazed diversions to the right.

In five minutes you'll come to a T junction with the stone piers of the Aqueduc de Doudon. Turn right, following the path below the aqueduct. At the end of the aqueduct you can climb up carefully to see the water flow.

From this end of the aqueduct you turn right over a little

embankment, where you'll see the entrance to a path diagonally forward and to your left. There's a low stone wall at its entrance, with a yellow blaze on the far side of it. Take this.

In 5–10 minutes you'll come to the pinkish-orange modern house where you first turned off **Ⓐ**. Continue straight past it. A few minutes later the path swings down left past the cemetery and back to the Moulin Cézanne. Turn right for the center of the village.

Middle Provence: Var and Verdon

The area encompassed by this section spreads from Europe's biggest gorge—the Grand Canyon du Verdon—east as far as the rugged country above Grasse and south toward the coast. It's a varied region, parts of it wrecked from the walker's point of view by the development sprawling north from the Mediterranean, other parts sublimely beautiful, with tracts of virtually uninhabited mountain forest stretching as far as the eye can see.

Some of Provence's most famous perched (and unperched) villages are here: Seillans, Bargeme, Cotignac. Disappointingly, the countryside around all these has become more or less fully suburbanized. But there are many other places, equally lovely, that have so far escaped the blight. Our favorite was Mons, an enchanting hilltop town rising out of the forest like something in the backdrop of a medieval painting, with all sorts of cultural and historical attractions on offer as well as several good restaurants, and yet—for most of the year—barely a tourist in sight (barely an inhabitant either, for that matter). Ampus,

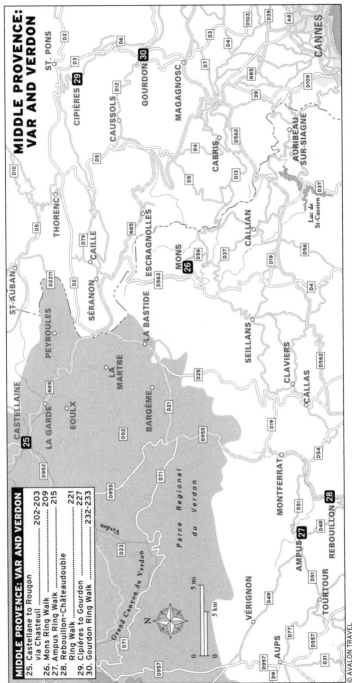

MIDDLE PROVENCE: VAR AND VERDON

VAR AND VERDON

© AVALON TRAVEL

Châteaudouble, and Cipiéres are almost as appealing (Ampus having the added bonus of a wonderfully low-key Michelin-starred restaurant). Even Gourdon, despite being a coach-tour magnet, remains a beguiling place, with a fascinating walk from it leading along the pipeline of an aquifer.

The Verdon Canyon is a spectacular sight. There are trails along it, but it's a major hike, and the time and effort it requires take it outside the scope of this book. Instead we've included a walk—Castellane to Rougon—that offers some superb, if at moments compromised (see the introduction to *Walk 25*) views of the canyon itself, as well as passing through the dramatic landscape around it.

We had hoped to find a walk to the Abbaye du Thoronet, oldest of the great three Romanesque monasteries in the region, but the dreariness of the immediate surroundings defeated us. Riez, on the other hand, an exceptionally handsome town set in lavender fields with some fine Roman ruins, was somewhere we should have included, and would have if we had had more time. We hope to rectify this in future editions.

BUS INFORMATION

You'll find all bus info for this area at www.transports.var.fr. The Conseuil Generale (the agency responsible for this site) claims it'll be putting schedules online soon, in which case you'll be able to click the "Horaires de ligne" link to see current schedules. At present you can get only the name of the bus company *(transporteur)* and its phone number, so until the schedules are posted your best bet is to call the local tourist office for current bus times.

Draguignan is the bus hub for the Ampus and Châteaudouble/Rebouillon walks. To get to Draguignan from Aix, Avignon, or Marseille, take the SNCF train (see *Planning Your Trip* for SNCF train information) to Les Arcs, and then the frequent *les Rapides Varois* bus to Draguignan, getting off at the last stop, about 20 minutes' ride, the *Gare Routiére* (bus station).

Along with regular scheduled buses, there's a request-service shuttle bus (le Petit TED) that you can call for transport between Draguignan, Ampus, Châteaudouble, and Rebouillon (and other local communities that we don't have walks in). It costs €2 a trip, and you must make your reservation no more than 15 days before your trip, but at the latest the day before you want the bus. The bus serves individuals, not groups. For more information go to www.dracenie.com/transports-dracenie/ted_petitbus.htm.

25 Castellane to Rougon via Chasteuil

5 Hours

The Grand Canyon du Verdon is the deepest, longest, most famous gorge in Europe. A whole sports and sightseeing industry has grown up around it, making it a problematic as well as an alluring place. You can drive along both sides of the top, and there are hiking trails down along the bottom. The latter require serious amounts of time and effort to complete (the most famous, the Sentier Martel, is 21 km), and for that reason falls outside the scope of this book.

But it *is* a spectacular natural phenomenon, half a mile deep in places, with the turquoise waters of the Verdon river glinting far down under the walls of white limestone, and we wanted to find a walk that would in some way include it. This one, which culminates in a grand view of the aptly named Point Sublime, where the gorge opens, was the most satisfactory of those we explored.

In many ways—most ways—it's a magnificent walk. Castellane is a handsome old town, towered over by a gigantic cliff with the chapel of Notre Dame du Roc perched on top. And Rougon is a very pleasant, laid-back mountain village. The countryside between them is as dramatic and beautiful as any part of Provence, with eagle's-eye views over the Verdon river, and at least one extraordinary rock formation—a kind of abstract Mount Rushmore called the Cadieres ("giants' seats") de Brandis—that looms above you a few kilometers outside Castellane. There's also a tiny, touching mountain chapel (St-Jean), and a perfect little hamlet, Chasteuil, to stop in for a picnic or, if you're up for a two-day itinerary, spend the night.

All of which makes for a great day walk. But we do have a couple of caveats. First, there's no way out of Castellane except along a quiet road, and there's a section after that, which though very pretty, is along an unshaded gravel track. Only two cars

passed us during the course of the half hour or so we were on it, but even this represented enough traffic to be mildly annoying. More important, though, is that the final approach to Rougon, where the canyon comes stunningly into view, appears to have been selected by the regional electric company as a showcase for the biggest pylons in its inventory, along with the most view-wrecking configuration of power lines it could dream up. You could try thinking of them as the great manmade monuments of our time, destined to become tourist attractions in their own right one day, but it's a little hard doing that with the wires humming overhead, as they do when the wind blows. Best just to put them behind you as fast as you can (it's only a matter of minutes before you're past them) and move on. And it has to be said that even with the power lines this vast fissured landscape is mind-blowing.

Check the weather before leaving; afternoon storms are not uncommon. We sat one out in Chasteuil before completing the second half of the walk. Plan on walking two hours from Castellane to Chasteuil and three hours from Chasteuil to Rougon.

FOOD

There's a pleasant Bistrot de Pays, **La Terrasse,** just as you enter the village of Rougon if you arrive by car, but our choice here would have to be **le Mur D'Abeilles,** a *creperie* off the main square, because of the superb mountain view from its rustic stone-walled terrace. Eagles and vultures wheeled across the valley below us as we lunched, and lightning zigzagged over the crests beyond. It's about as dramatic a setting as you could hope to eat in, and yet it lacks any of the pretension such a place might be expected to produce, retaining a completely laid-back ambience. The crepes also happen to be extremely good: light, crisp, savory ones filled with ham, eggs, artichokes, or cheese, and especially delicious sweet ones to follow (if you have room) with fillings of honey, stewed apple, *crème de marron* (chestnut puree), and various sorbets and ice creams. Prices are very modest, ranging around €3–8. It also has accommodation.

LOGISTICS
IGN Map Number and Name
#3542 OT—Castellane and #3442 OT—Gorges du Verdon

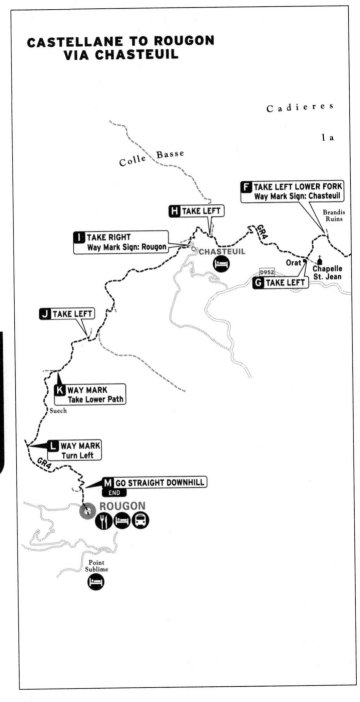

CASTELLANE TO ROUGON
VIA CHASTEUIL

Cadieres

l a

Colle Basse

F TAKE LEFT LOWER FORK
Way Mark Sign: Chasteuil

Brandis
Ruins

H TAKE LEFT

GR4

I TAKE RIGHT
Way Mark Sign: Rougon

CHASTEUIL

Orat

Chapelle
St. Jean

D952

G TAKE LEFT

J TAKE LEFT

K WAY MARK
Take Lower Path

Suech

L WAY MARK
Turn Left

GR4

M GO STRAIGHT DOWNHILL
END

ROUGON

Point
Sublime

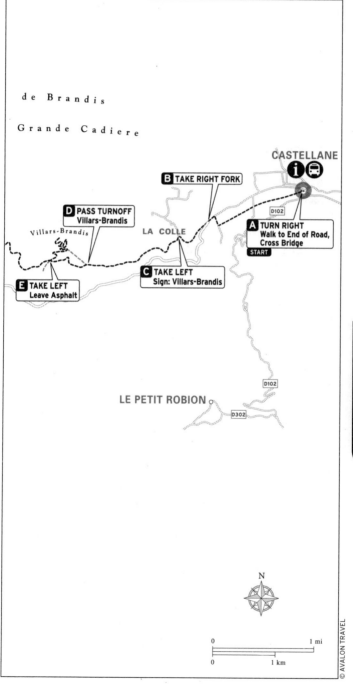

de Brandis

Grande Cadiere

CASTELLANE

B TAKE RIGHT FORK

D PASS TURNOFF
Villars-Brandis

Villars-Brandis

LA COLLE

D102

A TURN RIGHT
Walk to End of Road,
Cross Bridge

START

C TAKE LEFT
Sign: Villars-Brandis

E TAKE LEFT
Leave Asphalt

LE PETIT ROBION

D102

D302

N

0   1 mi

0   1 km

VAR AND VERDON

Tourist Information

Castellane:
  Phone: 0492/ 83 61 14
  Website or Email: www.castellane.org

Rougon:
  Phone: 0492/ 83 66 32
  Website or Email: www.rougon.fr (Rougon's *mairie*)
  Notes: Rougon is very small and has no tourist office, but you can address questions to the *mairie*.

Restaurants

Rougon:
  Name: Le Mur d'Abeilles
  See listing under Accommodations.
  Name: La Terrasse (Bistrot de Pays)
  Address: Rougon
  Phone: 0492/ 31 47 74
  Notes: Reservations recommended. Open all year. In addition to the restaurant, it sells small groceries and snacks.

Accommodations

Chasteuil:
  Name: Le Gîte de Chasteuil
  Address: Chasteuil, in the old schoolhouse, which has been renovated
  Phone: 0492/ 83 72 45
  Website or Email: www.gitedechasteuil.com
  Type of Lodging: *Chambres d'hôte* and *table d'hôte*
  Price: Room (with bathroom): €52 one person, €59 two people, €65–69 two people with two beds, €77 three people, €18 extra person bed and breakfast
  Notes: One of the proprietors is American, so English is well spoken. Make reservations, tell them you're on foot, and clarify that they will be making your dinner, as there's nowhere else to eat in Chasteuil. Vegetarian and other special diets are no problem; just make sure to let them know when you're making your reservation. Also let them know if you'll be wanting a picnic for your outbound journey the next day.

Rougon:
  Name: Le Mur d'Abeilles

Address: Rougon
Phone: 0492/ 83 76 33 or 0492/ 83 76 44 or 0687/ 77 38 30
Website or Email: www.rougon.fr (click on "Hébergement")
Type of Lodging: *Chambres d'hôte* and *gîte d'étape*
Price: €17 per person, €22 with breakfast, €36 demipension
Point Sublime:
Name: L'Auberge du Point Sublime
Address: Point Sublime
Phone: 0492/ 83 60 35 and 0492/ 83 69 15
Website or Email: www.logisdeprovence.com (On the home page under "Chercher un hôtel" click on "sur la carte." When the map comes up, click the icon by the town of Rougon.)
Type of Lodging: Logis de France hotel
Price: Rooms €51–57 per day, half pension €51–55 per day per person
Notes: Closed Oct. 15–Easter

Transportation

Bus
Name: Autocars Sumian Marseille/Castellane
Phone: 0442/ 54 72 82 or 0689/ 87 60 90
Frequency and Duration: One bus a day each way between Rougon and Castellane, but not *every* day. (See Notes.) At the time of this writing, the bus from Rougon to Castellane leaves Rougon at 11:30 and arrives Castellane at noon. Check with either the Rougon Mairie or the bus company closer to the time of your trip to confirm this bus, or otherwise be prepared to hire a taxi to return to Castellane.
Notes: Mon., Wed., Sat. except holidays Apr. 1–June 30 and Sept. 1–Oct. 30; every day except Sun. and holidays July 1–Aug. 31; Sat. only Nov. 1–Mar. 31, and by reservation only (call by 18:00 the day before you want the service). This bus comes from Marseille and Aix, ending at Riez, but connecting with the bus to Moustiers, Rougon, and Castellane. 3.5 hours from Marseille to Castellane, three hours from Aix.
Name: CDC Voyages
Phone: 0492/ 83 64 47
Notes: Point Sublime to Castellane, Sat., Sun., and holidays Apr. 15–30 Sept. 30; there's a *navette* (shuttle bus) twice a day each way July 1–Aug. 31 between Point Sublime and Castellane.

Name: Autocars Delaye
Phone: 0492/ 34 22 90
Website: www.autocars-delaye.com
Frequency and Duration: From Point Sublime to Castellane, twice a day (at the time of this writing, 10:00 and 18:30), half-hour ride
Notes: Every day in July and Aug., weekends and holidays only Apr. 1–June 30 and Sept. 1–15

Taxi
Name: Taxi Verdon
Phone: 0668/ 18 13 13
Notes: Year-round, eight-passenger vehicles
Name: F. Vincent
Phone: 0492/ 83 61 62 or 0611/ 26 97 31
Notes: Castellane based
Name: J. J. Guichard
Phone: 0492/ 83 60 80 or 0492/ 83 63 27
Notes: Castellane based

Miscellaneous Notes

Other than the *chambres d'hôte,* there's no commerce in Chasteuil. There used to be a snack bar in Chasteuil, but the people who ran it have retired.

Point Sublime is on the main road (D952), below Rougon. If you're going to walk down there, either to get a bus or stay at the hotel, take the GR 4 trail rather than the road; the trail is just under one km, but the road is about three times that.

WALK DIRECTIONS

In the main square of Castellane, with your back to the fountain, and facing the Grand Hôtel du Levant (the big hotel at the end of the square), go to the left of the hotel (the D952), and then turn immediately left into the little alleyway.

At the end of the alleyway you'll come to a quiet asphalt road; make a right on this **A**.

Walk to the end of this little road (blazed along here), about 1.5 km (15–20 minutes), crossing a little bridge with a green railing about midway. At the end of the road (where there's only a little alleyway straight ahead, and a fire hydrant on the right), turn right.

VAR AND VERDON

Walk about 150 meters/yards, when you'll reach the D952. Turn left on this, and then take the fork up to the right in about 100 meters **B**.

Walk up this road, passing through the hamlet of la Colle; 5––10 minutes past **B**, watch for a fork where the left prong is a bridge. Take this left **C**, signed Villars-Brandis before the bridge and Chasteuil just beyond it. (Have a look back toward Castellane along here.)

About 25 minutes past **C**, pass the first turnoff for Brandis **D**; 10–15 minutes later watch for the fork where the GR takes the left prong **E**, and take this, leaving the asphalt, which continues up to Villars-Brandis.

Ignore a downhill left fork in 20 meters, and in another minute ignore the right uphill wider prong of a fork. A minute or two later the narrow track joins a wider dirt track.

You have views of the Cadiéres de Brandis to the right here.

About 20–30 minutes past **E**, take the left lower fork **F** (way mark signed Chasteuil), where the right goes to the Brandis ruins.

About 15 minutes later you'll reach a little wayside oratory **G**. To visit the Chapel St.-Jean take the path left (3–4 minute walk to get up there), or for Rougon turn right.

In another half hour or so you'll pass a way mark and fork to Colle Basse **H**; 10 minutes later the path climbs up to the little village of Chasteuil at a track by a farm. Go left on this, and then take your first right **I** (about 75 meters) by the way mark signed to Rougon. The *chambres d'hôte* is down here on the right.

Continuing past the *chambres d'hôte,* ignore a fork downhill left in 40–45 minutes or so.

Almost an hour past the *chambres d'hôte,* the path makes a hairpin right turn, and in about 50 meters comes to a fork, both uphill, one straight on, the other to the left; take the left **J**. (In another 7–10 minutes you'll come to a fork with a narrower right prong; take the left prong uphill; the two meet again anyway.)

About 10–15 minutes past **J** you'll reach a way mark **K**. Take the lower of the two parallel paths here—the top one is very narrow and passes right in front of the way mark. The lower is wider (west-southwest), parallel.

Stay on the path that heads toward the big flat plain (Suech) with the electric line crossing it. Get ready for some major pylonage.

Near the end of the plain the track goes under the electric line and then curves away from it toward the right and then comes to a T junction at a way mark **L**. Turn left here.

You'll see some very unfortunate heavy-duty electric stuff here.

About a half hour of downhill past **L**, watch for a little road-side shrine on your left and a narrow path straight ahead where the main path makes a right-hand turn. Take this little path **M** (blaze on a tree ahead). Go straight downhill when it lets out on the bigger path again in a minute, and so into Rougon in another minute or two.

26 Mons Ring Walk

3 Hours

A welcome anomaly among the many perched villages of the southern Alpes de Haute-Provence, Mons remains unspoiled by sprawl or tourist shops, sitting in splendor on its forested rock, with its arcaded alleyways, hidden squares, and magnificent belvedere eerily empty, at least during any time of year you might go there to walk. The mystery deepens when you discover that there are several good restaurants in the village, as well as dolmens and Roman remains in the countryside around it, and a mind-boggling museum of matchstick replicas of famous ships made by a local truck driver who seems to have stepped straight out of a W. G. Sebald novel (he's still there, making them).

This longish ring walk descends straight from the village through shady woods all the way to the bottom of the valley, where the Siagnole river gushes up from underground springs through the culverts of an early 20th-century waterworks—an impressive sight and a good spot for a picnic. Throughout the woods you'll see the remains of old stone terracing: a farming method thought to have been brought from Italy to this part of France by Ligurian settlers after the Black Death wiped out the indigenous population (traces of Ligurian dialect can still be heard in the local variant of Provençal).

From the source of the Siagnole, the walk continues along the route of a Roman aqueduct. There are no remains of the aqueduct itself right here, but at one point you pass through an

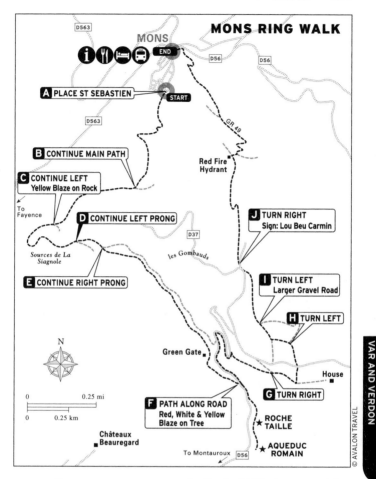

MONS RING WALK

MONS

END

A PLACE ST SEBASTIEN

START

D563

D563

B CONTINUE MAIN PATH

C CONTINUE LEFT
Yellow Blaze on Rock

To
Fayence

D CONTINUE LEFT PRONG

Sources de La
Siagnole

E CONTINUE RIGHT PRONG

D56

D56

GR 49

Red Fire
Hydrant

J TURN RIGHT
Sign: Lou Beu Carmin

D37

les Gombauds

I TURN LEFT
Larger Gravel Road

H TURN LEFT

N

House

0   0.25 mi

G TURN RIGHT

0   0.25 km

Green Gate

F PATH ALONG ROAD
Red, White & Yellow
Blaze on Tree

ROCHE
TAILLE

Châteaux
Beauregard

AQUEDUC
ROMAIN

To Montauroux   D56

© AVALON TRAVEL

VAR AND VERDON

extraordinary stone passageway, the Roche Taille, hewn straight
through a house-size boulder lying in the aqueduct's path. Look
closely at the walls: You'll see the stroke marks of the iron tools
used to carve out the rock—an intimate glimpse into the reality
of human sweat and labor underlying the monuments of Roman
engineering. A short stretch along an asphalt road (not busy) follows, and then the path goes back into woods and quiet farmland before climbing along a forest path back into Mons.

FOOD

There are several restaurants in Mons, and you could very com-
fortably stay in this attractive village long enough to try them
all. Each of the three we sampled was good. Our favorite was

perhaps the Bistrot de Pays **le Petit Bonheur,** hidden away in the silent central square. There are set *menus* at €18.50 and €22.50, with main courses at around €14 as well as very good pizzas and omelettes from €8. Appetizers are the strong point here: a beautifully presented terrine of courgettes and a completely delicious dish of fried, almond-crusted goat cheese. Main courses include confit of duck with apple, a robust casserole of rabbit with tiny but intensely flavorful mushrooms (served with garlicky green beans), and—for an inland restaurant—surprisingly fresh-tasting fish. Desserts are disappointing, especially the crème brûlée, but this is a very pleasant place to eat, inexpensive, and with some decent wines on offer (we had a good Gigondas). The only other people eating there that night were a couple of musicians, and a spontaneous concert of Jacques Brel songs—which attracted a group of village children who peeked in through the door and received occasional handouts of *frites* from the chef's wife—brought our evening to a thoroughly enjoyable end.

Almost equally pleasant is **Chez Barbaroux,** a cosy restaurant tucked in the alley behind the *boulangerie.* There's a €23 *menu,* or you can eat à la carte with main courses at about €13.50. Appetizers include a *panisse*—a wonderfully light, crisp, chickpea-flour griddle cake—and a gratin of aubergine with a finely concentrated eggplant flavor. Avoid the rather pallid boned and stuffed rabbit main course, and perhaps take advantage of a rare vegetarian option in the shape of a pasta with a thick, creamy artichoke sauce. The desserts include a crepe filled with melted chocolate that sounded better than it tasted and extremely good homemade ice creams.

Other possibilities in Mons include **Lou San Bastian,** a friendly restaurant on the main square at the end of the village (Place St. Sebastien, the parking area), serving substantial meals in great earthenware dishes for €12 and under, including a pungent ravioli with pistou, daube, mussel soup, an excellent fricasse of rabbit, and various crepes, and **L'Auberge Provençale** (we didn't actually eat here), serving *Pieds et Paquets* and other Provençal standards on its terrace looking out across the Siagnole valley.

LOGISTICS
IGN Map Number and Name
#3543 ET—Haute Siagne

Tourist Information

Address: Place Saint Sebastien
Phone: 0494/ 76 39 54
Website or Email: www.mairie-mons83.fr. See the email
address for the tourist office on the mairie's website if you want
to email them directly.
Hours: Hours change often, so check ahead. Currently
14:00-18:00 Mon.-Fri. out of season, with morning hours as
well in season.

Restaurants

Name: Le Petit Bonheur (bistrot de pays)
See listing under Accommodation
Closing Day: Wed. Also closed Oct. 26–Nov. 5 and
Feb. 1–Feb. 15
Name: Chez Barbaroux
Address: Rue Maurice Brunet
Phone: 0494/ 76 35 20
Closing Day: Sun. eve. and Mon. Closed out of season (approx
Oct.–Feb.).
Notes: No credit cards
Name: Lou San Bastian
Address: Place Saint-Sebastien
Phone: 0494/ 76 95 71
Closing Day: Thursday all day, and Friday lunch
Name: L'Auberge Provençale
Address: Place Saint-Sebastien
Phone: 0494/ 76 38 33
Closing Day: Wed.

Accommodations

For more accommodation, see the Marie's web site (listed above),
and click on "Hébergement, Restauration" on the left side of
their home page. Alternatively, see the tourist office's website, or
have them email you their Hébergement (lodging) list.
Name: Le Petit Bonheur
Address: Place de Centre
Phone: 0494/ 76 38 09
Website or Email: tbrouet@aol.com
Type of Lodging: Small hotel

Price: €45 for a double room
Notes: Closed Oct. 26–Nov. 5 and Feb. 1–Feb. 15

Transportation

Name: Transports Gagnard
Phone: 0494/ 76 02 29
Notes: From Draguignan take the #73 (Draguignan-Fayence-Grasse) to Fayence. Change to the #84 (Fayence-Mons) to Mons. Currently there's a 7:10 bus from the Fayence tourist office to Mons on Mon-Sat, and also a 17:00 from the Fayence piscine (pool) on Mon., Tues., Thur. and Fri. to Mons. From Mons to Fayence 7:50 Mon.–Sat., and 17:30 on Mon., Tues., Thurs. and Fri. Check these times with the tourist office (Mons or Fayence) or bus company when planning your journey.

WALK DIRECTIONS

Leaving from the main parking lot **Ⓐ** (Place St. Sebastien), head southeast toward the far end of the lot (the side that looks out over the mountains to the sea). Turn left at the stone wall there and head out the eastern corner of the lot, signed on a way mark to "Aqueduc romain," passing the L'Auberge Provençale on your right.

Follow the road downhill, bearing right downhill at the first fork, and then immediately turning right.

Cross the little parking area and get onto the stone pathway at the other end, passing under the L'Auberge Provençale.

Take this path downhill, straight ahead at first (ignore a fork back to the left shortly after entering the path), but becoming narrower and curvy and at least once splitting and rejoining a minute later. Follow the main path downhill, a fairly shady path. (The path zigzags and doesn't conform to the map here.)

About 20 minutes into the walk, you pass a path forking off sharply left (east-southeast), downhill, with big stones barring the entranceway **Ⓑ**. Continue on the main path (southwest).

About 10 minutes later *be aware:* The path forks, right uphill, left (rather sharply) downhill; take the left **Ⓒ**. (There's a yellow blaze on a rock.) (Ignore a fork about two minutes later, as both prongs meet again shortly.)

About 5–10 minutes past **Ⓒ** you reach the stream and a couple of minutes later come to a concrete bridge over it. You can see the water coming out at the left; this is the "Sources de La Siagnole," the source of the Siagnole river.

Just before crossing the bridge, there's a path up to the right toward a chain-link fence; climb up that and beyond the fence meet the wider path and turn left on it.

In another few minutes pass through a gate and the path forks beyond. Take the left prong ❶, flat and ahead.

In another minute the path forks again, right uphill, and left downhill and wider. Take the right fork ❷.

Stay on this path about 20–25 minutes past ❷ (there are some red and white blazes along here), when you come parallel to the road and pass a green gate. About 20 meters/yards farther on, drop to the road and cross it, turning right and walking along it for another 15 meters or so until you come to the path on the left ❸ dropping and paralleling the road. There are a red and white and a yellow blaze on a tree here.

Keep paralleling the road when the path forks. There are red and white blazes all along. In 5–10 minutes you'll come to a plaque with information about the aqueduct. Pass it and head downhill through the split rock, Roche Taille.

Retrace your steps to ❸ and then walk along the road. About 10 minutes past ❸, the road crosses a bridge over the Siagnole. Three minutes beyond the bridge, the road makes a hairpin left turn. In another 25 meters leave the road at a path on your sharp right, uphill, blazed red and white and yellow.

About 5–10 minutes later you'll come to a T junction ❹; turn right (blazed). A minute later, approaching a house, bear left with the path at a small fork (the right side actually goes straight, toward the house). This is plainly blazed.

In another couple of minutes the path comes out at a road. Cross directly over and take the asphalt track, which becomes gravel in 10 meters where you bear left. The path shortly resumes its asphalted surface, climbs rather steeply, and where it soon turns right, you turn left ❺.

In less than 10 minutes the path intersects a larger gravel road ❻; turn left on it.

In another five minutes or so the path comes to a fork signed Lou Touet, left downhill. ❼ Go right here, signed Lou Beu Carmin and crossing over a concrete culvert or bridge. Just beyond this the gravel track forks again; take the left prong.

Stay on this path for about 15 minutes, and when you come to a red fire hydrant on your left, turn right off the path, onto a smaller path (blazed). In about 25 meters the path makes a sharp left turn where another path continues straight. Follow the path left here. Then almost immediately it bends sharply right where, again, another path continues straight ahead. Stay on the path turning right.

A steady climb along this path brings you into Mons about 20 minutes later. Turn left where the path comes out on the asphalt road and then leave the road when you come to the first left, passing to the right of the fountain (La Plus Loin Fontaine) and straight up that road into Mons.

27 Ampus Ring Walk
3 Hours

We stumbled on Ampus, a sleepy, unspoiled village with a starred Michelin restaurant, after trying to find walks around the better-known villages of this part of the Var region, such as Seillans, Bargemon, and Cotignac. The latter are all very quaint in themselves, but their outskirts have been developed to the point that you wouldn't want to walk near them. By all means drive through and stop for a drink in their reliably picturesque central squares. But for a real walk through rolling farmland and quiet woods with fascinating historic landmark sites along the way and a fabulous meal at the end, Ampus is definitely the place to come.

Circling northwest from the village, the walk climbs through woods where you can take a spur to view the prehistoric dolmen of Marenq (a stone-covered open chamber thought to have functioned as an altar)—perhaps not the most spectacular example of its kind but worth the short detour. There's a rather long bit along a road after this, but it's an extremely quiet road through pretty farm country. From there a farm track leads you past the Romanesque chapel of Notre Dame de Spéluque, begun in 1090, to mark a victory over Saracen invaders by the people of Ampus. This is private property—it actually belongs to the nun who lives in the farmhouse just before it. If you're lucky enough to run into her at a quiet moment, as we were, she might show you inside this austerely exquisite building (be sure to leave a

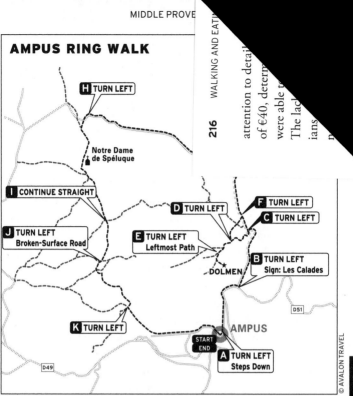

WALKING AND EATI

216

attention to detai
of €40, determ
were able t
The lac
ians

AMPUS RING WALK

H TURN LEFT

Notre Dame de Spéluque

I CONTINUE STRAIGHT

D TURN LEFT

F TURN LEFT

C TURN LEFT

J TURN LEFT
Broken-Surface Road

E TURN LEFT
Leftmost Path

DOLMEN

B TURN LEFT
Sign: Les Calades

D51

K TURN LEFT

AMPUS

START
END

D49

A TURN LEFT
Steps Down

© AVALON TRAVEL

donation for its upkeep). But it's pretty just from the outside too, half-hidden in its thicket of white lilacs.

Coming back into Ampus you'll see signs directing you along a stretch of the town's historic watercourse, a 15th-century canal that was used for irrigation, mills, laundry, and drinking water. Clear water still rushes through it (it powered the street lights at one time), and the little tour is a delightful way of reentering the town.

FOOD

The place to eat here is the wonderful **La Fontaine**. There are other choices (including a cheap but decent pizzeria, **Lou Darnaga**) but La Fontaine has a Michelin star—a rarity in this area—and the food is absolutely delicious.

It's a tiny place, a light, charming, wood-paneled Proven-çal room painted with ivy leaves, and with space for no more than about a dozen diners. The atmosphere is relaxed (no need to dress up), the cooking rooted in the unassuming cuisine of the region, but done with a degree of care, imagination, and

...that sets it apart. There's a set *menu* each day ...ined by whatever is freshest in the market. We ...o get a reservation in April without great difficulty. ...k of choice in the *menu* may be a problem for vegetar-...though fresh fruit and vegetables feature far more promi-...ently in the dishes than they do in most other restaurants down here, and in our case a more than satisfactory main course was made out of the vegetable side dishes.

A refreshing rosé sangria got things off to a very good start, along with an *amuse-bouche* comprising a chickpea-flour crepe and a dip of crushed grilled almonds with garlic and olive oil—a startlingly good combination. The appetizer, a *melee* of *haricots verts,* mâche, and courgettes in a *pistou* of tomato and walnut, was a good test of the chef's abilities. In lesser hands a dish with that many distinct ingredients (seasoned, further, with both cooked and raw onions *and* sesame seeds) would have collapsed in a heap. In this case, however, the different flavors and textures managed not only to remain intensely themselves, but also to complement each other in all sorts of fresh and dynamic ways. Salmon followed, in a light mousseline of asparagus made with the poaching juices of the fish: again a study in freshness and the matching of intense, distinct flavors (we'd just begun to see bundles of giant green asparagus in the markets, and we were hankering for some). The meat course was boned duck, superbly succulent and gamey, and filled with a stuffing flavored with sage and violet olives. An eggplant *marmelade* accompanied this, its sweet and savory smokiness echoing and varying that of the duck itself. The dessert, beautiful to look at (as was everything else), was a creamy, heavenly white mousse of *lait à l'orgeat* (barley milk), afloat on a *soupe* of minted strawberries and pistachios, served with golden curls of what seemed some sort of miraculous sweet, crisped air. An excellent dry Côtes de Provence rosé—a Château Rasque 2005—from the small but choice wine list added to the bill, which was higher than we would normally spend on lunch, but worth every cent.

This was an unforgettable meal, its several courses perfectly judged so as to leave one well fed but without any of the all-too-common feeling of having overindulged or been cajoled into spending money on pretentious, tricksy food. It was perhaps the best dining experience we had in all of Provence.

LOGISTICS
IGN Map Number and Name
#3443 OT—Aups / Salernes

Tourist Information
Name: Bureau de Tourisme d'Ampus
Address: Montée des Lauves
Phone: 0494/ 76 72 66
Website or Email: www.mairie-ampus.fr
Notes: The tourist office is open only June–Sept. At other times you can visit the *mairie* (office in the main square, place de la Mairie) or contact it through its website or at 0494/ 70 97 11 (open 9:30–12:30). You can also contact the regional tourist office in Draguignan, which we've found very helpful.
Name: Office de Tourisme Intercommunal de la Dracénie
Address: 2, avenue Carnot, Draguignan
Phone: 0498/ 10 51 05
Website or Email: www.dracenie.com
Notes: Draguignan is the regional administrative hub; its website contains information on the smaller villages.

Restaurants
Name: La Fontaine d'Ampus
Address: Place de la Mairie
Phone: 0494/ 70 98 08
Closing Day: Open Thurs.–Sun. all year
Name: Lou Darnaga
Address: Place Neuve
Phone: 0494/ 60 19 84

Accommodations
For more accommodations see the Ampus Mairie's website (above); under "Les Services" click on "Hébergement."
Name: La Farigoule
Address: Ampus
Phone: 0494/ 50 68 79
Website or Email: www.lafarigoule-var.fr
Type of Lodging: *Chambres d'hôte*
Price: €65 for a double room, including breakfast
Notes: Open Apr. 1–end of Oct.

Transportation

Bus

Name: Les Rapides Varois

Phone: 0494/ 50 21 50

Frequency and Duration: Two or three buses each direction most weekdays, no Sun. or holidays; Draguignan to Ampus about 30 minutes

Notes: From Draguignan Gare Routiére (bus station) take the #45 to Ampus.

Name: TED Petit Bus

Phone: Free phone number inside France 0800/ 65 12 20, regular number 0494/ 50 94 40

Website or Email: www.dracenie.com/transports-dracenie/ted_petitbus.htm.

Notes: Call to make your *rendez-vous* anywhere from 15 days ahead, to as late as the day before you want the service. Call the free number during reservation hours, 8:00–12:00 and 14:00–17:30 Mon.–Fri. Trips cost €2. If you're using the TED bus to connect with a regular bus, ask the TED driver to give you a *billet* when you get off the bus. This is good for 45 minutes after your TED bus trip.

Taxi

Name: MIP

Phone: 0494/ 50 44 20 or 0609/ 30 82 06 or 0805/ 80 51 22

Website or Email: www.mip-prestige.com

Miscellaneous Notes

Masses are held at Notre Dame de Spéluque at 11:00 each Tues., Thurs., and holidays.

WALK DIRECTIONS

From the center of Ampus, facing the fountain and the *mairie* and with your back to the La Fontaine d'Ampus restaurant, bear right, signed Toutes Directions onto the rue St. Joseph.

In about 20 meters/yards, take the steps down on your left **Ⓐ**, and go straight ahead on the road there. There's a yellow blaze on the pylon to your right here.

Five minutes downhill brings you to a T junction at a bigger road; turn left on it, crossing over a rather sizable bridge (le pont le Ratton).

Take your first left (another two minutes) signed Les Calades **B**. There's also a way mark with a dolmen graphic pictured on it here. (*Note:* The first left after the bridge as shown on the IGN map has been supplanted by an ugly new house with boulders in front.)

In 10–15 minutes pass the driveway of a *gîte* with a metal gate, and then make a hairpin left. Two minutes' steep climb later watch for a dirt track **C** off to the left as the road curves right, signed by the wooden way mark with the dolmen graphic. Turn left here for the spur to the dolmen.

In about three minutes the path meets another path **D**. Go left here now (but later you'll come back and go the other way).

A minute later the path forks in three; take the leftmost path **E**, and bear left again two minutes later, coming to the dolmen in another minute.

Retrace your steps to **D**, but instead of turning right at the intersection, bear left (fluorescent green blaze on the right past the intersection). In 2–3 minutes you'll come to a crossroads. Go straight across and in less than a minute reach the road (now dirt) and turn left **F**.

Follow the dirt road until you come to a T junction in 6–8 minutes **G**, signed for Turquet here on your right. Turn left onto a little asphalt road.

After nearly two kilometers (20–30 minutes) on this road (about 100 meters past a little sign, La Treille) ignore a sharp fork backward left. Then as the road bends right, across from a yellow blaze on a phone pole, take a dirt track off the left of the road **H**. This comes out on a T junction with a dirt road in about a minute; turn left here. Almost immediately the road forks; bear left.

In about five minutes you'll reach the entrance to the chapel Notre Dame de Spéluque.

After visiting the chapel, return to the road and turn left, continuing on the way you were going.

The path immediately crosses a dry streambed and enters a field, where it divides. Go left. As it exits the corner of the field in about 80 meters it divides again; go left (southeast) on a pleasant woodland path.

In 10 minutes or so you'll come to an intersection with a stone shrine, the Oratoire St.-Hubert **I**. Go straight across, entering a much smaller path through boxwood and juniper scrub.

In about five minutes the path begins to descend, bending sharply to the right (a yellow "X" warns you not to go left here), soon passing above a house (ignore another sharp left here—it's really just a bit of terracing) and coming out at a T junction with a small, broken-surface road ❶; go left here.

In about 70 meters, where the road hairpins to the left, you'll see a large track going off to the right and a smaller one going downhill, just to the left of this. Take this downhill track (yellow blaze here).

This yellow-blazed trail winds down to the bottom of the valley, meandering through pine scrub and in about 10 minutes crossing a small iron footbridge before continuing uphill on the other side.

Be alert: After 3–5 minutes of steep climbing you'll come to a little crossroads of paths; go left (east) ❷. In another five minutes, after passing some houses (one with a loud dog, which you studiously ignore), you'll come to a T junction with a small asphalt road; turn left onto the road.

In a few minutes you'll pass a sign on the right for Centre Ville. Continue forward, passing a little stone chapel on your left. This route into town will take you along the *chemin de l'eau,* the town's historic watercourse.

A few minutes from the chapel, just after the blacktop begins bending sharply to the right, look for a stone shrine on your left, dedicated to St. Francis of Assisi. Follow the *chemin de l'eau* as it goes off to the left here, straight into town, with a stop at a little belvedere on the way.

28 Rebouillon–Châteaudouble Ring Walk

4.5–5 Hours

Like Ampus, these two villages are off the main tourist trails of the Var, and they are all the more appealing for it. A splendid gorge, carved by the river Nartuby, connects them.

Châteaudouble hangs dramatically at the edge of a 500-foot cliff. There are remnants of two castles here (hence the name), and the usual medieval priorities of defense, fortification, secret alleys for escaping invaders, and general inaccessibility express themselves in the usual walls, towers, and gateways that seem so

REBOUILLON-CHÂTEAUDOUBLE
RING WALK

CHÂTEAUDOUBLE

H TURN RIGHT
Leave Path

G TURN RIGHT
Stone Steps

D51

D955

F TURN LEFT
Leave Track

E TURN LEFT

A TAKE RIGHT PRONG

D TURN LEFT

REBOUILLON

START
END

C TURN RIGHT
Uphill

B TURN RIGHT
Dirt Road

N

D955

○ **LA GRANEGON**

0   0.5 mi

0   0.5 km

© AVALON TRAVEL

VAR AND VERDON

charming today. Rebouillon is an unusually configured village, built in a great semicircle around its green.

Leaving Rebouillon, the walk climbs through olive groves to the shady Vallon de la Font de Maurel, coming out at woods and heathland of the plateau known as les Malines. It's very peaceful up here—except when the army starts doing artillery practice in the nearby military camp of Canjuers, when it can get a bit thunderous. A steep descent, passing the 16th-century Chapelle St-Jean, takes you to the river below Châteaudouble, from which an even steeper ascent (part of it along a beautifully made *rue calade*—stone street) takes you up to the village.

From here the trail rolls gently downhill through the gorge and then along the wooded banks of the Nartuby itself which, in spring, turns from a near-dry stream to a sparkling forest river as it approaches Rebouillon, with dramatic torrents and some very inviting pools along the way.

FOOD

There are two restaurants in Châteaudouble: the **Restaurant du Château,** which might be worth trying though the menu looks a bit flossy, and our choice, **le Tour**, where you can eat decent (if somewhat heavy) Provençal home cooking from *menus* of €23 or €33 on a pleasant terrace overlooking the gorge.

The enormous appetizers could easily make a lunch in themselves: a good salad of marinated smoked salmon with an unusual cumin flavor, or the excellent *assiette provençale,* which comes with a red pepper tart, a delicious tapenade, some *jambon cru,* and a miniature omelette. The main courses may leave you somewhat disinclined to embark on the second half of the walk—or at least grateful that it's all downhill. These include a daube of boar, a filet of beef with morels, a tasty but ridiculously large shank of lamb braised with wild mushrooms and served with generous amounts of courgettes and *pommes dauphinoise* and a *tian* of green beans. Against our general rule of avoiding seafood in inland restaurants, we tried the sole *en papillote*: an elaborate production involving large amounts of tin foil and a not-very-thrilling piece of fish. Desserts too—baked apple, an apple tart—were so-so. But in general it's an attractive, congenial place for a relaxing lunch. There's nowhere to eat in Rebouillon.

LOGISTICS
IGN Map Number and Name
#3543 OT—Draguignan

Tourist Information
Name: Châteaudouble Mairie
Phone: 0494/ 70 90 02
Website or Email: chateaudouble@wanadoo.fr
Notes: Châteaudouble is a tiny town without a tourist office. However, you can email the *mairie* for answers to any questions you may have.
Name: Office de Tourisme Intercommunal de la Dracénie
Address: 2, avenue Carnot, Draguignan
Phone: 0498/ 10 51 05
Website or Email: www.dracenie.com
Notes: Draguignan is the regional administrative hub; its website contains information on the smaller villages.

Restaurants
Name: Le Tour
Address: Place Beausoleil
Phone: 0494/ 70 93 08
Closing Day: Wed., closed Dec. 15–30

Accommodations
Name: Restaurant du Château
Address: Village center, Châteaudouble
Phone: 0494/ 70 90 05
Website or Email: p.bafico1@tiscali.fr
Type of Lodging: *Chambres d'hôte*
Notes: Two double rooms, €75 one large with bath, €65 one with only a shower, breakfast included

Transportation
Bus
Name: Autocars Bleu Voyages
Phone: 0494/ 67 22 56
Frequency and Duration: One early-morning bus to Draguignan, one or two from Draguignan later in the day, not on Sun. or holidays; from Draguignan about 20 minutes to Rebouillon and 35 to Châteaudouble
Notes: From the Gare Routiére (bus station) in Draguignan, take the #80.
Name: Bus TED
Phone: Free phone number inside France 0800/ 65 12 20, regular number 0494/ 50 94 40
Website or Email: www.tedbus.com; info about the TED bus also at www.dracenie.com/transports-dracenie/ted_petitbus.htm
Notes: This "request bus" service is the TED Petit bus. There are TED Petit bus stops in both Châteaudouble and Rebouillon. The Châteaudouble stop (stop 1, La Place) is at the northwest end of town, just past the Restaurant du Château (which is on your right); there's a TED bus stop sign there. The Rebouillon stop is stop 8 on the same route. The buses run 6:00–20:00, not on Sun. or holidays.

Call to make your *rendez-vous* anywhere from 15 days ahead to as late as the day before you want the service. Call the free number during reservation hours, 8:00–12:00 and

14:00–17:30, Mon.–Fri. Trips cost €2. If you're using the TED bus to connect with a regular bus, ask the TED driver to give you a *billet* when you get off the bus. This is good for 45 minutes after your TED bus trip.

WALK DIRECTIONS

From the parking lot at Rebouillon, walk along the road with the river (Nartuby) to your left and a high stone wall to your right. Past the big iron gate on your right, turn right at the corner in front of the arch. Walk up this road and about 30 meters/yards before the little church, turn left where you see some steps.

Climb the steps, and after them, where the concrete ends there's a fork with two narrow dirt paths; take the right-hand one **Ⓐ**.

Climb the path, in about two minutes from **Ⓐ** meet the road (D955) and cross over it, climbing up a little path that comes in about 30 meters to a little asphalted road in an olive grove. Turn right on this.

Climb up here, passing a cemetery on your left. As you continue to climb, with a stone wall on your left, stay left at a fork about 5–7 minutes past the cemetery. Always keep to the main path. Again, stay left (straight) uphill a minute later when there's a flat path off to the right (a yellow blaze on a rock here). A few minutes later the path comes out on a dirt road **Ⓑ**; turn right.

Stay on this road for a little more than a half kilometer (7–10 minutes) and watch for a substantial dirt track forking off the road to the left uphill, which narrows considerably in 10 meters as it climbs uphill to the right of an olive grove. Take this **Ⓒ**.

Stick to the main path always, and in about a half hour past **Ⓒ** the path comes out at a larger dirt track **Ⓓ**; turn left. Stay on this path (which soon becomes stone, as it bends left, where you ignore a path off to the right) for another 10 minutes or so, until you come to a T junction **Ⓔ**; go left.

Stay on this path (ignoring a path off to the right in about 20 minutes) until you come to a way mark on the right in a little under an hour. Pass the way mark, bearing left, and again 10 meters later, stay left (straight).

Less than five minutes later at a crossroads of several tracks, leave your track and turn left **Ⓕ**, and then at the fork in less than 10 meters, take the right, narrower downhill prong.

This little downhill path comes to a fork (almost a T

junction) in 10–15 minutes; turn right, rather steeply downhill, passing the 16th-century Chapelle St.-Jean in under a minute and turning left just beyond it.

Bear right downhill at the next fork in about a minute. Keep going downhill to the road (D955), which you reach in a few minutes. Cross over and cross the bridge on the other side, bearing right on the path beyond it.

Climb to the top of the path, where it meets the road (D51). Turn left and walk on the road, through the little tunnel, and about 80 meters beyond the tunnel (and across from some recycling bins) at a pedestrian crossing, take the set of stone steps **ⓖ** on your right, up to the village. Turn right into the village.

Leaving Châteaudouble

If you began in Rebouillon, go back down the stone steps **ⓖ**. If you're starting from Châteaudouble, to find the steps take the road out of town, passing the Restaurant du Château on your right, and about 10 meters farther on take the left downhill between two buildings, which leads to the steps **ⓖ** behind the building on the right. Go down these.

From **ⓖ**, cross over the main road (D51) to the little road ahead of you and take that downhill. There's a way mark at the intersection signed Les Avals.

Five minutes from **ⓖ** ignore a driveway up to the right and continue on the road, which bends left here, gently downhill.

Follow this road for about 45–50 minutes, and then as the road makes a hairpin left turn, leave it for a small path off to the right **ⓗ**.

In 10 minutes or so, the river comes into view and you come to a small T junction, where the left fork drops to the river; turn right, though, following to the left of a green chain-link fence, and then the path turns left and crosses a little concrete bridge over the stream.

About 10 meters beyond the bridge, the path comes to another little T junction; turn left (back toward the river).

About 10 minutes later there's a fork where both prongs are ahead; take the right upper one, and in less than a minute come to a bridge, cross over it, and turn right at the gravel road at the end of it.

In another minute or so cross over another gravel road

crossing your path, and continue downhill on the other side, on a path that immediately narrows (you're now walking parallel to the river on the other side). You can also walk on the lower path you can see below you (closer to the river, but still above it).

About 20 minutes past the bridge, the culvert path (lower path) ends at a house (with a corrugated roof). Jump over the culvert before reaching the house, and turn left on the path on the other side of the culvert (going away from the house). Climb up this path, which in about 20 meters comes out just before **A**; turn right to reach **A**, and then retrace your steps back to the parking lot.

29 Cipiéres to Gourdon
3.5 Hours

If you're staying in this area and want something more bucoli-cally rural than the Gourdon Ring Walk, this is the walk to take (it's a one-way itinerary; see *Logistics* for how to get a bus or taxi back).

Though not far from Gourdon as the crow flies, Cipiéres is in another world altogether, well off the tourist track, set on a knoll above an upland plain—the Plateau de Calerne—that seems to have protected it so far against the northward sprawl from the Riviera. It's a quiet, pretty, farming village with a very congenial central square and an anomalously huge 17th-century château at its northern edge.

Leaving the village, you soon enter the heathlike Plateau de Calerne where, after putting a couple of regrettably placed power lines behind you, you're in a semi-wilderness of woods, stone walls, little streams, and rocky pastures full of grazing, bleating, bell-tinkling sheep (along with the occasional sheep-dog). There's a spur to see a fine *borie,* and then, as you ap-proach the steep cliffs at the edge of the plateau (a favorite haunt of paragliders), increasingly fabulous views all the way to the Mediterranean. The final approach to Gourdon, zigzagging down these cliffs, is wonderful.

You can call the *à la demande* shuttle bus to get from Grasse (the closest SNCF train station) to Cipiéres, have lunch, and then walk to Gourdon and stay there overnight (or return to Grasse from Gourdon if you wish; see *Logistics* under

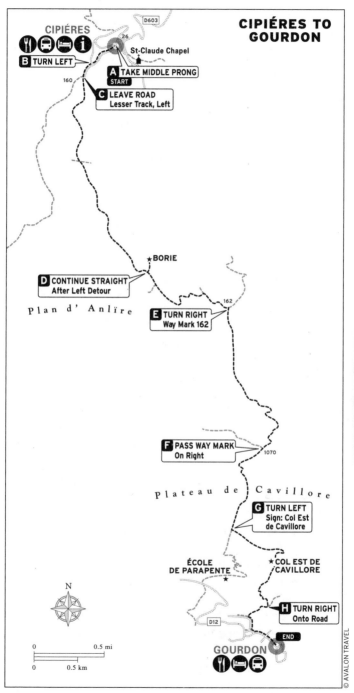

CIPIÉRES TO GOURDON

D603

CIPIÉRES

26

St-Claude Chapel

B TURN LEFT

A TAKE MIDDLE PRONG
START

160

C LEAVE ROAD
Lesser Track, Left

★ BORIE

D CONTINUE STRAIGHT
After Left Detour

Plan d' Anlïre

162

E TURN RIGHT
Way Mark 162

F PASS WAY MARK
On Right

1070

Plateau de Cavillore

G TURN LEFT
Sign: Col Est
de Cavillore

ÉCOLE
DE PARAPENTE

★ COL EST DE
CAVILLORE

★

H TURN RIGHT
Onto Road

D12

END

GOURDON

N

0   0.5 mi

0   0.5 km

VAR AND VERDON

Walk 30 for that). Or base yourself in Gourdon and take either a taxi or the *à la demande* bus to Cipiéres, have lunch, and walk back to Gourdon (either way, see *Logistics* for more transportation details).

FOOD

There's only one restaurant in Cipiéres, **Les Ormeaux,** appealingly situated in the quiet center of this attractive old village. It's a relaxing place to eat, with an outdoor terrace as well as pleasantly shadowy indoor seating, and even though the cooking is not the greatest, enough care is taken to assure you of a satisfying meal.

Main courses à la carte are €11–13, or there's a €20 three-course *menu*. Goat cheese salad or a fresh-tasting and photogenic pink and beige–striped terrine of fish was followed by a choice of chicken brochettes with fennel, beef tournedos, or lamb cutlets. Avoid the papery chicken; the beef and lamb, however, were fine, if a little tough. All were served with beignets (fritters) of courgette, which looked quite a bit better than they tasted, and a gratin of eggplant, which also raised expectations that its undercooked contents didn't quite fulfill. Desserts were nothing special, except for a surprisingly delicious homemade nougat ice cream. None of this perhaps sounds terribly tempting, but it really isn't bad, and the friendliness of the service and the laid-back charm of the setting (especially if you eat outside), more than make up for a certain mediocrity in the food itself.

LOGISTICS
IGN Map Number and Name
#3643 ET—Cannes/Grasse and #3642 ET—Vallée de l'Estéron

Tourist Information
For Gourdon tourist information, see Walk 30.
  Name: Cipiéres Mairie
  Phone: 0493/ 59 96 48
  Notes: Cipiéres is tiny and has no tourist office. If you speak French you can call the *mairie* with any questions you might have, but it doesn't have enough staff to operate as a tourist office.

VAR AND VERDON

Restaurants

For Gourdon, see Walk 30.
  Name: Les Ormeaux
  Address: Cipiéres village center
  Phone: 0493/ 59 95 09
  Closing Day: Mon.

Accommodations

For accommodation in Gourdon, see Walk 30.

Transportation

Check with the Gourdon tourist office for transportation questions; see Walk 30.
  Bus
  Name: TAM
  Phone: 0800/ 06 01 06
  Notes: This is a request-service bus *(service à la demande)*. Call for a reservation; the latest you can make your request is 16:00 the day before you wish to travel. The phone number above is a free call inside France, but if you want to call before you get to France, the number is 0497/18 64 82.
  Taxi
  Name: Taxi Gourdon
  Phone: 0624/ 26 41 12 or 0493/ 42 93 49
  Name: Taxi Roger
  Phone: 0673/ 69 69 11 or 0493/ 36 28 40
  Notes: This is based in the town of Caussols.

WALK DIRECTIONS

In the main square of Cipiéres, with your back to the restaurant and the fountain, cross the square aiming slightly toward your right, and head up the steps beyond the way mark 26, with three signs signed to Chemin des Collets.

Keep climbing the steps until you come to a double concrete track; turn right uphill on that. In about 20 meters/yards the track ends at a three-way fork; go across (the middle fork) **Ⓐ**.

In another 20 meters take the steps to the left just before a gated driveway.

Follow this path for a few minutes until it comes out at a little

asphalt road with a line of cypresses above a stone wall; turn left
B (about 10 minutes from the start of the walk).

Keep straight on the road 20 meters later, when four other options (driveways and dirt tracks) present themselves. Soon you'll
pass a red and white blaze on your left, and then the asphalt
turns to gravel track with a sign, Chemin d'Ardou. In another
30 meters leave the gravel road for a lesser track on the left at
way mark 160 (signed Chemin des Collets) **C**.

About 20 minutes later, between two pylons the route is
crossed by a farm track; cross over.

Follow this path for about a half hour, until you come to a
way mark **D**. We continue straight ahead here, but first detour to the left (sharply left and back) to visit the *borie* 100
meters along.

Resuming your forward trajectory at **D**, 2–3 minutes later
you come to a wide dirt track; go left on it.

About 15 minutes later (ignoring a track to the left about 10
minutes past **D**) you'll reach way mark 162 **E**. Leave the road
here and take the slightly lesser path to the right.

In another couple of minutes ignore a track bearing right
(confirmatory blaze on a stone wall a minute later).

About 40 minutes later (IGN map point 1070), you pass a de-
funct way mark on the right **F**, and another 20 minutes later
come to a way mark **G** signed ahead for Circuit de Cavillore,
where we turn left instead, signed Col Est de Cavillore.

There's no shortage of yellow blazes to guide you along here.

About 10 minutes past **G**, you'll pass another way mark (Col
Est de Cavillore) on your left, signed for Gourdon.

Follow the path downhill for about a half hour until it comes
out at a way mark and a little road. Turn right on the road **H**.

In about two minutes you'll come to a T junction with another road; turn left.

Follow this road downhill, and in three minutes or so, just as
the road turns right toward the bigger road (D12), leave it for a
little trail on the left by a way mark.

When this lets out on the big asphalt road (D12), turn left
and so into town in another few minutes.

30 Gourdon Ring Walk

3.5 Hours

The development north of Nice sprawls far inland, but it does eventually ease off, and the dramatically perched village of Gourdon marks one of the points where it stops. Despite being given over entirely to gift shops, the village itself retains considerable charm, with vast views all the way down to the coast (even as far as Corsica on a clear day), and a château with a museum containing, among other things, a Rembrandt self-portrait and Marie-Antoinette's writing desk.

Our walk here is a little different—a departure from our usual avoidance of all things man-made, a large part of it being in close proximity to a monumental piece of industrial engineering. This is the Aqueduc du Foulon, a pipeline built along the steep sides of the Loup valley to bring water from the Alpes Maritimes to Grasse. The walk is fascinating and fun but perhaps not everybody's idea of a day in the country.

Leaving Gourdon along a zigzagging rocky path known as the Chemin du Paradis (the name is earned by the wildflowers alone: In May pink Valerian blossoms from every cranny in the rocks), you turn off, following the GR 51 trail alongside the dramatic course of the pipeline itself. The heroic nature of this engineering feat becomes apparent as you start entering the series of tunnels hewn through the rock for its path. *Note:* These tunnels, though not more than 150 meters long, are cold and very dark. We didn't have a flashlight with us, but there were moments we wished we did.

In keeping with the industrial theme here, there's a stretch above a much more modern industrial complex, Les Englades— ugly as hell, but far enough away not to be too bothersome. Shortly after this the walk becomes more rustic, climbing into the pleasant trees and *garrigue* of the Bois de Gourdon, before turning east for a spectacular reentry into Gourdon.

FOOD

Touristy villages such as Gourdon tend to produce restaurants more dedicated to the quick buck than the patient art of good cooking and one approaches the task of choosing somewhere to eat with trepidation. But with help from some local foodies

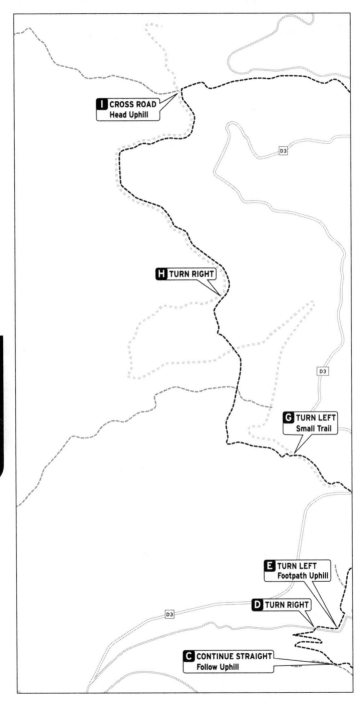

VAR AND VERDON

I CROSS ROAD
Head Uphill

H TURN RIGHT

G TURN LEFT
Small Trail

E TURN LEFT
Footpath Uphill

D TURN RIGHT

C CONTINUE STRAIGHT
Follow Uphill

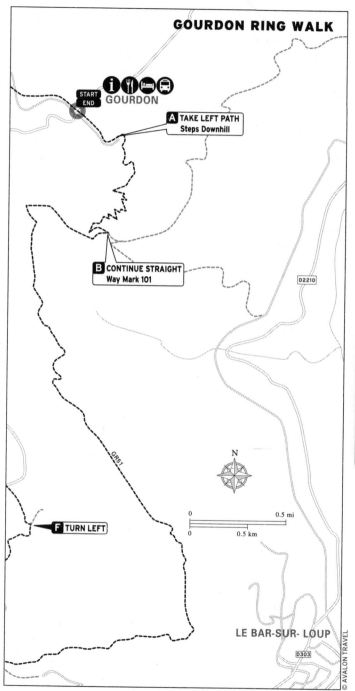

GOURDON RING WALK

START END GOURDON

A TAKE LEFT PATH
Steps Downhill

B CONTINUE STRAIGHT
Way Mark 101

D2210

N

GR51

F TURN LEFT

| 0 | 0.5 mi |
| 0 | 0.5 km |

LE BAR-SUR- LOUP

D303

VAR AND VERDON

© AVALON TRAVEL

we were able to find two decent restaurants to recommend, one plain and cheap, the other a little fancier.

La Bergerie pizzeria is in the coach park below the village, an unprepossessing setting that prepares you for its modest pricing (wood-fired pizzas for around €10, daily *plats* such as cod with peppers or entrecôte with cèpes for a few euros more), but not for its surprisingly good food. The large, crisp-crusted pizzas are terrific—the Sicilian especially, with its fat capers and green olives, and the Montagnard, generously tiled over with *jambon cru*. There are excellent salads—niçoise, smoked duck, and so forth, for €3–11. And judging from our sampling of the daily *plats*—a half baby chicken served with stuffed tomatoes and a rich, smoky ratatouille—there's no reason to limit yourself to the pizza side of the menu. The homemade strawberry and apple tarts were pretty good too.

At the other end of the spectrum is **le Vieux Four,** a little wood-beamed parlor to the left as you walk into the village. The €36 *menu* changes daily, always a good sign as far as the freshness of the ingredients goes. The presentation here is somewhat fussy and the portions are tiny, but the food is certainly fresh and prepared with zealous attention to the bringing out and balancing of flavors. Slices of chorizo and radish made a startling accompaniment to little warm seafood pastries in our *amuse-bouche*. Tuna carpaccio was combined with *pistou,* tomatoes and roasted pine nuts in one delicious appetizer (the other, a gazpacho, was an over-complicated production involving a saucer, a cast-iron pot, and a glass jar that made it seem more like a science project than something you'd want to eat). After a long wait, excellent—but again tiny—main courses arrived: some choice pieces of succulent local lamb, a beautifully cooked piece of hake *(colinet)* served on a minestrone of peas and white beans, for the vegetarians a thimbleful of exquisite artichoke risotto. The desserts were similarly poised between fuss and finesse, the best of them an apricot *pain perdue* (a sort of high-class bread-and-butter pudding) with a sweet iced yogurt nicely setting off the tartness of the apricots. If you're off desserts you can opt for a cheese plate instead, and be pleasantly surprised by its quantity—five or six first-rate Provençal cheeses—as well as its quality. By the end you do feel well fed, but a little more concession to the spirit

of abundance wouldn't have hurt. The bill arrives clipped in a miniature clothespin.

Note: Like all the other restaurants in the village, these are primarily lunch places. Le Vieux Four opens at night only on weekends and La Bergerie only on Saturday nights out of season (in season it's open nights).

LOGISTICS
IGN Map Number and Name
#3643 ET—Cannes/Grasse

Tourist Information
Address: Place Victoria
Phone: 0493/ 09 68 25
Website or Email: www.gourdon-france.com
Hours: 11:00–18:00 every day

Restaurants
Name: Le Vieux Four
Address: Rue Basse
Phone: 0493/ 09 68 60
Closing Day: Opening stated as "open every day (maybe)"
Name: La Bergerie
Address: Just below the town, on the main road
Phone: 0493/ 42 94 54
Closing Day: Mon., out of season open only at lunch and on Sat. night
Name: L'Epicurieux
Address: Rue principale (the main up-and-down street of Gourdon)
Phone: 0493/ 77 66 97
Notes: Sandwiches and homemade ice cream, nice-looking small meals at lunchtime. When we were there, it had no sign indicating the name of the restaurant.

Accommodations
See the Gourdon tourist office's website for additional listings. Lodging right inside Gourdon is scarce; the tourist office website has more listings in nearby towns.
Name: Château de Gourdon

Address: Gourdon village center
Phone: 0661/ 34 21 12 or 0493/ 09 68 02 (Call this number to speak to someone in English.)
Type of Lodging: Apartments for 2–10 people, fully equipped, usually rented by the week, but if it has any empty ones (fairly likely outside July and Aug.), it'll rent by the night or two.
Price: €60–65 per night
Name: SCI Polus
Address: Gourdon village center—rue de l'Eglise
Phone: 0493/ 09 68 89
Website or Email: sainte.catherine@wanadoo.fr
Type of Lodging: Apartment for 2–4
Price: €65 for two people, €95 for four people
Notes: This apartment is listed (and linked to the photos of and contact for it) on the Gourdon tourist office website, but no price is given on the site.

Transportation
Bus
Name: Envibus
Phone: 0489/ 87 72 00
Website or Email: www.envibus.fr; the site has an English option, and you can see everything you need here: routes, schedules, and more.
Frequency and Duration: Five Envibus (*navettes,* or shuttle buses) a day from Châteauneuf to Gourdon, and seven a day from Gourdon to Châteauneuf; 15-minute ride
Notes: Grasse is the nearest SNCF (train) station, 14 km from Gourdon. From either Nice or Grasse, take the Nice–Grasse #500 bus to Châteauneuf and change in Châteauneuf for the Envibus, line 12 bis (Ligne 12 bis), to Gourdon. The Envibus runs Mon.–Sat. all year.

WALK DIRECTIONS

From the car park just above the traffic roundabout below the town, walk uphill, and just outside the actual village (where you can't bring a car any farther), find the path (steps downhill) on the left Ⓐ (east northeast). You'll see way mark 102, signed Chemin du Paradis. Follow this increasingly pretty mule track, continuously downhill.

VAR AND VERDON

After 40 minutes or so of leisurely walking, you'll come to an intersection at way mark 101 and some big pipes **B**. Carry on straight ahead, coming almost immediately to your first tunnels.

Follow the pipe for about an hour (ignoring a path downhill left about 45 minutes past **B**, at which point it goes into the ground and a concrete path leads straight ahead uphill **C**. Follow this uphill for about 10–15 minutes, when the path comes out at another road (gravel to the left, asphalt to the right); turn right here **D**.

A few minutes later, as the road bends right, leave it for a little footpath off the road left uphill **E**, with a wooden sign, Bois de Gourdon. After a minute or two of climbing, you'll come to a T junction with a narrow dirt track; turn right on this.

Follow this path for about 10–15 minutes, when it comes out at a wider dirt track; bear left here, and then in about 20 meters/ yards you'll reach a T junction with a cart track (rough concrete); turn left **F**.

A few minutes later come out on the asphalt road (D3). Cross over and take the little footpath that leads up to a graveled parking lot. Wrap around left at the parking lot, onto a gravel road uphill west-northwest, signed Piste Bois de Gourdon and passing through the iron bar that bars the road to cars.

In 2–3 minutes take the smaller trail left **G** (counterintuitive), which bends around to the right in 15 meters or so, and then bends left and comes to a T junction by a wooden signpost; turn right.

Stay on this trail, climbing, ignoring deviations, including a track crossing over our trail about 10 minutes after taking the left turn at **G**.

A few minutes later our trail crosses over the bigger "piste track" again. Cross straight over (and soon pass beehives on your left). About five minutes later the trail comes out on the "piste track" again; turn right **H**.

About 10–15 minutes later pass another metal bar and pass under a stone cross to the left. Keep on the main track, downhill.

In another 10 minutes or so you'll pass an old sheep trough on the left. The road is asphalt now. A few minutes later you pass a way mark, and 10 minutes after that this road comes out on a bigger road **I**; cross over the road and head uphill on the road to the right of a stone road, and in about 15 meters, as the road bends left, leave it for the dirt path on the right, by a way mark signed for Gourdon (note the old iron cross on the right just as you enter the path).

Shortly this comes out on the road; turn left and so into Gourdon.

The Narrow-Gauge Train des Pignes

The Train des Pignes is the sole survivor of four narrow-gauge (one meter) railway lines built in the Alpes Maritimes during the 19th century. The old steam engines used pine cones for fuel, hence the name, though some say it's so named because one had time to jump off and gather pine nuts *(pignes)* and get back on again without slowing the course of the train.

The inspiration of a Dignoise engineer who proposed a railway to connect the sea and the countryside, the line was eventually accomplished by spacing the rails a meter apart (rather than the usual 1.4 meters) to facilitate the sharper turns required by the challenging terrain; thus the term "narrow-gauge." The first stretch, between Digne and Mezel, was completed in 1891, with the final stretch to Nice completed 20 years later, encompassing 25 tunnels, 16 viaducts, and 15 or so bridges in its 150 kilometers.

The 3.5-hour journey from Nice to Digne passes through some beautiful mountain scenery along the way and stops at some of the loveliest towns and villages in all of Provence. Many

THE NARROW-GAUGE
TRAIN DES PIGNES

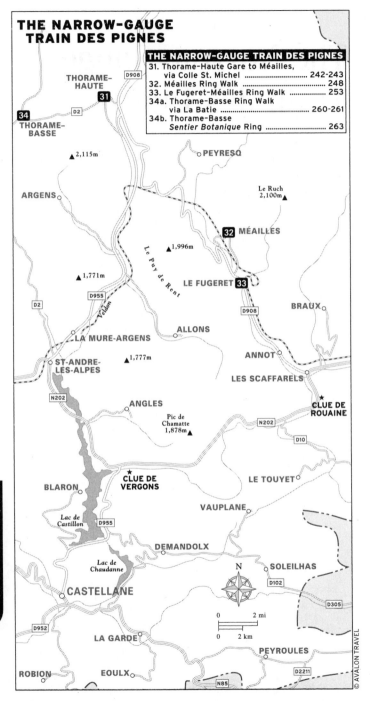

THORAME-
HAUTE

D908

31

34

D2

THORAME-
BASSE

▲ 2,115m

PEYRESQ

Le Ruch
2,100m ▲

ARGENS

MÉAILLES

32

▲ 1,996m

Le Puy de Rent

LE FUGERET

33

▲ 1,771m

D955

D2

BRAUX

D908

Verdon

LA MURE-ARGENS

ALLONS

ST-ANDRE-
LES-ALPES

▲ 1,777m

ANNOT

LES SCAFFARELS

N202

ANGLES

Pic de
Chamatte
1,878m ▲

CLUE DE
ROUAINE ★

N202

D10

CLUE DE
VERGONS ★

LE TOUYET

BLARON

VAUPLANE

Lac de
Castillon

D955

DEMANDOLX

Lac de
Chaudanne

SOLEILHAS

N

D102

CASTELLANE

D305

0   2 mi

0   2 km

D952

LA GARDE

PEYROULES

ROBION

EOULX

D2211

N85

of these are within walking distance of each other, opening up the very appealing prospect of ring walks that use this tiny, delightful, dependable railway as a part of the itinerary. These were some of the most enjoyable walks we did, the train part adding an element of pure fun.

Entrevaux, Annot, and Touet-sur-Var are among the more splendid towns on the line; all are well worth visiting. The best places for walking, however, are farther north. We've concentrated on the section between le Fugeret and Thorame-Haute Gare (station), with the stunning village of Méailles in between. It's a quiet, remote-feeling area, with some small-scale farming going on, a little Nordic skiing in winter, and not much else. We've included ring walks from two of the villages themselves, along with the walks linking them to each other. One of these involves an optional visit to a deep, dark cave requiring a powerful flashlight, while the other crosses a ravine where there's a possible danger of rock slides, so be warned.

We've also included a couple of walks in an exceptionally pretty sheep-farming area around the village of Thorame-Basse. This isn't actually within walking distance from Thorame-Haute Gare (the train station), so you'll need to get there by car. It's well worth the visit.

31 Thorame-Haute Gare to Méailles, via Colle St. Michel

3 Hours

Thorame-Haute station, several kilometers from Thorame-Haute itself, is a sleepy spot with a church, a hotel/restaurant, and a few faded old buildings attesting to busier times on this splendid old railroad. You'll feel as if you're disembarking in the middle of nowhere.

This leg of our railroad itinerary is a steady climb along an old forest track, much of it in the shade. The landscape is austere at first: steep, stony mountainsides crowding in on each other. But after an hour or so it opens out into the alpine pastures around the village of Colle St. Michel. In May these are a deep lush green, strewn with blue forget-me-nots and yellow cowslips.

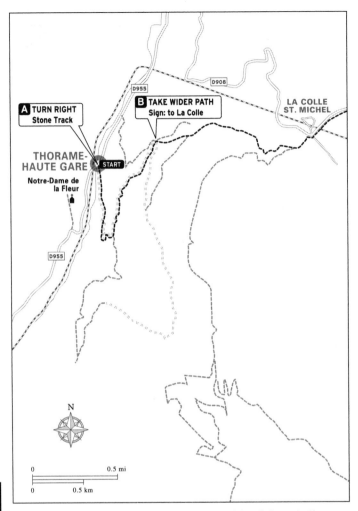

Cuckoos abound, and you can hear the tinkle of sheep bells. The village itself isn't especially old or picturesque (it's a Nordic ski station in winter), but it has an extremely pleasant, tranquil atmosphere and would be a fine place to spend a night if you don't feel like pushing on to Le Fugeret (there's nowhere to stay at Méailles, but you can catch the train there).

The walk onward, from Colle St. Michel to Méailles, is one of the most beautiful walks in this region. It's also very easy, sloping gently downhill almost all the way. After a kilometer or so on the paved (but very quiet) road, the trail leads off through woods that soon open out into the unspoiled valley of the Vaire

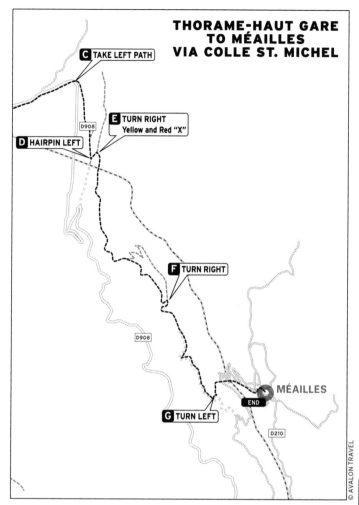

THORAME-HAUT GARE
TO MÉAILLES
VIA COLLE ST. MICHEL

C TAKE LEFT PATH

D908

E TURN RIGHT
Yellow and Red "X"

D HAIRPIN LEFT

F TURN RIGHT

D908

MÉAILLES

END

G TURN LEFT

D210

© AVALON TRAVEL

river. As you wind down through the sheep pastures and sweet-smelling broom, you'll see an extraordinary line of cliffs running the length of the opposite side of the valley, rising and dipping like a stretch of the Great Wall of China. The village of Méailles merges into it so imperceptibly it takes a moment to realize you're no longer looking at a natural rock formation. It's a very pretty village, well worth the 15-minute climb from the station to visit it. In the past it was a thriving farming community, but there are only two working farmers here now, and most of the other houses are *residences secondaires,* empty till their owners flee here from Nice in the summer.

At present there's nowhere to stay in Méailles itself. Your options are to take the train back to Thorame-Haute Gare, or proceed—on foot or by train—to Le Fugeret (another hour's walk), where there are places to eat and stay (and where you can also get the train again).

Plan on 2 hours to Colle St. Michel, and 1.5 from there to Méailles.

LOGISTICS

There is no lodging in Méailles, and food only on weekends. Stay overnight in Colle St. Michel, or catch the train again at Méailles station and go on to Le Fugeret or Annot. Annot is a good-size town with plenty of lodging.

For Méailles information, see Walk 32.

For Le Fugeret information, see Walk 33.

IGN Map Number and Name
#3541 OT—Annot

Tourist Information
There's no tourist office, but you can contact the Thorame-Haute Mairie at 0492/ 83 90 86.

Restaurants
Colle St. Michel:
 Name: Auberge l'Oustelet
 See listing under Accommodations.

Accommodations
Colle St. Michel:
 Name: Auberge l'Oustelet
 Address: Colle St. Michel; see Walk Directions.
 Phone: 0492/ 83 23 80
 Type of Lodging: Auberge/*gîte d'étape*
 Price: €15–25 per room, €25–44 for two people, breakfast €6, demipension €35–46, full pension €50–58
 Notes: Three rooms for 2–4 people, closed Nov. 15–Dec. 15
 Name: Gîte d'Étape de la Colle Saint-Michel
 Address: Colle St. Michel
 Phone: 0492/ 83 30 78

Website or Email: http://collesaintmichel.free.fr
Type of Lodging: *Gîte d'étape*
Price: €20 per person per night including breakfast, half pension €30, full pension €38, reduced prices for kids
Notes: Eight rooms for 2–4 people, four *dortoirs* for 6–8 people, sauna, whirlpool tub, mountain bike rentals, bar, and two fireplaces, English spoken, closed Nov. 15–Dec. 30

Transportation
General Train Logistics
Name: Chemins de Fer de Provence
Phone: 0497/ 03 80 80 (Nice)
Website or Email: www.trainprovence.com (English option available)
Frequency and Duration: Every day all year, 3.5 hours, four or five trains per day each way
Notes: Nice–Digne line. We found the train tends to run a little late, but don't count on it. See website for schedule. Buy your ticket in the station or on the train. Get there early during tourist season.
Name: Thorame-Haute Gare (train station)
Phone: 0492/ 89 02 55
Website or Email: www.trainprovence.com
Frequency and Duration: From Nice to Thorame about 2.5 hours, four or five trains each direction per day
Notes: There's a bus connection from Thorame-Haute station to the village of Thorame-Haute about 10 minutes away. The bus also goes to the villages of Beauvezer, Villars/Colmars, Colmars-les-Alpes, and Allos. There's not a connection for every train, only three a day each way. If you're going to do the Thorame–Basse walks (Walk 34) you can use this bus connection to go at least part of the way; see Walk 34 for more details on this bus connection.

Miscellaneous Notes
If you do go north from Thorame-Haute, there's an interesting shop just outside Beauvezer selling local artisanal products, the **Maison de Produits de Pays du Haut-Verdon;** on the Route de Colmars (D908), 0492/ 83 58 87, open Fri., Sat., and Sun. out of season, every day during school vacation, closed mid-Nov.–mid-Dec.

TRAIN DES PIGNES

WALK DIRECTIONS

Coming out of the front of the station, with the Notre-Dame de la Fleur church on your left and the hotel/restaurant across from you, make a right turn before you get to the road, and walk down along the tracks until in about 100 meters/yards the tracks intersect the asphalt road.

Turn right on the asphalt road and walk down to the first right off it (about 50 meters), a stone track; there's a stone chapel on the little hill here at the turning. Take this **Ⓐ**.

In about 2–2.5 km (around 45 minutes or so, but depending largely on your rate of climbing), as the road makes a hairpin right turn, you can notice two trails off it to the left: a very small leftmost one, and a wider one steeply uphill. Take the wider one **Ⓑ**, signed to La Colle.

After about 10 minutes' steep climb a path comes in from the right. In another 20 minutes you'll meet with a path coming from the right, and five minutes later come to the asphalt road. Turn right on the asphalt road, passing the *gîte d'étape* on your left. Walk down the road a few minutes and you'll see the sign pointing left for the Auberge Oustelet.

From Colle St. Michel

Come out the driveway from Auberge Oustelet and turn left on the asphalt road (D908). Pass extensive terracing on your left.

In 10 minutes ignore the turnoff to Peyresq (D32) on the left; 3–4 minutes later, as the road bends right and there's a metal guardrail on the left, watch for a left-turn blaze and take the gravel left-turn path **Ⓒ** downhill just past the guardrail (red and yellow blaze on a tree).

After about 8–10 minutes' downhill walk, ignore a fork off sharply left. You'll see a yellow and red blaze immediately ahead on a tree.

Five minutes later you come to a fork: Make the hairpin left **Ⓓ**, rather than continuing straight ahead (yellow and red blaze and sign for Méailles on a tree), and about 75 meters later, watch for a smaller path dropping on the right **Ⓔ**; take this (yellow and red "X" on a tree where the path you're leaving continues ahead).

You can see the arches of the train bridge ahead.

About 35 minutes past **Ⓔ** you come to a T junction (with a house below) **Ⓕ**; turn right.

After another 20–25 minutes as the path zigzags downhill, watch for a shortcut way mark pointing left and take it **G**. Five minutes later you cross a bridge and then cross over the road (D210) and pick up the trail on the other side. Follow the signs, crossing the road a few more times like this, arriving at the Méailles station/*arrêt* about 10 minutes past the bridge.

To reach Méailles village from the station (about 15 minutes farther), stand between the tracks and the train station, with your back to the station, turn right, and follow the gravel road away from the station. Where it meets the asphalt road, turn right on the road and immediately see the blazed path on your right. It's a narrow asphalted path and leads all the way up to the village of Méailles.

32 Méailles Ring Walk
1–2 Hours Each Way

The countryside above Méailles looks ideal for walking: lush meadows rising to the forested slopes of a high ridge. The area IGN map shows a perfect-looking ring walk, going up the west side of the ridge, traversing its length, and then coming down on the east side. We tried doing this and nearly ended up spending a rainy night on the ridge: The east-side trail shown on the map is virtually impossible to find and extremely hard to follow even if you do (this was confirmed by some locals we spoke to later). So we can't, alas, recommend that walk.

What we have instead is a there-and-back itinerary up the west side, one that, we hope, is varied and interesting enough to make up for the always less-than-thrilling prospect of returning along one's own tracks.

After a fairly steep, lengthy climb past the meadows and up through the rocky scrub above the Ravin du Maouna, you come out at the outcrop at the west end of the ridge, known as the Rocher du Brec. From here you can go around to the other side of the ridge and visit a remarkable cave, the Grotte de Méailles. Neanderthal and Bronze Age remains have been found in this natural tunnel, which penetrates more than 100 meters into the cliff. There are stalactites and calcite domes at various spots, and a pool, the "lake of fairies," about halfway along. We should confess here that we saw none of the above. Our flashlight

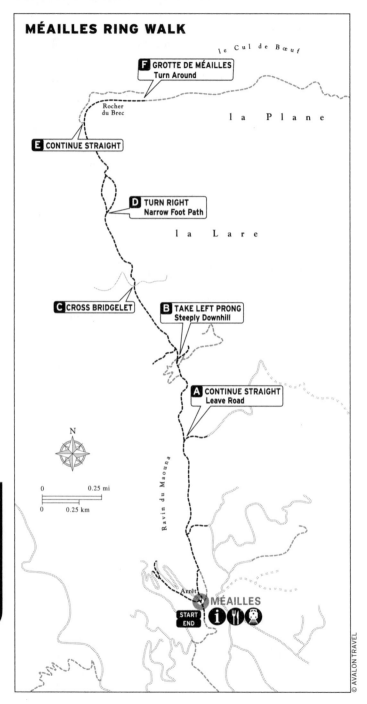

MÉAILLES RING WALK

le Cul de Bœuf

F GROTTE DE MÉAILLES
Turn Around

Rocher
du Brec

l a   P l a n e

E CONTINUE STRAIGHT

D TURN RIGHT
Narrow Foot Path

l a   L a r e

C CROSS BRIDGELET

B TAKE LEFT PRONG
Steeply Downhill

A CONTINUE STRAIGHT
Leave Road

N

0   0.25 mi

0   0.25 km

Ravin du Maouna

Arrêt

MÉAILLES

START
END

turned out to be not nearly powerful enough, and sheer chicken-hearted terror got the better of us after only a few yards in. By all accounts (including the official IGN *Promenades Randonnees* guide to the area), there are no particular dangers or difficulties, but a *powerful* flashlight—preferably two or three—with good batteries is essential, as it's pitch black once you turn the corner. Also, the ground slopes steeply downhill and is fairly slippery, which—depending on your temperament—can be rapidly conducive to panic. So be warned, and be sure not to leave anything behind in this pristine but fragile little ecosystem. You should also let someone in the village know that you're going there.

Back at the Rocher de Brec, you can either go straight back to Méailles, or you can wander along this side of the ridge. It's a bit vertiginous in places (and there are some natural chasms in the rock that you need to avoid falling into), but the views are terrific, and there are some great spots for a picnic. The lovingly restored village of Peyresq (now a center for scientific conferences) is visible across the valley as your path turns to the right (east), though it blends so well into its surroundings it can take a while to spot it. Farther along, look out across the valley and see if you can figure out why the particular configuration of bulges and hollows in the hillsides opposite have been named the Cul de Boeuf (bull's ass)....

The optional spur walk can be any length you want it to be; we went another hour or so farther past the cave (remember to double your time for the round trip if you decide to press on).

FOOD

There's a small café in Méailles, said to open its doors occasionally during the high season. Otherwise your only option here is **La Pizza de Méailles,** a friendly pizzeria, which also happens to be very good. It's only open on weekends and you need to reserve as it's extremely popular. The regular pizzas—thin-crusted and wood-fired—go for €6.50–9.50 and feature various tasty combinations of cèpes, *pistou,* crème fraîche, salmon, cantal cheese, Merguez sausage, and artichokes. It also does a "double" pizza for €16, a deep-dish extravaganza with everything in it but the kitchen sink. We tried the Double Delice Orientale; there was enough of it to feed a small army but frankly the singles were much better, particularly the *pistou* pizza, a simple but delicious combination of fresh tomato, cantal cheese, and homemade *pistou*. The house rosé is nice and dry here, but avoid the red.

LOGISTICS
IGN Map Number and Name
#3541 OT—Annot

Tourist Information
Name: Méailles Mairie
Address: Mairie (village center)
Phone: 0492/ 83 32 55
Website or Email: mairie.meailles@wanadoo.fr

Restaurants
Name: La Pizza de Méailles
Address: Méailles; see Walk Directions.
Phone: 0492/ 83 29 86
Closing Day: Open weekends only—evenings Fri., lunch and dinner Sat., lunch Sun.; also open holidays

Accommodations
There is no lodging in Méailles. Le Fugeret has the *gîte d'étape,* or go on to Annot, which has plenty of lodging.

Transportation
Train
Website or Email: www.trainprovence.com (English option available)
Frequency and Duration: From Nice to Méailles about two hours, four or five trains each direction per day

WALK DIRECTIONS
From Méailles train station, standing between the tracks and the train station and with your back to the station, turn right and follow the gravel road away from the station. Where it meets the asphalt road, turn right on the road and you'll immediately see the blazed path on your right. It's a narrow asphalted path and leads all the way up to the village of Méailles.

Arriving at the top you'll be facing the side of the church;

turn left along the main street through the village. Continue along this road out through the end of the village (it's the only road leading northward out of the village).

A couple of hundred meters/yards past the last houses ignore a turnoff to the right.

In another 600–700 meters, where the road bends right (toward a line of trees), leave the road at a gravelly area **Ⓐ** and you'll see the trail.

In a little less than 10 minutes, you'll come to a big rock area where there's no clear path. Basically keep straight here, slightly on a diagonal right, and you can see a pine tree up the other side that has a yellow blaze on it. Pass the tree on your right, and you'll see a yellow arrow pointing right on a boulder in front of you. Keep following the blazes (and also the little rock cairns) as you climb up this rocky area. Cairns mark the way all along here.

You walk across a large (about 100 meters/yards in length) rock outcrop, and at the end/top, the gravel path resumes: There are a little cairn and a fork, both ahead, the left one narrower and more steeply downhill: Take that **Ⓑ**.

At the bottom, turn left, crossing over a streambed, and then bear right up a broad expanse of rock. At the top bear left (yellow blaze on pine tree ahead).

Keep climbing, guided by blazes and, especially, cairns. You're more or less carrying on *ahead*—definitely no major turns. Generally in a northwest direction, the way it *looks* that you go *is* the way you go, and there are cairns all the way along.

At a certain point (10 minutes or so from **Ⓑ**) it feels as if you're on a rock "avenue," as opposed to the rather undefined areas you've been traversing. (The trail becomes easier to follow from this point.) At the top of this (about 15 minutes past **Ⓑ**) the path turns left (west), with a yellow blaze on a tree ahead, and a cairn on the left side of the path.

Five minutes or so past the avenue you cross a tiny bridgelet over a stream/trench **Ⓒ**. (A couple of minutes later the path narrows slightly and enters some trees—ignore the fork left just beyond, as they meet up later.)

Ten minutes past **Ⓒ** watch for a big cairn and a left-hand-turn blaze on a tree. Leave the wider path here for a narrower footpath on the right **Ⓓ**, leading into a little stand of pine trees. (You can go left here, but it's the ATV trail; the right goes through the woods, is nicer, and is properly blazed now for walkers.)

Stay on this for another 15–20 minutes until you arrive at a crossroads and way mark **Ⓔ**. Go straight here, signed to the Grotte (cave).

What you'll be doing here is going down under the Rocher du Brec (the name of the rock outcrop here). In about 15 minutes you'll reach a wide sandy area and the mouth of the Grotte de Méailles **Ⓕ** underneath the overhanging rock ledge.

After exploring the cave, retrace your steps to **Ⓔ**, from where you can continue onto the spur, or return to Méailles the way you came.

For Longer Spur Walk

Note that there are many places to picnic along here, but be aware that there are some deep, overgrown chasms you could fall into if you aren't careful. Be especially attentive if you have children with you. Follow the trail as long as you like, but in terms of doing the full loop as marked on the IGN (which we tried and failed to do), note that there's no marked trail coming down the other side, and by all accounts it's quite easy to get lost, unless you have a guide.

As you approach the crossroads at **Ⓔ** from the cave, turn left at **Ⓔ**, signed Le Cougnas.

In 2–3 minutes, as the path walks along the edge of a steep drop-off, and just before it makes a right turn, look out across the valley ahead of you (north-northwest) and see if you can pick out the village of Peyresq; it's plenty big enough to see, but it blends in so beautifully that you probably wouldn't notice it unless you're really looking for it.

The path basically follows along the edge of the cliff. Roughly 40 minutes past **Ⓔ** the path gets quite narrow. At the time of this writing, there were yellow plastic ties on bushes. It's a very narrow track through grass, always pretty close to the edge.

About 15 minutes later, you'll pass a yellow blaze on a rock on the ground and then come into a roundish open area, roughly 25 meters across. You can just see the town below. You've reached the top here, a nice place for a picnic.

33 Le Fugeret–Méailles Ring Walk

2–3 Hours

In the absence of anywhere to stay in Méailles, your nearest option is Le Fugeret, just more than an hour's stroll to the south (or one short stop on the Train des Pignes). It's a modest place, a bit flyblown from the flocks of sheep that pass through from time to time, but not unattractive, with a lively little *place* and a fine church with 12th-century foundations.

The walk connecting Méailles station and Le Fugeret is very simple: a woodland trail along the east side of the Vaire valley, more or less paralleling the road (D210), though high enough above it for the light traffic to be largely unnoticeable. The last kilometer goes along the road itself.

TRAIN DES PIGNES

© AVALON TRAVEL

The actual Le Fugeret–Méailles Ring Walk can be used as a longer, more adventurous way to get from Méailles to Le Fugeret, or else as an additional ring walk from either Le Fugeret or Méailles itself. It's a very pretty, somewhat strenuous walk, passing along old farm trails up into the mountainous country above Méailles. The first part follows the uphill path above the D210 (see above). Not long after leaving Méailles you'll see a sign warning of possible rock slides ahead. Rather alarmingly, the trail takes you right across the spot where these apparently occur. This is the Ravin de l'Ubac, one of the large scoops of crumbling scree that give many of the mountains around here their odd look of being constructed out of cheap, low-grade stone. Since this is a trail maintained by the local commune, we assume this passage is safe, but it *was* a little scary to cross. From here, after rounding the top of the Paumelle, you come down a pleasant path that leads through one of the few remaining *châtaigniers*— chestnut farms—that used to be common in this area before a blight killed off most of these magnificent trees. Fine views open up as you continue down the valley, crossing the train line before reentering Le Fugeret.

FOOD

The *gîte d'étape* in Le Fugeret does pizzas and other main courses, but it was closed each time we were there; there's a café that serves snacks, and up a farm track above the village there's a *ferme/auberge*, **La Rouie,** which might be worth trying if you're here for more than a night.

The new place in town is the **Bar Restaurant La Fontane.** It's a modest place in every sense, and was undergoing various teething troubles when we went, but it's pleasant and inexpensive, and the couple running it are working hard to make a go of it. You can have a dish of the day for €9, or a €15 three-course *menu*. Generous salads—one with *lardons,* eggs, croutons, and tomato heaped over the lettuce, the other an equally hearty *niçoise*— were on offer as appetizers, followed by a substantial and well-prepared plate of sautéed cod that was supposed to come with a béarnaise sauce. The sauce never arrived but the dish was good enough to make one curious to know how it would have tasted. Desserts were ice cream or a run-of-the-mill *île flottante.*

LOGISTICS
IGN Map Number and Name
#3541 OT—Annot

Tourist Information
Name: Le Fugeret Mairie
Address: Place de la Mairie (village center)
Phone: 0492/ 83 20 16
Website or Email: le.fugeret.mairie@wanadoo.fr

Restaurants
Also see listings under Accommodations.
Name: Bar Restaurant La Fontane
Address: Le Fugeret village center
Phone: 0492/ 83 05 23 or 0665/ 17 65 33
Closing Day: Evenings Sun., open for lunch every day, open for dinner by reservation only

Accommodations
Name: Le Gîte Saint Pierre
Address: Place de la Mairie (Le Fugeret village center)
Phone: 0492/ 83 34 36 or 0664/ 65 27 22
Website or Email: www.gîtesaintpierre.fr
Type of Lodging: *Gîte d'étape*
Price: In a room: €22 per person including breakfast, €35 half pension, €48 full pension; in the *dortoir:* €20 per person including breakfast, €33 half pension, €46 full pension; kids under 10 get 20 percent discount on all prices
Notes: Three rooms with two beds, two rooms with three beds, one room with four beds, one room with six beds, one *dortoir* with 14 beds. It can do special dinners by reservation, such as *fondue savoyarde,* raclette, and others; see the website.
Name: La Rouie
Address: In the countryside not far from Le Fugeret; call for directions, but it may not have anyone who speaks English. This is a farm; you must make a reservation.
Phone: 0492/ 83 25 90
Type of Lodging: *Ferme/auberge*
Notes: We weren't able to get up to La Rouie, but several people told us about it. If you're intrepid, you might want to try it out.

Transportation
Train
  Phone: 0492/83 20 16 (Le Fugeret station)
  Website or Email: www.trainprovence.com (English option available)
  Frequency and Duration: From Nice to Le Fugeret about two hours, four or five trains each direction per day

WALK DIRECTIONS
Méailles Station to Le Fugeret– 1–1.5 Hour

Standing between the tracks and the train station, with your back to the station, turn right and follow the gravel road away from the station. Where it meets the asphalt road, turn right on the road and you'll immediately see the blazed path on your right. It's a narrow asphalted path and leads all the way up to the village of Méailles.

Arriving at the top, you'll be facing the side of the church; turn right, passing the church on your left. Pass the bar on your left and head downhill, blazed.

At the first fork past the bar (10 meters/yards) bear left and follow the road all the way downhill, where you'll see the old village *lavoir,* still in use. Turn right and head down the road, passing an iron cross on your left. (Note the name of the pizza place (La Pizza de Méailles) on your right, across a parking lot.)

Stay on this road until it forks in a couple of minutes ❶ (another mounted iron cross to your left and behind). Turn right. In a few minutes you'll pass the "leaving Méailles" sign, there's a left turn that you ignore, and immediately after that the road forks; bear left.

In another few minutes the asphalt ends at a little chapel, Notre Dame du Rosaire. Pass to the left of it, continuing straight ahead on the dirt track.

In five minutes or less, watch for a right-turn blaze on a tree on the right of the path, and just beyond the blaze you'll see a very small footpath on the right ❸: Take that.

Stay on this path for about 20 minutes, when you'll come out at a little asphalt road (D210) ❷. Turn left on the road and in about 5–10 minutes you'll reach an intersection ❶ of the D210 and D908. Turn left and follow the road into Le Fugeret, reached in five minutes or so.

TRAIN DES PIGNES

To get to the Le Fugeret train station: With your back to the *mairie* and the *gîte d'étape,* turn left onto the main road and walk down to the intersection where you'll find Avenue de la Gare; pass the cemetery on your left, then the World War I memorial on your right. Stay on this road, which leads to the station in another few minutes.

Le Fugeret to Méailles– 1–1.5 Hour

With your back to the *mairie* and the *gîte d'étape,* turn right. Follow the road out of town until, a few minutes past the outskirts of town, you come to an intersection with the D908 to your left and the D210 to your right. Take the right **Ⓐ**.

In about 5–8 minutes the road bends right and you come to the ruins of a house on the right of the road. About two minutes farther uphill you'll see a little track off the road on the right (the first right after the ruin), uphill. Take this **Ⓑ**.

(*Note:* If this little track is closed off, take the official path instead, which is the next right off the road, a smaller track about 75 paces beyond **Ⓑ**.)

Stay on this path for 20–30 minutes, when you join a larger path on which you bear left **Ⓒ**.

In another 400 meters or so (about five minutes), the path comes out by a chapel on your left and an asphalt road. Take this road downhill.

In about 200 meters it comes out on another little asphalt road. Turn right (ignoring a right turn immediately beyond), and pass the sign for Méailles on your left.

In another 200 meters follow the road as it bends left **Ⓓ**. (Note: This is where you'd turn right to continue the Le Fugeret Ring Walk without going into Méailles.)

Follow this road uphill, passing the pizzeria on your left in another 100 meters or so, and just beyond that, reaching the *lavoir.* Bend sharply left uphill at the *lavoir,* following the road uphill until it comes out at the church.

Pass around the front of the church, and then turn right and look for the blaze indicating the path on the left that leads down to the train station.

Le Fugeret Ring Walk– 2 Hours

With your back to the *mairie* and the *gîte d'étape,* turn right.

Follow the road out of town until, a few minutes past the outskirts of town, you come to an intersection with the D908 to your left and the D210 to your right. Take the right **Ⓐ**.

In about 600 meters (6–8 minutes) the road bends right and you come to the ruins of a house on the right of the road. About two minutes farther uphill you'll see a little track off the road on the right (the first right after the ruin), uphill. Take this **Ⓑ**.

(*Note:* If this little track is closed off, take the official path instead, which is the next right off the road, a smaller track about 75 paces beyond **Ⓑ**.)

Stay on this path for 20–30 minutes, when you join a larger path on which you bear left **Ⓒ**.

In another 400 meters or so (about five minutes) the path comes out by a chapel on your left and an asphalt road. Take this road downhill.

In about 200 meters it comes out on another little asphalt road. Turn right (ignoring a right turn immediately beyond), and pass the sign for Méailles on your left.

In another 200 meters turn right **Ⓓ** (*Note:* You'd follow the road as it bends left here if you wanted to go up to Méailles village or to the Méailles train station. It's signed on a wooden sign for Le Fugeret–Gîte).

In five minutes or so pass a left turn, and in another 100 meters or so the asphalt ends at a house and the track turns right **Ⓔ**, dirt now. Stay on this track, ignoring a right fork off in a minute or so (yellow and red "X").

About five minutes later, note that the route leaves this main track on a lesser path **Ⓕ**. On the main track there's a red and yellow "X" on a tree and a Prive sign; on the correct path is a red and yellow blaze ahead.

About a half kilometer (5–7 minutes later), be alert on the right for a right-turn blaze on a tree: The path you've been on continues straight, but you turn right **Ⓖ** on an equally narrow path that crosses high over a streambed.

Soon you'll pass a Falling Rocks icon sign and beyond that come to a big wide area of gray rock or scree, the Ravin de l'Ubac. Continue straight across, at a very slightly downhill diagonal. It's something of a scramble, but just take it slow. You may see footsteps of other people forming the suggestion of a path. From about midway over it gets easier, as there's a bit of a flat ledge. In any case, it only takes a couple of minutes to get across.

In about 10 minutes you'll reach an area where the path is somewhat unclear. What it does is make a U-turn to the left. Another minute farther on the path makes a hairpin right turn. (There *are* a couple of blazes along here.)

About 10 minutes later, you'll come to an intersection of paths, with signposts downhill right (Le Fugeret—Gîte) and uphill left (La Rate and Annot) ❽. Take the downhill right path toward Le Fugeret.

About 15–20 minutes later you'll pass through a chestnut orchard of the farm le Chastel, and in another 10 minutes the path bends around left, joining another track coming in from the right ❾. Keep to the right again when the track forks in 15 meters.

In another couple of minutes, just after a left bend in the road, leave the road for a gravel track on your right ❿.

About five minutes later, as the path is about to wind right and uphill through a gate next to a stone wall (toward some dilapidated farm sheds), leave it, dropping down to the little path parallel to it on the left.

This little path leads downhill and in a couple of minutes crosses over the railroad track, soon letting out on a little asphalt road. Turn left on this, following it down to the T junction (under the train track) ⓚ and turn right. In less than a minute you come to another T junction (the main road). Turn right here to go into Le Fugeret, or left onto Avenue de la Gare to go to the train station.

To continue to the station, after making the left onto Avenue de la Gare, pass the cemetery on your left, then the World War I memorial on your right. Stay on this road, which leads to the station in another few minutes.

34 Two Ring Walks from Thorame-Basse

2 Hours and 1–1.5 Hour

THORAME-BASSE RING WALK
VIA LA BATIE– 2 Hours

In the course of a frustrating search for walks in the area north of St-Andre-les-Alpes (which includes the lovely alpine villages of

TRAIN DES PIGNES

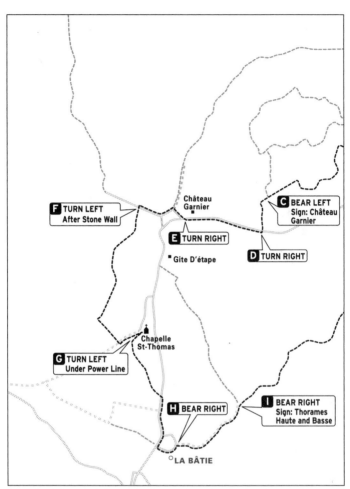

F TURN LEFT
After Stone Wall

Château
Garnier

C BEAR LEFT
Sign: Château
Garnier

E TURN RIGHT

D TURN RIGHT

Gite D'étape

Chapelle
St-Thomas

G TURN LEFT
Under Power Line

H BEAR RIGHT

I BEAR RIGHT
Sign: Thorames
Haute and Basse

LA BÂTIE

TRAIN DES PIGNES

Beauvezer and Colmars), we noticed a green, English-looking val-ley to the west of the D908, with the strangely named villages of Thorame-Haute and Thorame-Basse on a signpost pointing off into a rolling, pastoral landscape. Though there's a train station, Thorame-Haute Gare, several miles south of here, neither of these villages rated more than a line or two in any of our guidebooks.

But when we finally got around to exploring them we found them—and the quietly industrious farm country sur-rounding them—to be delightful places. Thorame-Haute, as it turns out, is a well-preserved old village with some fine buildings and an excellent artisanal butcher in its general store. The better walking, however, is a few miles down the

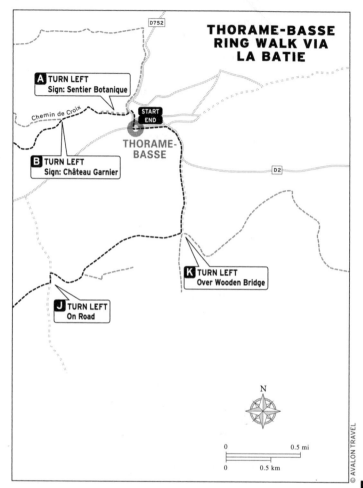

THORAME-BASSE RING WALK VIA LA BATIE

D752

A TURN LEFT
Sign: Sentier Botanique

Chemin de Croix

START
END

THORAME-BASSE

B TURN LEFT
Sign: Château Garnier

D2

K TURN LEFT
Over Wooden Bridge

J TURN LEFT
On Road

N

0   0.5 mi
0   0.5 km

© AVALON TRAVEL

road, at Thorame-Basse, where there also happens to be an excellent Bistrot de Pays.

The village itself is less pretty than its neighbor, but it's very pleasant nonetheless, a sheep-farming center, with a good rustic smell (the sheep are regularly herded through its streets) and a couple of reasonable places to stay.

Of our two walks here, this is by far the best. It's longer, but not terribly strenuous, passing under the stark mountains through a refreshingly grassy and open countryside of dovetailing sheep meadows, with woods of pine and larch *(meleze)*, streams, and old farmsteads along the way. There's a small honey factory in the village of Château Garnier, which you can visit if you call ahead. A

little farther on you'll pass the Romanesque Chapelle St-Thomas with its 12th-century fresco (you'll need to get keys beforehand, from the *mairie* in Château Garnier). From here the path continues in a more or less idyllic fashion through the farming hamlet of La Batie, with its turkeys and guinea fowl and flower-filled pastures, before leading you gently back to Thorame-Basse.

THORAME-BASSE *SENTIER BOTANIQUE* RING— 1–1.5 Hour

This is an easy walk, which is sometimes all that's wanted, climbing the little hill known as Piegut, just outside the village. After passing some brick markers for the Stations of the Cross, the path passes the modern Chapelle St-Jean and becomes a *sentier botanique*: a botanical trail with several fascinating and informative placards about the local flora and fauna along the way (you might want to bring a dictionary). For a little more exercise, take the spur leading to the top of the hill, where there's a fine view over the valley, and a ruined medieval watchtower with some moderately interesting stonework.

FOOD

The lovely village restaurant, **Le Café de la Vallée,** is a true Bistrot de Pays in both name and spirit. The food is wholesomely prepared from mostly local ingredients and at the same time full of delightful, imaginative surprises.

There's a €14 two-course lunch *menu* and a €19 three-course dinner *menu,* or you can eat à la carte, with main courses at €12–€14. We were a large party when we ate here; we tried more or less everything on the menu and everything was good. Appetizers included grilled shrimp in a light, delicious almond aioli; a salad of tomato and warm goat cheese with a blood-orange dressing; good oak-smoked salmon; and a plate of *cochonnailles*—charcuterie—from the prizewinning artisanal butcher in nearby Thorame-Haute, in which a juniper-seasoned pâté stood out.

For the main course there was a choice of local lamb grilled with herbs, duck breast with honey from the nearby Château Garnier beehives, and a Thai curry of scallops and *rouget* (red mullet). You can call ahead for children's meals and vegetarian options, which in our case consisted respectively of a much-appreciated omelette with *frites* and a so-so ratatouille served

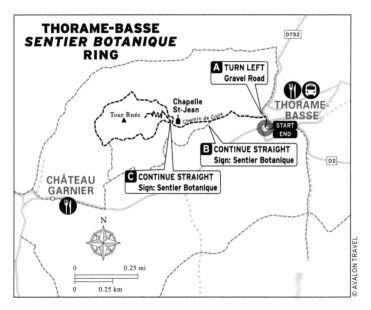

with a very good cornmeal *galette.* This being sheep country, there was also the hard-to-love Provençal favorite, *pieds et pa-quets.* One of our party ordered it, the rest having long ago sworn off. The little lamb's trotter with its accompanying bundle of tripes came strongly seasoned with tomato and savory, and was surprisingly good: meatier and less gelatinous than usual.

Best of all were the desserts, excellent lemon tart, a startlingly fresh mandarin sorbet, and a wonderful tangy, unsweetened mousse of *fromage frais* in a raspberry coulis.

A good Château Rousset Coteaux de Pierrevert 2003 added €14 to our bill, but was well worth it, the house wine being nowhere near up to the standards of the excellent cooking.

LOGISTICS
IGN Map Number and Name
#3541 OT—Annot

Tourist Information
There's no tourist office in the Thorames, but you can try their *mairies* (if you speak passable French). Otherwise, the tourist office in Colmars handles the region generally, including the Thorames. Visit its website, and for specific questions you can send email from its website: www.colmars-les-alpes.fr.

Name: Thorame-Haute Mairie
Phone: 0492/ 83 90 86
Name: Thorame-Basse Mairie
Phone: 0492/ 83 92 97
Hours: 8:00–12:00 Tues. and 13:30–17:00 Thurs.

Restaurants

Name: Le Café de la Vallée (Bistrot de Pays)
Address: Thorame-Basse village center
Phone: 0492/ 89 14 31
Notes: Fulfilling the Bistrot de Pays mission, along with being a restaurant it is also a bar, *depôt de pain* (bread outlet), newspaper distributor, tourist information point, and regional products outlet.

Accommodations

Name: Château Garnier
Address: Château Garnier, past the little village center (which basically consists only of the *miellerie,* which sells all manner of honey-based products); see the walk map
Phone: 0492/ 83 92 80 or 0492/ 83 92 73
Website or Email: gite.chateau-garnier@laposte.net
Type of Lodging: *Gîte d'étape*
Price: €1 to join association, then €12 per person per night, €27 half pension, €34full pension, €5 breakfast, €13 dinner
Notes: 40 places in 10 rooms of four beds (bunks) each, washing machine, English spoken
Name: La Ferme du Villard
Address: Thorame-Basse village center
Phone: 0492/ 83 92 53
Website or Email: www.cordoeil.com
Type of Lodging: *Chambres d'hôte,* also *table d'hôte*
Price: €31 for one person, €45 for two
Notes: The Pougnet family, who own the Camping Villard empire, also own the Cordoeil organic beer company. A relatively recent enterprise, in 2006 they made their organic Cordoeil beer entirely on the premises, from barley and hops grown here on their own farm. Along with the *chambres d'hôte,* they do *table d'hôte* and have a little brasserie where they serve their beer.

Transportation

Train/Bus

Name: Thorame-Haute Gare (train station)

Phone: 0492/ 89 02 55

Website or Email: www.trainprovence.com (English option available)

Frequency and Duration: From Nice to Thorame about 2.5 hours, four or five trains each direction per day

Notes: There's a bus connection from Thorame-Haute station to the village of Thorame-Haute about 10 minutes away from the station, and then it's another five minutes from there to Thorame-Basse. You can use this bus connection to get from the Thorame-Haute station to the village of Thorame-Basse, but then you would have to hitch a ride out to Thorame-Basse, which shouldn't be difficult. There's almost no one on the road, but people who do pass would be fairly likely to give you a ride. It's so beautiful out that way that this is one time the inconvenience of hitching is really worth it.

Bear in mind that the bus connection isn't made for every train, only for three trains (each way) per day, so check this ahead of time. You can either email Chemins de Fer from the website (www.trainprovence.com), or you could call the Thorame-Haute station, or you could call the bus company (HVV, or Haut Verdon Voyages, 0492/ 83 95 81, www.haut-verdon-voyages.com) directly. This bus service is called Correspondances Val d'Allos (because it connects the villages of the Allos Valley, which is to the north of Thorame-Haute, with the train station). Thorame-Haute village is the stop closest to the train station. The same company also runs a bus Sat. only all through the year, from the Thorame-Haute station *(gare)* to both Thorame-Haute and Thorame-Basse. At the time of this writing, runs to the station from Thorame-Basse were at 9:00 (15-minute journey, includes stop at Thorame-Haute), and from the station to Thorame-Basse at 11:45, arriving Thorame-Basse 15 minutes later.

Miscellaneous Notes

Keys to the St. Thomas chapel you pass on the main ring walk are available from:

- Juliette Roux: 0492/ 83 90 43

- Michele Tyran (the walk route passes her house in Château Garnier, and she runs the *gîte d'étape*): 0492/ 83 92 80. The *gîte d'étape* is very near the chapel, so you might arrange to pick up the keys at the *gîte d'étape*.

- Mdm. Chailan at the honey-production center (Miellerie Chailan) in Château Garnier. Again, the walk route passes through Château Garnier (and right by the honey "factory"), so you could try to arrange to pick up the keys there: 0492/ 83 92 86.

WALK DIRECTIONS
Thorame-Basse Ring Walk via La Batie

With your back to the village *lavoir* (old village laundry) and facing the *mairie,* turn left and take the uphill road on your left signed to La Valette. Follow this road uphill, passing the church/clock tower on your right, and just beyond that, turn left **Ⓐ** onto a gravel track (signed Sentier Botanique). The gravel ends in about seven meters/yards, and the road is asphalted.

Soon the asphalt ends; continue ahead on a dirt track, which passes some stone Stations of the Cross markers (empty).

Across from the stage 8 marker, there are a fork and a way mark **Ⓑ**: turn left, signed on the way mark Château Garnier.

Follow the path for about 25 minutes, when you come to a fork with way marks **Ⓒ**; bear left, signed to Château Garnier.

The path comes out at the asphalt road in a few minutes. Turn right **Ⓓ**, passing an interesting sawmill on your right and a little farther on the honey "factory."

About 80 meters past the honey factory, before the bell tower/steeple, take the right turn that leads into Château Garnier **Ⓔ**.

Come to the *lavoir* on your right (delicious cold water, as usual at these fountains), and turn left, signed on a way mark to La Batie. In less than a minute turn right at the church (way mark signed Cheval Blanc).

Pass another *lavoir* on the left and then a stone wall with an *oratoire* built into it. Take the first left after that **Ⓕ**, a nicely shaded wide dirt farm track (just before a stone building on the left).

The path crosses the river, and then there's a nice view up to the ruined medieval tower back behind you on the hill to the left, and then of the St. Thomas chapel ahead on the left.

About 15 minutes from its start, this track ends at a gravel road leading directly to the chapel. Go left on this.

If you've gotten the keys ahead of time and go inside, remember (as a note on the door requests) to turn off the lights and give two turns of the key.

After visiting the chapel, if you're stopping at the *gîte d'étape,* go out the chapel's driveway to the road and turn left on it, which takes you to the *gîte d'étape* in a couple of minutes.

Otherwise, go back along the gravel road the way you came, but not as far as the farm track you came in on. Instead turn left on the first farm track you come to **G**, under the power line.

In five minutes or so, you'll reach an asphalt road and turn right on it. Follow it for a few minutes, a little way into La Batie, turning left when you reach the *lavoir* on your left.

The asphalt ends in about 40 meters and dirt track takes over. In a minute or so you come to a fork; bear right **H**.

In another 5–7 minutes the path forks again **I**. Bear right, signed Thorames Haute and Basse. (The left is signed to Château Garnier and is where the path from the *gîte d'étape* comes in.)

When you reach the river in another few minutes, you cross the bridge straight ahead. On the other side, follow the main path, which bears left.

Stay on this path for about 10 minutes, until it comes out at a bigger gravel road at a way mark **J**. Turn left on the road, follow it for about 40 meters, and then turn right on the path at the pylon, signed on a way mark to the Thorames.

Ignore a smaller farm track leading ahead about 2–3 minutes later, bending left on the main track instead.

About 5–10 minutes later, the path comes to a T junction with another gravel road **K**; turn left, crossing over a little wooden bridge.

Stay on this path, which comes out on the asphalt road (D2) just at the edge of town five or so minutes later. Turn left, and so into town, passing the Cordoeil brewery/brasserie and *chambres d'hôtes* on your way.

Sentier Botanique Ring

With your back to the village *lavoir* (old village laundry) and facing the *mairie,* turn left and take the uphill road on your left signed to La Valette. Follow this road uphill, passing the church/ clock tower on your right, and just beyond that, turn left **Ⓐ** onto a gravel track (signed Sentier Botanique). The gravel ends in about seven meters/yards, and the road is asphalted.

Soon the asphalt ends; continue ahead on a dirt track, which passes some stone Stations of the Cross markers (empty).

Across from the stage 8 marker, there are a fork and a way mark **Ⓑ**: Keep on straight here, signed Sentier Botanique. (At the fork at stage 13, you can go either way.)

Just beyond the Chapelle St.-Jean the path forks again, a three-way fork **Ⓒ**.

To take the spur to the tower, take the middle of the three forks at **Ⓒ**, signed Sentier Botanique. Continue uphill, but take the gentler zigzagging path that goes up to the right soon after you start climbing, rather than continuing on the steep gully that goes straight up the hill. The path leads you all the way up to the tower, a modest medieval ruin with some interesting stonework on the inside, and very pleasant views over the valley.

Return to the three-way fork **Ⓒ** the way you came.

From here **Ⓒ**, to continue on the *sentier botanique,* take the rightmost fork of the three.

In about a half hour (if you're stopping to read all the placards) you come to a fork signed Château Garnier to the right; ignore it.

The *sentier* returns to Chapelle St.-Jean; return to town the way you came.

Northeast Kingdom: The Mercantour

Sospel and the Roya valley mark the eastern frontier of Provence. The area is as wild and rugged as it gets, and in many ways it's about as good as it gets too. You can feel the close-ness of Italy in the ornate buildings with their wonderfully daft trompe l'oeil facades, as well as in the food, which takes what for many will be a welcome turn toward pasta and fresh vegetables.

A small (though not narrow-gauge) train line, the aptly named Train des Merveilles, links three of our four destinations here: Sospel, Saorge, and La Brigue, each of which is high on our list of places most worth visiting: Sospel for its tumbledown baroque houses straddling the Bevera river, Saorge for its austere splendor high above the Roya, La Brigue for its Italianate charm and the glorious paintings in the nearby chapel of Notre Dame des Fontaines. We don't have walks between them (the distances are too great), but you can use the train to get from one to an-other in much the same way as in the previous chapter.

The fourth destination, Casterino, in itself just a cluster of

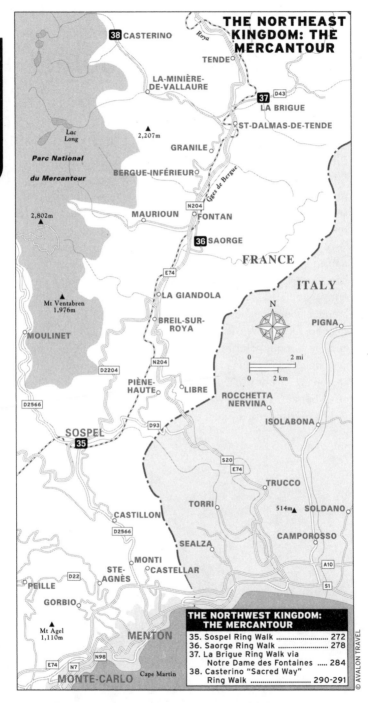

THE MERCANTOUR

THE NORTHEAST KINGDOM: THE MERCANTOUR

Roya

38 CASTERINO

TENDE

LA-MINIÈRE-DE-VALLAURE

37 D43

LA BRIGUE

ST-DALMAS-DE-TENDE

Lac Long

▲ 2,207m

GRANILE

Parc National du Mercantour

BERGUE-INFÉRIEUR

Ġes de Bergue

2,802m ▲

MAURIOUN

N204

FONTAN

36 SAORGE

FRANCE

Mt Ventabren 1,976m ▲

E74

LA GIANDOLA

ITALY

N

BREIL-SUR-ROYA

PIGNA

MOULINET

N204

0   2 mi
0   2 km

D2204

PIÈNE-HAUTE

LIBRE

ROCCHETTA NERVINA

D2566

ISOLABONA

SOSPEL

35

D93

S20

E74

TRUCCO

CASTILLON

TORRI

514m▲ SOLDANO

D2566

CAMPOROSSO

SEALZA

A10

MONTI

STE-AGNÈS

CASTELLAR

PEILLE

D22

GORBIO

S1

Mt Agel 1,110m ▲

MENTON

E74   N7

N98

Cape Martin

MONTE-CARLO

THE NORTHWEST KINGDOM: THE MERCANTOUR

© AVALON TRAVEL

small hotels, represents one of the high points in this book. Its position makes it an ideal point of embarkation for a walk in the Mercantour National Park. This is one of the wildest areas left in Western Europe; a mountain region of unspoiled beauty, with marmots, ibexes, chamois, and numerous birds of prey thriving within its well-protected borders. It is also a place of immense cultural interest, the haunting, eerie landscape of its so-called Vallee des Merveilles containing a vast number of extraordinary Bronze Age rock inscriptions.

Our walk here was certainly one of the most rewarding and exhilarating we did. It doesn't hurt that you can also eat exceptionally well in Casterino itself.

TRAIN INFORMATION

The "Train des Merveilles" is a sub-line of the regular Nice–Cuneo line (line #5, also known as the Nice–Breil/Roya–Tende line). The schedule for that line (i.e., line #5) shows all the trains covering the stations of the towns in this chapter, except Casterino, which isn't on a train line. The "Train des Merveilles" itself runs weekends and bank holidays in May, then everyday from June 1–September 30, and again on weekends in October. It also runs a few days in November. The difference with the Train des Merveilles—which is a "train touristique"—is that they have commentaries (in both French and English) on the towns the train passes through, and they recommend cultural visits within the towns. You can get off wherever you want, and get back on later in the day.

You can see the current #5 train schedule, and also the brochure (in English) for the Train des Merveilles at this website, which is an excellent site for information on the entire area: www.royabevera.com. Choose the English option by clicking on the British flag. The same schedules are available on the Sospel Tourist Office's website.

35 Sospel Ring Walk
2 Hours

The dilapidatedly handsome town of Sospel, full of Italianate buildings with crazily improbable trompe l'oeil facades, straddles the Bevera river by way of an 11th-century toll bridge (complete with stone toll booth), a collection point along the old salt road

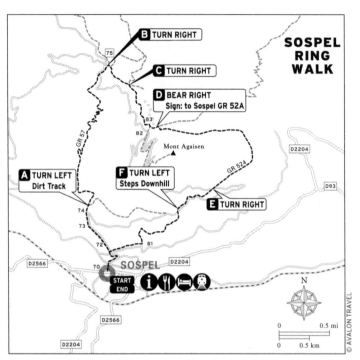

that led from Nice to Piedmont and Lombardy. The town's strategic importance continued well into the 20th century, when fortified bunkers were built around it as part of the ill-fated Maginot Line. One of these, the Fort St-Roch, is now a museum of the Resistance. Others, including the Agaisen blockhouse, can be visited during the course of this ring walk. A few miles southwest of the Roya valley (and linked to it by the very charming Nice–Cuneo rail line, otherwise known as the Train des Merveilles), Sospel would make a congenial base for explorations of this area.

Though not especially long, the walk involves a fairly stiff climb up to the ridge of Mont Agaisen, the mountain directly overlooking town. It's a peaceful, pleasant trail, passing abandoned vineyards with old stone terraces and then turning through woods along the crest. You'll pass right by one fortification in the woods—a gun emplacement—and there are others to visit at the summit of Mont Agaisen if you have the time. Those we saw were striking for their curvy, almost groovy '30s design. A gentle descent along the GR 52A, with fine views of the town and its ring of mountains, brings you back to Sospel.

FOOD

There are several pleasant places to eat in this delightful town. **La Mordagne,** on the north side of the river, offers Savoyard specialties such as *tartiflette* (a gratin of potatoes, onions, bacon, and reblochon cheese), various stuffed galettes, and—best choice if you're feeling hungry—hearty and delicious fondues, served for a minimum of two people, at €14–18 per person. Some specialty meat fondues (for which you cook the meat in hot oil at the table) are available by reservation.

Of the two or three pizza places, **Le Picoune** seemed by far the best. The pizzas, cooked in a wood-fired oven in the middle of the restaurant, are great value at €10–12 apiece. The salads, made with fresh market greens, are exceptionally good (someone had gone to the trouble of *peeling* the fava beans in our niçoise salad), and—unusually for France—the pastas are made with real zest and conviction, our favorite being a steaming bowl of saffron-flavored papardelle with courgettes. You feel the heart-warming proximity of Italy. There's even a decent homemade tiramisu.

But our first choice here is the decidedly French **Bel Aqua,** the restaurant of the Hôtel des Étrangers. Like many hotel restaurants, the atmosphere is a degree or two below congenial, but any chilliness is more than made up for by the exceptionally good cooking. There's a €23 Menu Regional and a €33 Gourmand *menu*, or you can eat à la carte, where some interesting vegetable dishes are to be found. A sort of sophisticated Provençal home cooking prevails, with generous portions of complex but unfussy food. We started with an intense confit of eggplant accompanied by roasted pepper in an anchovy sauce, and a dish of roasted asparagus cooked with thyme and caramelized onions: a delicious combination. For our main course, passing over the hare's leg fricassee and the snail ravioli, we shared fresh sardines served with a delicate *tian* of rice and vegetables, a wonderful dish of fresh artichokes cooked with fava beans and a little bacon, and a beef daube of a flavorful tenderness that made us realize how rudimentary our previous sampling of this Provençal standby (basically an olive-flavored stew) had been. The excellent desserts included some exotic-sounding confections such as a clementine soufflé and a raspberry gratin, both good, though our favorite was the more conventional, cookielike *sablet,* heaped with apple and cream. The proprietor, Jean-Pierre, has sidelines in two other happy areas: He knows what he's doing when it comes to wine—you're in good hands when it comes to the "recommended" bottles marked with asterisks on the wine list—and he's president of the local walking association (he runs the *gîte d'étape* behind the hotel) and knows all the best walking not only around Sospel but throughout the entire *département.* A bottle of Deschants St-Joseph (M. Chapoutier 2003) made a fine accompaniment to a meal that, with its skillful and inventive cooking, and relatively modest price, amply justified the restaurant's Michelin "Bib" status for good value.

LOGISTICS
IGN Map Number and Name
#3741 ET—Vallées de La Bévéra et des Paillons
Note: We strongly recommend having the IGN map for this walk, as the routing around way marks 83 is too intricate and compressed for us to map in full detail. Having said that, the IGN map doesn't conform exactly to the reality on the ground at that juncture either. Moreover, rather than the usual single way mark per number, there are in fact *three* way marks numbered 83, all in this one confusing area. We were lost here for more than an hour, but we hope that by following the written directions at that point, you'll be spared a similar experience. We'd appreciate any feedback on this, which you can email us at our website www.walkingandeating.com.

Tourist Information
Address: 19, avenue Jean Médecin
Phone: 0493/ 04 15 80
Website or Email: www.sospel-tourisme.com

Restaurants
Name: Bel Aqua (at the Hôtel des Étrangers)
See listing under Accommodations.
Closing Day: All day Tues. and lunch Wed., closed Nov. 1–Mar. 3
Name: La Mordagne
Address: Place Garibaldi
Phone: 0493/ 04 01 30
Closing Day: Open lunch and dinner Wed.–Sun.

Name: Le Picoune
Address: 16, avenue Jean Médecin
Phone: 0493/ 04 00 06
Closing Day: Open daily. Closed Mon. and Tues. in winter.

Accommodations

There is also plenty of *chambres d'hôte* accommodation in Sospel. See the tourist office's listings.

Name: Hôtel des Étrangers
Address: 7, boulevard de Verdun
Phone: 0493/ 04 00 09
Website or Email: www.sospel.net
Type of Lodging: Logis de France hotel
Price: €60/€70 single rooms, €68/€90 double rooms
Notes: Closed Nov. 1–Mar. 3

Name: Le Mercantour
Address: Behind the Hôtel des Étrangers
Phone: 0493/ 04 00 09
Type of Lodging: *Gîte d'étape*
Price: Obligatory demipension (you eat at the Bel Aqua, so it's a great deal), €45 per person
Notes: The *gîte d'étape* (and the deal) is available *only* to walkers.

Name: La Friguiéra
Address: 1.5 km outside Sospel, in la Vasta, which is in the direction of Moulinet (west from Sospel); marked on IGN map
Phone: 0493/ 04 12 33
Type of Lodging: *Gîte d'étape*
Price: €16–18 per person per night, €30–35 demipension
Notes: 19 places in a big old traditional house, one room with double bed and bunks, three *dortoirs* for four, five, and six people. Open all year, but Nov. 1–Mar. 31 takes only groups of 10 or more. It's a popular place and gets booked up ahead of time, so try to make your reservation early. Family-style cooking. English spoken.

Transportation

Train

See train info in chapter introduction.

Name: Sospel train station

Phone: 0493/ 04 00 17

Frequency and Duration: About six trains per day in each direction between Nice and Sospel, 50-minute journey

Notes: The trains of line #5 leave Nice for Breil-sur-Roya and some go through Ventimiglia; make sure not to get on one of those, as they miss Sospel (though as it's just one station south of Breil, you could get a train back down from Breil).

Miscellaneous Notes

Market days are Sunday morning for local products, in the Place du Marché, and Thursdays for the "regular" market, in the Place des Platanes.

The Bar du Marché, on the corner near the car bridge, does a great lemon *pressé* (fresh lemon juice and water).

WALK DIRECTIONS

Cross to the far (north) side of the car bridge (Pont de la Liberation) and cross over the road at its end, coming to a way mark (70) on your left. Walk up this road (signed to Baissede Figuiérat GR 52), and take your first left (about 100 meters/yards).

At the intersection of Boulevard Charles de Gualle and Montée du Serret (zebra crosswalk here), turn left, and then bear left past the little park (don't take the flight of steps next to the park) and then turn left up another, broader set of steps.

At the top of the steps, across from the school (Groupe Scolaire) with the clock, cross over the road, turn left and then immediately right (at the way mark 72) onto Chemin de Cantamerlon. In about five minutes you'll pass way mark 73 on your right. Stay on the road.

In another minute or two, as the road makes a hairpin right turn, leave the road for the gravel path on the left, at way mark 74.

In about 25 meters, when the path forks again **Ⓐ**, take the left, a narrower, dirt track.

Continue on this path, uphill, ignoring lesser deviations and following blazes, for about 40 minutes when the path's *lacets* enter an oak wood, and about five minutes later the path comes out on a road. Join this road, carrying on straight ahead, uphill.

In a few minutes leave the road for a path on the right, sharply back and uphill **Ⓑ**, at way mark 75. In about 50 meters the path forks at *another* way mark 75; take the right, signed Col de l'Agaisen. (Ignore the "X" blaze on the tree. The path is blazed yellow.)

In 5–10 minutes you'll come to a crossroads **C**. Turn right.

This is a new trail, a variant from the GR 52, which it leaves at **C**, taking you past impressive World War II fortifications.

Less than 10 minutes from **C**, the path comes out at a small asphalt road. Turn left on it and then follow it downhill, and as the road makes a hairpin right, you'll see two way marks (both 83) on your left. Leave the road at this hairpin bend, turning left off it, and from here choose whether you want to continue up to the blockhouse or not.

If you want to make the detour up there, at the way mark 83 then on your right, take the narrow downhill path, signed to Cantamerlo and Sospel. Reaching the asphalt road, turn left, immediately coming to a fork and way mark 82. At the fork (both prongs asphalted), take the left uphill prong and follow the road for about 800 meters to reach it. From there you can take the concrete road by the metal gate for another 200 meters to reach the peak and more of the old defences.

If you're skipping the blockhouse, as you turn left off the hairpin bend, drop down to the way mark 83 that's now on your left, and turn *right* at the way mark, signed to Sospel GR 52A, La Puella, and Col du Pérus.

In less than a minute, you'll reach a *third* way mark 83 and a fork **D**; bear right, signed Sospel GR 52A.

About a half hour after **D** the path comes out on a small asphalt road **E**. Turn right and in about 10 meters take the very narrow footpath on the left. In another few minutes bear right again when you again reach the asphalt road.

A few minutes later watch on the left side of the road for steps going downhill. Take these **F**.

Follow the blazes back toward Sospel, and when you reach the asphalt road again (about 20 minutes) at way mark 81, turn right on the road, follow it back to the steps in front of the school, and retrace your way into town in another five minutes or so.

36 Saorge Ring Walk
1.5–2 Hours

The stunning village of Saorge must have looked forbidding to the marauding armies of the medieval period. It was certainly supposed to, with its slash of stone walls high above the Roya valley, not to mention the near-inaccessible verticality of all approaches from below. At one time it was known as the "lock of the valley." Nowadays, of course, we read this bellicose architecture as the height of picturesque charm, and Saorge's covered stone alleys, shimmering tile cupolas, and its tall (sometimes five stories) narrow old houses place it among the most charming of the charming. But it does retain a certain uncompromising aura. Though well preserved, it has yielded remarkably little to gentrification (there's almost nowhere to stay, amazingly, since the *gîte d'étape* closed a few years ago), and its geography has largely precluded modern development.

The mountainous countryside beyond the village is magnificent, and this walk takes you straight into it. Leaving town

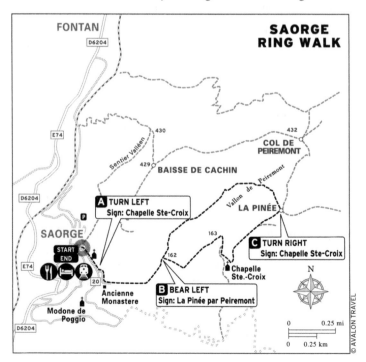

via the 17th-century Franciscan monastery, which—if you can catch it at a time when it's open—has allegedly fine frescoes and woodcarvings (there's also an 11th-century church nearby, the Madona del Poggia, but this is private), your path takes you along a secluded valley, once farmed, now full of abandoned terraces covered over with bright yellow broom. Climbing, you encounter the pleasant surprise of a sheep farm that has actually come back to life—a one-man enterprise with no road and only solar panels for electricity (the owner hikes into town for flour and cooking gas). The views over this ruggedly beautiful section of the Provençal Alps grow steadily more impressive as you climb to the ruined *bergerie* and *abreuvoir* (sheep trough) of la Pinée. From here you can go on climbing to extend the walk, or continue down the other side of the hill you've been circling, passing the old chapel of Ste.-Croix and a scattering of restored houses where an appealingly hippyish spirit prevails: again no roads, and—so far—none of the giant electricity pylons that ruin so much of the landscape in this region. This was one of our favorite places.

FOOD

There's a very good *epicerie* here, **La Petite Epicerie** (closed Tuesdays) where, on weekends, you can get delicious food to go: rotisserie chickens, cakes and olive breads, and various local specialties such as *barbajuan* (stuffed fried dumplings) and *tourte saorgienne*—a tart filled with chard. On Fridays it also does a *plat a emporter* (main dish to go), and if you've timed your walk for a weekend and the weather is good, our suggestion would be to assemble a picnic here.

The **Bellevue** has beautiful views, and the food isn't bad either. There are daily specials and *menus* at €17.50 and €28 featuring appetizers such as its own version of the *tourte saorgienne* and homemade ravioli with cèpes or *pistou,* followed by roast quail with thyme or grilled *langoustines* with rosemary, or a pleasant, cumin-accented *cari* (curry) of free-range chicken. You can also eat à la carte with main courses at around €14.50. The ravioli is excellent, and along with our curry we had an enjoyable, if tough, coq au vin, served with yet more of the ravioli. The atmosphere is somewhat sterile, but it's an acceptable place if you're in the market for a full meal.

There was one other restaurant that looked quite promising, **Lou Pountin,** on rue Lieutenant Revelli. It was closed both times we were there (it was April), but we'd love to hear any reports on this restaurant at our website www.walkingandeating.com.

LOGISTICS
IGN Map Number and Name
#3841 OT—Vallée de la Roya

Tourist Information
There's no actual tourist office for Saorge, but the *mairie* and also the local bookshop seem to manage this function between them.

Name: Saorge Mairie
Address: Avenue du Docteur Davéo
Phone: 0493/ 04 51 23
Website or Email: www.saorge.fr
Name: Librairie de Cairos bookshop
Address: Avenue du Docteur Davéo
Phone: 0493/ 04 51 60

Restaurants
Name: Le Bellevue
Address: 5, rue Louis Périssol
Phone: 0493/ 04 51 37
Closing Day: Evenings Mon. and all day Tues., closed Nov. 12–Dec. 31 and Jan. 8–Feb. 2
Name: Lou Pountin
Address: Rue Lieutenant Revelli
Phone: 0493/ 04 54 90
Closing Day: Wed. May–Oct. and Mon.–Thurs. Nov.–Apr.
Name: La Petite Epicerie
Address: 68, rue du Lieutenant Revelli
Phone: 0493/ 04 51 27
Closing Day: Tuesdays, and out of season Wednesdays as well

Accommodations
There used to be a *gîte d'étape,* but since that closed a few years ago, there's no lodging "establishment" in Saorge. The easiest solution is probably to take a late-afternoon or early-evening

train up to La Brigue or Tende, where lodging is easier to come by. If you really want to stay in Saorge, there are a few *gîtes* that offer weekend rates, and they will also do those rates for two nights midweek. You can look at the *gîtes* online at www.gîtes-de-france-alpes-maritimes.com and then call the gîtes-de-france-alpes-maritimes office (English spoken) to book this two-day arrangement, because you can't do it online unless it's for a weekend. The gîtes-de-france people will also look up the available *gîtes* in Saorge *for* you (there are five, ranging in price for a two-day stay €78–174). Another way to see what's available in Saorge is on the extremely informative www.royabevera.com site. From its home page (don't choose the English option or this won't work):

- Click the "Héb./Rest." tab on the top of the page.

- Click the magnifying-glass icon ("chercher") to search by village.

- In the "ville" drop-down menu choose "Saorge."

Here all the options will be listed, and you can click on each one to get its complete information.

Name: Gîtes-de-france-alpes-maritimes

Phone: 0492/ 15 21 30

Website or Email: www.gites-de-france-alpes-maritimes.com
This is an apartment in the village that was advertising itself with a sign:

Name: Apartment for rent

Address: 85, rue Louis Perissol

Phone: 0493/ 04 55 97

Type of Lodging: Apartment inside village

Price: €80 a night in high season (two-night minimum)

Notes: Two bedrooms with double beds and one infant bed, €15 for supplemental bed in living room; this place looked nice.

Transportation

See the **Train** notes in the chapter introduction.

To get to Saorge (which shares a station with Fontan), take the train from Nice to Breil-sur-Roya and then change for Fontan/Saorge. The trip takes about two hours, depending on your connection at Breil. Trains are frequent. If you're going from Sospel to Saorge, there are five trains a day. Some are direct and take about a half hour; others change in Breil and take closer to an hour.

From the station (which is Fontan/Saorge) you can walk up to town on the road, a 20 minute walk, or take the old footpath from the station, about an hour. The footpath is signed, and marked on both the IGN and our map. Basically, it is: way mark #431 at the station, to #430, where you can either turn right onto the "Sentier Valléen" into town, or continue on to way mark #429 at Baisse de Cachin and there turn right and drop down into Saorge from there. Also, see our suggested alternative Saorge walk route under Miscellaneous Notes below.

If you don't want to walk, you can get the TAD *transport à la demande* bus from the train station to the village. Again, this information is on the www.royabevera.com site (but don't click on the English option, as it won't work for this info). To get the request bus, which costs €1.30 per ride, you call the free number (0800/ 06 01 06; at the latest the day before you wish to travel) and tell the staff your name and the route you're interested in (Fontan/Saorge Gare to Saorge village), and they'll send a bus to pick you up. The central reservation office is open 10:00–17:00 Mon.–Fri. Buses run 7:30–12:30 and 14:00–19:30 Tues.–Sat., not on holidays.

Miscellaneous Notes

The Franciscan monastery is allegedly open approximately 10:00–12:00 and 14:00–17:00 or 18:00 every day except Tues. (though it wasn't when we were there), phone: 0493/ 04 55 55; you can also go to the website www.monum.fr and type in "saorge" to get information on the monastery.

Another excellent variation for the Saorge walk (you'll need the IGN map) would be to leave from the train station and follow the trail to the village of Saorge (way mark #431 at the station, to #430, then at #429) instead of turning right to continue into the village, instead turn left and head up to 432 at Col de Peiremont. From 432 turn right and follow the trail to la Pinée, which is ⓒ on our regular walk. We did not have a chance to do this route, but after seeing the landscape from the vantage point of the walk we did do, this route seems as if it would be splendid, and it would be one of our first choices for an update.

WALK DIRECTIONS

From the parking lot (marked with the "P" parking lot symbol on the IGN map), walk up through town passing the *mairie* on your left, then the phone booth and fountain on your right; bear left uphill at the fork just beyond the fountain, and then again at the rue L. Jean Revelli (where you go up and then down the other side). Pass Le Bellevue restaurant on the right.

Pass a fountain and a *lavoir* on your left, coming to the fork at the end of town and way mark 20 **A**: take the left uphill, signed Chapelle Ste-Croix.

Follow this cobbled street uphill, and in a couple of minutes when it forks again, go up either way to the monastery. Continue uphill past the monastery on the cobbled road and then between tall stone walls.

There are views of Soarge bell tower behind you as you climb—beautiful little path full of flowers.

In 15 minutes or so reach a fork at way mark 162 **B**; bear left uphill, signed La Pinée par Peiremont, yellow-blazed trail.

In an hour or so, reach two way marks (433) "La Pinée" at an *abreuvoir* (sheep trough) **C**. If you want a higher view you can go up either of the two uphill paths here as far as you feel like—apparently the view extends even to the Alps—then come back to **C**.

From **C**, turn right downhill at a sheep trough (la Pinée), signed Chapelle Ste-Croix.

In about five minutes or so, pass a ruined stone farmhouse on your left (note the vaulted-ceiling animal quarters downstairs), and another 15 minutes beyond that, reach the Chapelle Ste.-Croix.

Five minutes later you'll pass way mark 163 on your right.

About 15–20 minutes later, rejoin the route at **B** (way mark 162 and a sheep trough), and retrace your steps back into town, another 20 minutes or so.

37 La Brigue Ring Walk via Notre Dame des Fontaines

2 Hours

In itself this isn't the most dramatic of walks—a simple there-and-back (although you can have a slight variation on the way back by visiting the Pont du Coq) along an informative nature trail,

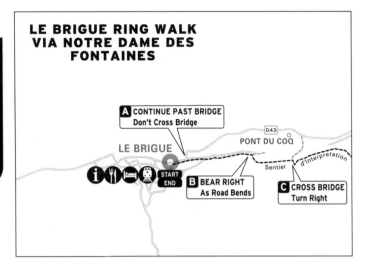

LE BRIGUE RING WALK VIA NOTRE DAME DES FONTAINES

A CONTINUE PAST BRIDGE
Don't Cross Bridge

LE BRIGUE

PONT DU COQ

D43

Sentier   d'Interpretation

START END

B BEAR RIGHT
As Road Bends

C CROSS BRIDGE
Turn Right

mostly through woods, with good views here and there—but La Brigue is a very pleasant, out-of-the-way village (it's off the main Roya valley road, so it avoids much of the tourist traffic. Bounded by the mountains of the Marguarais Massif, and the swift-flowing Levense river (a tributary of the Roya), it has a number of fine buildings, including the Gothic church of St. Martin, where you can see some gory altarpieces by Ludovico Brea.

But the real point of the walk is that it takes you to the little church of Notre Dame des Fontaines, where some of the most extraordinary works of art in all of Provence are to be found. These are the frescoes by the 15th-century Piedmontese painter Giovanni Canavesio. They depict the Passion of Christ and the Last Judgment in a series of stunningly complex, formalized, brilliantly colored tableaux. Though little known, Canavesio clearly understood how to organize large amounts of highly dramatic, turbulent material in a way that instantly transfixes the viewer. The Last Judgment is as horrible as you could wish, the suicide of Judas as gruesome, but the real genius is in the scenes from the life of Jesus: amazing studies of earthly and spiritual power in violent contention. If you read any French it is well worth buying the explanatory pamphlet on sale in the church, which details some of the murderous historical intrigues underlying the original commission (and slyly incorporated into its execution). But even if you don't, these are riveting works of art.

To see them you need to make an arrangement with the

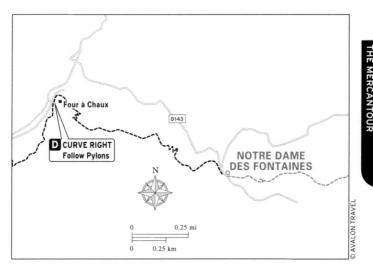

tourist office staff, who will open the church for you in the afternoon and provide you with a certain amount of English-language guidance, if you want it. Try to go on a sunny day: The lighting in the church is very poor (it was even worse at the time the frescoes were actually painted, begging the question of how exactly they were seen) and in fact the tourist office won't always open it at all if the weather isn't good.

Other points of interest on the walk include a splendid old ruined distillery and an extremely unusual 13th-century bridge, the Pont du Coq, which makes a right-angled turn halfway along. There are different theories about the purpose of this, the leading one being that it was to discourage cavalry charges.

FOOD

The delightful **Hôtel Mirval** has a good restaurant in a windowed terrace above the river. The €18 demipension *menu* (which you can have whether you're staying there or not) starts with a choice of homemade terrine, canelloni *à la niçoise,* lasagna with *pistou* or a soup of the day (in our case an excellent minestrone served with, again, *pistou*). Main courses were either trout fresh from the nearby Vivier, or a daily special, which was roast beef accompanied by an extremely good ratatouille (worth mentioning as this quintessentially Provençal dish can often be a disappointing slop of half-raw eggplant and unripe tomato). A chilled lemon tart on an admirably crisp piece of pastry arrived for dessert—but you can opt for cheese if you prefer. There's also a €23 Menu de Terroir offering all the above along with other choices such as rabbit with olives or entrecote with a pepper sauce. We sampled the *assiette terroir* from its appetizer list; the combination of the local *tourte* (a pastry filled, in this case, with potato and chard), roasted pepper with anchovy, and stuffed vegetables, all sounded too good to pass up. It wasn't bad, but it didn't quite live up to its promise until the delayed arrival of a delicious hot *feuillete* (flaky pastry) filled with cèpes, which certainly justified the slightly higher price tag. We had the Vacqueyras: It was from the cooperative in Beaumes-de-Venise, rather than an individual domaine, and rather mediocre.

There's also a tiny restaurant, **La Cassolette,** just along the road from the main square, that has a good local reputation and is worth trying. There's room for only about a dozen people in its cosy *salle,* crammed with toy roosters, so be sure to reserve. There's a daily *plat* for €9.50 and a rather complicated series of *menus* going upward from €18.50. An appealing brand of Provençal home cooking, enhanced by strong Italian accents, prevails (La Brigue belonged to Italy until 1947). We had excellent homemade gnocchi with *pistou, sugelli* (a local pasta shaped a bit like a child's ear) in a tomato sauce, and one of the meaty salads so beloved by the French—this one filled with a rather good "ham" of dried duck. Our choice of *plat* was a substantial and heart-warming dish of veal *escalope* covered in a sauce of wild cèpes and served with more gnocchi. Cheeses followed and then cherry pie and *crème caramel;* both were excellent, though by then the slight discomfort of the Provençal megalunch had set in. A very pleasant Esterol rosé helped (as did the best cappuccino of the trip, made, not surprisingly, with Italian coffee), except that under its influence we neglected to check our bill, only realizing later that we had been served (and charged for) one or two things that we hadn't ordered. The cause of this was almost certainly the absurdly labyrinthine set-*menu* system rather than dishonesty, but here, as everywhere, you do need to keep an eye on these things.

LOGISTICS
IGN Map Number and Name
#3841 OT—Vallée de la Roya

Tourist Information

Address: 26, avenue Général de Gaulle
Phone: 0493/ 79 09 34
Website or Email: www.patrimoine-labrigue.org
Hours: 9:00–12:00 every day and 14:00–17:30 Mon.–Sat.
Apr.-Oct., reduced hours out of season; see website
Notes: Closed Tues., and sometimes they're not there
afternoons Mon. and Wed. because they're at the chapel
(Notre Dame des Fontaines).

Restaurants

Name: Hôtel Mirval
See the listing under Accommodations.
Name: La Cassolette
Address: 20, avenue Général de Gaulle
Phone: 0493/ 04 63 82 or 0617/ 32 87 92
Closing Day: Open for lunch every day except Mon., also
evenings Fri. and Sat.

Accommodations

Name: Hôtel Mirval
Address: 3, rue Vincent Ferrier
Phone: 0493/ 04 63 71
Website or Email: www.lemirval.com
Type of Lodging: Logis de France hotel
Price: Low season €42/50/59 for a single/double room, three-
person room €65/74, four-person room €69; demipension
€45/49/54 per person (double occupancy), demipension
€66/73/78 for single; €32 kids under 10; prices higher in
season
Notes: Open Apr. 1–Nov. 1
Name: Le Pra Reound
Address: Chemin St. Jean
Phone: 0493/ 04 65 67
Website or Email: www.gîtes-de-france-alpes-maritimes.com;
on the opening page type in "5596" in the box that says "Vous
connaissez le numero"
Type of Lodging: *Chambres d'hôte*
Price: €34 one person, €46 two people, €13 additional person
Notes: Independent structure with six nice, simple, clean

rooms, with bathrooms. Clean kitchen at end of the building. Owner's farm next door. You can cook yourself, or order in from La Pizzeria Brigasque (0493/ 04 73 31).

Transportation
Train
See train notes in the chapter introduction and also in the Saorge Logistics. La Brigue is 20 minutes' ride north of Saorge, and all the train information is the same as for Saorge. All the trains that stop at Saorge also stop at La Brigue, except one in the late afternoon (about 17:00, and if that's the time you're leaving Saorge, you can take the train to Tende, the stop after La Brigue, then catch the next southbound train shortly thereafter, and take it for the four-minute trip to La Brigue).
Taxi
Name: Taxi Franck
Phone: 0493/ 04 62 92 or 0686/ 16 22 94
Notes: Day and night

Miscellaneous Notes
For Notre Dame des Fontaines, make visit requests through the tourist office. Apr. 1–Oct. 31: Unguided visit 14:00–17:00 Mon., Wed., Fri. and 14:00–17:30 Sat. and Sun., €1.50; visits with commentary (in French) 10:00–12:00 Thurs., Fri., Sat., €3.50; the guide can usually speak some English. Winter hours: Unguided 14:00–15:00 Mon., Wed., Fri., Sat., Sun.; with commentary 10:00–12:00 Thurs., Fri., Sat. Closed afternoons Tues. and Thurs. all year.

WALK DIRECTIONS
Walk out of town with the river to your left. Continue past the bridge Ⓐ (don't cross it) that leads to the D43 (to Notre Dame des Fontaines and Morignole), still with the river to your left, and in another half kilometer or so (about 5–7 minutes), you'll pass a way mark on your left Ⓑ, signed Notre Dame des Fontaines.

Immediately after the way mark, follow the road as it bends right, and 20 meters/yards beyond the way mark there's a green metal gate on the right, leading to a grassy area with benches on it. The asphalt ends here. Go straight ahead; don't bend left with the dirt track that leads to a picnic table and big pylon. Instead go straight ahead—you'll see a wooden signpost about 20 meters ahead of you, which you'll pass to your right, reaching the first interpretation table and beginning to climb.

Five minutes later ⬤, cross a wooden bridge with a way mark; turn right here for Notre Dame des Fontaines, or make a short detour to see the Pont du Coq. To visit the Pont du Coq, turn left here at ⬤ and go two minutes downhill. Come to a way mark, turn right, and in another two minutes come out at the bridge. Cross over and have a look at it from the road. Or you can visit it on the way back, and instead of returning to the trail afterward, you can follow the road (D43), which is very quiet, back into La Brigue.

Continuing from ⬤, about 25 minutes later pass the old distillery Four à Chaux ⬤. Curve around right, following the pylons.

Follow the trail for another 40 minutes or so, until it comes out on the road (D143). Turn right and follow the road to the chapel.

38 Casterino "Sacred Way" Ring Walk

5 Hours

This demanding, exhilarating day walk is one of the most rewarding in all of Provence, climbing along an ancient military road from the little mountain hamlet of Casterino (really just a few small hotels and a horse-riding operation) up into the stunning, protected wilderness of the Mercantour Park, where gentians, yellow violets, pansies, forget-me-nots, and other wildflowers abound, marmots sit perched on almost every rock, and there's a good chance of seeing rare animals such as ibexes (we did).

Every bit as extraordinary as the scenery are the Bronze Age rock inscriptions on the glacier-polished stones in the remote high valleys under Mont Bego. More than 40,000 of these hieroglyphic marks have been found, and this walk brings you to some of the more famous among them, including the cluster on the extended passage of tabletlike flat stones known as the "Sacred Way."

Most of these inscriptions are in some way expressions of a

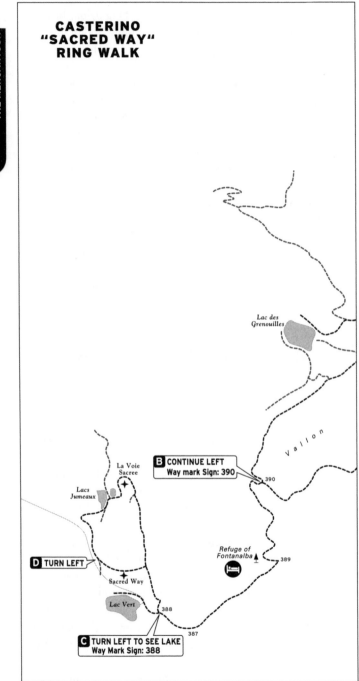

CASTERINO
"SACRED WAY"
RING WALK

Lac des Grenouilles

Vallon

B CONTINUE LEFT
Way mark Sign: 390

390

La Voie Sacree

Lacs Jumeaux

D TURN LEFT

Refuge of Fontanalba

389

Sacred Way

Lac Vert

388

387

C TURN LEFT TO SEE LAKE
Way Mark Sign: 388

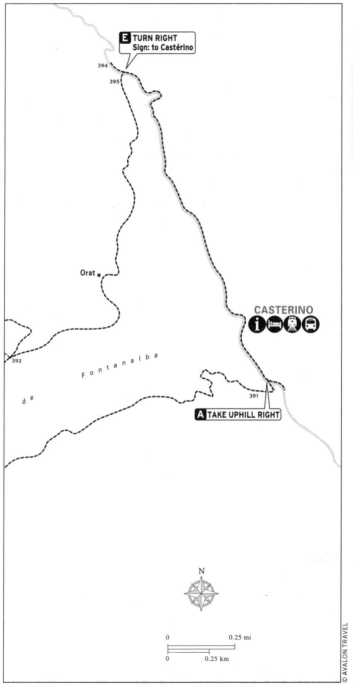

cattle-raising (possibly bull-worshipping) culture. The basic pictorial element is of the oblong body of a cow or bull topped with wide horns (at first glance it looks like simply the horned head, but once you grasp that it's in fact an aerial view of the whole animal, sometimes with legs and tail sticking out to the side and back, the images make more sense). Sometimes these are configured into a team of oxen yoked to a plow; sometimes you'll see them in proximity to a rudimentary figure of a man with an ax; sometimes the "body" is divided into a grid-like pattern thought to represent the boundaries of grazing properties in the surrounding valleys; sometimes it is metamorphosed into a human head (the most famous of these, the Sorcerer, is in another area of the Mercantour). Though not sophisticated or "beautiful" in the way of cave paintings, these are fascinating, highly expressive artifacts. Not much is known about them, but the area—full of clear streams and blue-green pools—is thought to have been a sacred site, with Bego perhaps representing some fertility god of thunder and lightning, and the engravings possibly marks left by pilgrims. Aside from some helpful signs here and there, the place remains wild, retaining a palpably charged atmosphere.

You can return to Casterino the way you came, or for a longer walk (involving a stretch at the end on a little-used asphalt road), you can circle around the other side of the alpine valley you climbed on the way up. There is a private mountain refuge shortly after you enter the park, where it may be possible to eat, though it was closed when we went. Otherwise the hotels will provide you with a picnic lunch (there are no shops in Casterino).

It probably takes about five hours' actual walking time, but with looking at things, allow a full day.

FOOD

High standards of cooking are maintained at the family-run hotel/restaurant **Les Melezes** high up here in the mountains. You can eat from the €18 Menu Pensionnaire, with daily specials such as fresh asparagus soup followed by a beautifully prepared chicken *basquaise* with peppers and tomato. Or à la carte you can choose from various grilled meats or a perfect fresh trout with fennel. There are good homemade pastas—*arrabbiata* or with morel mushrooms and cream—fondues of meat and cheese, and a spectacular raclette (€30 for two people) served with heaped plates of charcuterie, pickled mushroom, and boiled potatoes. Very good side vegetables accompany the main dishes—particularly the serving of lemon-perfumed spelt that came with our trout. And the desserts—a blueberry tart, a confection of iced mascarpone and honey—were wonderful. The wine list features, among other things, a very good Bandol rosé, Domaine du Pey-Neuf 2005, for €24.

LOGISTICS
IGN Map Number and Name
#3841 OT—Vallée de la Roya

Tourist Information
There's an information point for the Mercantour Park in Casterino, open only in the summer. The best tourist-information access is from the excellent www.royabevera.com site, which covers this entire region. The site is well-organized and packed with information. English option.

Name: Chalet de Casterino

Phone: 0493/ 04 89 79

Website or Email: www.parc-mercantour.com (general website for the park)

Notes: Information point for the Mercantour Park, open June 15–Sept. 15

Restaurants
Name: Les Melezes

See listing under Accommodations.

Accommodations
Name: Hôtel les Melezes

Address: Casterino

Phone: 0493/ 04 95 95

Website or Email: www.lesmelezes.fr

Type of Lodging: Logis de France hotel

Price: Rooms €42/50, demipension €57/60 per person, €72/75 full pension; extra adult in room, €35 demipension, €50 full pension; kids €23/34 demipension, €31/41 full pension

Name: Refuge de Fontanalbe
Address: Inside the park
Phone: 0493/ 04 89 19 or 0493/ 04 69 22)
Type of Lodging: *Gîte d'étape,* basically
Price: €30 demipension
Notes: Open mid-June–mid-Sept., although in the first part of June it may let you stay by reservation only. Nice place, with *dortoir* sleeping arrangements. It also makes picnics.

Transportation

If you're arriving on the train, in July and August there are four *navettes* (shuttle buses) a day from the St. Dalmas de Tende station (the station between Saorge and La Brigue) to Casterino. However, since it's very hot in July and Aug. (though admittedly quite a bit cooler up in Casterino than elsewhere in Provence), you'll likely be arriving in some other month. You have two options in this case. One is to take a taxi; the other is to hitchhike. There's only one road to Casterino, the little D91, and when you get off the train at the St. Dalmas de Tende *arrêt* (station), you're on it. The road doesn't go anywhere except to Casterino (there's a little outpost halfway, at the lake of Mesches, and a *gîte d'étape* a km from the lake) so you're likely to do well with your thumb.

Taxi
  Name: Taxi Tende (Philippe)
  Phone: 0616/ 52 72 07
  Name: Taxi Franck
  Phone: 0493/ 04 62 92 or 0686/ 16 22 94
  Notes: Operates out of La Brigue
  Name: Taxi Breil
  Phone: 0493/ 04 94 43

Miscellaneous Notes

There's a museum of the Merveilles in Tende. For more information see www.museedesmerveilles.com

WALK DIRECTIONS

Turn right out the Hôtel-Restaurant Les Melezes and walk down the road, passing the Hôtel Chamois d'Or and then the Chalet d'Accueil and the signboard about the park on your right.

Pass a dirt path uphill right just beyond the signboard, and take the next uphill right another 20 meters/yards beyond that **Ⓐ**. There's a way mark here, 391, signed Refuge de Fontanalba.

Stay on this yellow-blazed trail as it climbs above the Vallon de Fontanalba until you come to way mark 390 **Ⓑ**. (This took us an hour and 40 minutes, but we were moving slowly.) Continue uphill left toward the signboards at the Mercantour Park entrance.

About 20 minutes past **Ⓑ**, you'll reach way mark 389 (at the Refuge Fontanalba), and 15 minutes or so later, way mark 387. Continue over the bridge.

In another couple of minutes you'll see way mark 388 on your left **Ⓒ**, signed to Lac Vert. To see the lake (a short detour and a nice picnic spot), turn left onto this small footpath, arriving at the lake in 5–10 minutes, and when you're ready, retrace your steps back to **Ⓒ** and turn left on the path.

In 15 minutes or so you'll see a little way mark pointing right for the rock engravings *(gravures).* From here until you return to this path (after **Ⓓ**, you'll see the rock engravings; first the "Sacred Way," but beyond that there are several other well-signed clusters. Please stay on the paths, and don't touch the inscriptions or climb on the rocks.

Climb up across from—not on—the long stone tablet (the "Sacred Way").

Turn left after the "Sacred Way." Check out the table of orientation, and then continue downhill, passing a service hut on your right. Just beyond there is the path, by another small way mark. (You'll see the two pools known as Twin Lakes—Lacs Jumeaux.) Turn right, signed "Parcours de découverte."

About 15 minutes later, watch for a little way mark at a fork by the stream **Ⓓ**. The downhill right is signed for Lac Vert; take the left uphill, signed "Parcours de découverte."

In about five minutes (but as with all these timings, it really depends how long you're stopping to look at the engravings), come out at a wider path (the same path you took on the way up); turn right, passing a little stone hut on your right (there's a salt lick here for the ibex, two of whom were there when we passed). Five minutes later pass way mark 388 **Ⓒ**.

Beyond here, bear left at way mark 387.

About 25 minutes later you'll reach **Ⓑ** again. Here you can either go back the way you came or, if you'd like to take a different way back (longer), turn left here and cross the stone bridge.

In 20 minutes there's a spur on the left (way mark 392) for the Lake of Frogs (Lac des Grenouilles) a 15-minute walk that we were too tired to explore. Otherwise, keep on straight here.

About 40–50 minutes later the path comes out on a small, little-used road **Ⓔ**. Turn right, signed to Casterino, reaching Casterino in another half hour.

INDEX

ACCOMMODATIONS INDEX

RESTAURANTS INDEX

PHOTO CREDITS

ACKNOWLEDGMENTS

We would like to thank the following people for the part they played in bringing this book to fruition:

Camilla Panufnik, Catherine Audard, Nicole Czechowski, and Suzanne Spiegelberg for their great kindness in helping us organize ourselves.

Lady Hamlyn for her incredible generosity in lending us her house.

Mme. Mousie Stephan at the Cucuron Library for her friendliness and advice.

Linda Lorentz for so much practical guidance.

Alan Brooks and Cheryl Taylor for the gift of their precious time and glorious companionship.

Lachlan Brooks for fun, good spirits, and patience.

Donna White-Davis for taking the plunge and for her always loving and creative care of our kids.

Our friends and family who joined us in our travels and made them so much brighter: Susan Lasdun, William Lasdun, Lisa Class, Blaise Lasdun, Lavinia Greenlaw, Martha Kearney, Chris Shaw, Michael and Jacob Hofmann, Barbara Hofmeister, Stephen Romer, Jenny and Mitch Druckman.

Bill Newlin, our publisher, for his staunch support, and our editors Kevin McLain and Cinnamon Hearst for their keen eyes and excellent advice.

www.moon.com

For helpful advice on planning a trip, visit www .moon.com for the **TRAVEL PLANNER** and get access to useful travel strategies and valuable information about great places to visit. When you travel with Moon, expect an experience that is uncommon and truly unique.

HANDBOOKS | METRO | OUTDOORS | LIVING ABR